DATE			

HB
884
.S25
1984

Salas, Rafael M.
Reflections on
population

D1435245

Books by Rafael M. Salas

People: An International Choice
The Multilateral Approach to Population (1976)
(translated into Arabic, Chinese, French, Japanese, Russian and Spanish)

International Population Assistance:
The First Decade (1979)
(A Look at the Concepts and Policies Which Have Guided The UNFPA in Its First Ten Years)
(translated into Arabic, French, Japanese and Spanish)

Reflections on Population (1985)
(translated into French, Japanese and Spanish)

Direct inquiries to Pergamon Press

REFLECTIONS ON POPULATION

RAFAEL M. SALAS
United Nations Fund for
Population Activities

Second Edition

PERGAMON PRESS
New York • Oxford • Toronto • Sydney • Paris • Frankfurt

Pergamon Press Offices:

U.S.A.	Pergamon Press Inc., Maxwell House, Fairview Park, Elmsford, New York 10523, U.S.A.
U.K.	Pergamon Press Ltd., Headington Hill Hall, Oxford OX3 0BW, England
CANADA	Pergamon Press Canada Ltd., Suite 104, 150 Consumers Road, Willowdale, Ontario M2J 1P9, Canada
AUSTRALIA	Pergamon Press (Aust.) Pty. Ltd., P.O. Box 544, Potts Point, NSW 2011, Australia
FRANCE	Pergamon Press SARL, 24 rue des Ecoles, 75240 Paris, Cedex 05, France
FEDERAL REPUBLIC OF GERMANY	Pergamon Press GmbH, Hammerweg 6, D-6242 Kronberg-Taunus, Federal Republic of Germany

Library of Congress Cataloging in Publications Data

Salas, Rafael M.
    Reflections on population.

    Bibliography: p.
    Includes index.
    1. Developing countries--Population. 2. Population
assistance--Developing countries. 3. United Nations
Fund for Population Activities. I. Title.
HB884.S25   1985   304.6'09172'4   85-3458
ISBN 0-08-032406-1

Printed in the United States of America

This book is dedicated
to all the participants
in the 1984 International
Conference on Population.

CONTENTS

FOREWORD

The Charter of the United Nations calls for "the creation of conditions of well-being" for all peoples. When those words were writ-
ten nearly 40 years ago, the new global problems that today affect
the developed and developing countries alike could hardly be envisaged. One of the most urgent of these global problems is population. By the year 2000, the global population is expected to reach
6.1 billion. The awesome reality of this number of people who will
inhabit our earth in the relatively near future has a direct bearing
on virtually every political, economic and social issue now confronting us.

The United Nations Fund for Population Activities became operational in 1969. The author of this book, Mr. Rafael M. Salas, has
served as Executive Director of the Fund since that time. It has
become the largest multilateral population assistance programme
and has proven to be a dynamic organization responsive to the
needs of the developing countries. Today it supports programmes
throughout the developing world. When the Population Fund was
first established population initiatives and interest in them were
largely limited to a few developing countries. Now the interest and,
what is most important, the commitment of governments have
taken wide root. We can take a measure of satisfaction that, for
the first time, the overall world population growth rate has
declined. Yet, the problem remains enormous and unavoidable. It is
without doubt one of the most difficult issues that Member States
and the United Nations have to deal with on a national and international basis. Religious, ideological and cultural values are involved as well as intensely personal and human considerations.

The International Population Conference will be held in Mexico
City this summer. Mr. Salas will serve as Secretary-General of the
Conference and has felt that there should be a clear exposition and
understanding of the issues to be dealt with. He has sought to provide this in the present book. Its great value lies both in its timeli-

ness and its success in focussing attention on the scope and complexity of the problem. It does not lecture and it offers no easy answers. But by stating the facts clearly and honestly it serves as a catalyst for the creative thinking and statesmanship that are essential if population is to be dealt with in such a way as to contribute to a peaceful, equitable and just world. The present book can serve as an invaluable blueprint for the work that lies ahead.

It is essential now to give the most serious thought to the quality of life which can be assured for those who will inhabit the earth at the end of the century. The present book serves as a challenge to all to meet this requirement. This is an essential part of the commitment of the Member States of the United Nations to promote social progress and better standards of life in larger freedom, a commitment which must be seen now in terms of what the world population will be in the year 2000.

New York, February 1984

Javier Pérez de Cuéllar
Secretary-General
of the United Nations

PREFACE

I am writing this book in my capacity as the Executive Director of the United Nations Fund for Population Activities. It is a sequel to *International Population Assistance: The First Decade*, published in 1979, in which I defined and described the workable population concepts that governed the Fund's operations for ten years in the various functional areas of population programmes. That volume showed how UNFPA's policies evolved over a period of time and how its self-instituted principles of neutrality, flexibility and innovation in rendering assistance were, in fact, the essential policy approaches that have made the Fund the largest multilateral source of population funding that it is today.

After five years and with the International Conference on Population in mind, I felt that an additional volume was needed to characterize the work of the UNFPA with the developing countries up to 1984 and to relate these experiences to the issues before the Conference. Reflections on the Fund's work can assist the reader in thinking about the future of population.

Chapter I is an overview of the significant developments in population up to the year of the Conference. Chapters II through VII discuss the main issues before the Conference and generally reflect the arrangement of the document to be before the Conference concerning the recommendations for the further implementation of the World Population Plan of Action. They are divided into an *Introduction* which describes the demographic situation pertinent to the issues (a complete list of reference sources for the Introductions in Chapters II through VII is provided on page 129) *Excerpts from Statements* which are extracts from my policy statements on behalf of UNFPA; and *Issues for the Future* which point to relevant policy considerations for the population programmes of countries. Within each section of these chapters, the excerpts have been arranged in an analytic rather than chronological order, with the aim of facilitating the flow of the arguments presented. Dates following each excerpt refer to the date on which the statement was given. (A complete list of these statements is contained in Appendix E.) Chapter VIII contains my reflections on the future of population assistance.

Appendix C to this volume contains the five *State of World Population Reports* issued from 1980 to 1984. The *Reports* for 1978 and 1979 were reprinted in *International Population Assistance: The First Decade.* Appendix D comprises seven of my statements which, primarily due to their focus on the population issues of particular importance to the major regions of the globe, have been reproduced here in their entirety.

Demographic and other statistics in the excerpts from statements, in the statements reprinted in full, and in the *State of World Population Reports*, which were based on the most current figures available at the time of issuance, have been retained as originally presented. Continuing refinements in the data base alter neither the nature of the problems faced by countries nor the measures required to meet them. Unless otherwise stated, demographic figures used in the introductions to chapters II through VII have been based on "Demographic Indicators by Countries as Assessed in 1982", prepared by the Population Division of the United Nations Department of International Economic and Social Affairs. Other sources of information were utilized and adapted in the preparation of this volume; all sources are listed on p. 129.

This volume can serve as a convenient reference guide for the 1984 Conference. In deliberating and preparing statements on the issues during the Conference, Conference delegates can refer, as needed, to material under such headings as fertility and the family, mortality and health policy and others.

The policies treated in the text are obviously more limited than the issues before the Conference since they were primarily derived from the population programmes of developing countries as assisted by UNFPA. In reading the text, one should be aware that some issues which textbooks, encyclopaedias and studies usually consider a normal part of the subject of population are not treated in this volume. This reflects the absence, or unevenness in the treatment of these issues by countries, in what they generally consider—at least up to the time of this writing—relevant areas for international population assistance.

To make use of UNFPA policies as part of the conceptual approach in analyzing the *Review and Appraisal of the World Population Plan of Action* and the *Recommendations for the further implementation of the World Population Plan of Action*, one might consider the following steps:

First, to relate the provisions of the World Population Plan of Action as a whole and then the various sectoral areas with those that have been covered by the UNFPA policies, noting which of the related policies will prospectively remain valid and those that will need consideration for future implementation;

Second, to assume that the provisions of the World Population Plan of Action that are substantially similar to those covered by UNFPA policies reflect the population and socio-economic factors prevailing in the developing countries and acceptance by countries of these factors;

Third, to take UNFPA statements as evidence of the past experiences of developing countries in thinking about the provisions of the World Population Plan of Action; and

Fourth, to foresee in the suggestions for further implementation of the World Population Plan of Action, the necessity of continued financial support for the population programmes both nationally and globally by using the UNFPA experience as an indicator of the assistance that should be extended to national programmes to achieve long-term population goals.

The first English-language edition of this book was issued in July 1984 in order to make it available to the participants in the International Conference on Population held in August 1984. This second edition of *Reflections on Population*, printed after the Conference, includes demographic data later available, my statements as Secretary-General of the Conference (Chapter IX), the Eighty-Eight Recommendations of the Mexico City Conference and the Mexico City Declaration on Population and Development (Appendix A), and the text of the World Population Plan of Action (Appendix B).

The ultimate hope behind this book is that it will be relevant beyond the 1984 Conference. It is a faithful record of the experience of UNFPA and the assisted countries in population policy-making. It will serve its purpose if it can be one of the bases for generating thought and ideas that will be required for the future.

New York, January 1985

Rafael M. Salas
Executive Director

ACKNOWLEDGEMENTS

In the preparation of this book, I have been helped by many people.

I am particularly grateful to several UNFPA staff members who helped in the drafting of many of my statements, excerpts from many of which are provided in this volume—T.N. Krishnan, Alex Marshall, Sethuramiah L.N. Rao and Jack Voelpel, and to Mr. Krishnan who was instrumental in the drafting of my *State of World Population* reports.

The senior staff of the Fund provided many valuable suggestions for the final manuscript, but I would particularly like to acknowledge the critical appraisals of Mr. Krishnan, Catherine Pierce, Mr. Rao, Jürgen Sacklowski, Jyoti Singh and Arumugam Thavarajah and their contributions to the final manuscript.

Fay Cox, Marion Walrond, Mirey Chaljub and Jean Butler typed the various drafts with great conscientiousness and skill.

Finally, I would like to express my special appreciation to Jack Voelpel who with Jeff Hester saw the manuscript through from beginning to end and was primarily responsible for editing of the project.

Chapter I

THINKING ABOUT POPULATION, 1984

The International Conference on Population will be held in Mexico City in August 1984. The occasion offers a particularly appropriate time for rethinking population—both reflecting on the past and assessing future directions of population policies and programmes.

Ten years ago, in August 1974, the international community met in Bucharest, Romania, for the first intergovernmental political meeting on population. The major achievement of the World Population Conference, in addition to focussing worldwide attention on the subject of population through the United Nations-designated World Population Year of 1974, was the adoption by consensus of the World Population Plan of Action (WPPA).

This document, which became one of the major international sectoral development strategies, is today the most comprehensive international statement ever adopted on population and its interrelationships with socio-economic development. The Plan has served as the guidepost for the formulation and implementation of population policies and programmes by national governments and has been the basic framework for technical co-operation in population among countries.

As a conceptualization of population issues and their integral relationship with economic and social factors, the Plan has withstood the test of applicability to all countries, developed and developing alike. Certainly, it would be hard to find a better measure of its success than the fact that, among developing countries today, there is a universal commitment to population policies and to programmes to implement them.

In the ten years that have elapsed since the 1974 Conference, much has been learned about the complex interrelationships between population and socio-economic factors. Demographic change and the new issues and perceptions which emerge from population trends necessitate a periodic review of national and international strategies in population. Goals must be continually reassessed and accomplishments as well as failures alternatively measured. Thus, at the 1984 International Conference on Population, the international community, while reaffirming its commitment to the principles and objectives of the Plan of Action, will foreseeably adopt modified approaches and more comprehensive policies to enable a more effective implementation of population programmes. These policies will ensure that the Plan remains a valid framework for national and international efforts in the population field.

Within the United Nations system of population assistance, the United Nations Fund for Population Activities is the focal point. In its fourteen years of operation, UNFPA has extended more than $1 billion in population assistance to almost all of the developing countries and to a number of territories that have population programmes and has thus become the world's largest source of multilateral assistance in population. The policies that have been adopted and enunciated by UNFPA have evolved from the collective experience of UNFPA and the recipient countries.

Throughout this period, UNFPA has been continuously engaged in an effort consistent with the goals and objectives of the World Population Plan of Action to refine and strengthen the conceptualization of population policies and to adapt and respond to the significant and substantial changes in the perception of population problems by all countries. These changes in perception are derived primarily from an analysis of demographic trends such as the documented decline in the global fertility rate and its variation in regions and individual countries, and such developments as the unprecedented growth of cities in the developing countries and the accelerated movements of people within and outside national boundaries. In responding to these changes, UNFPA has constantly been generalizing ideas from its assisted programmes so that its assistance to countries remains consistently relevant to national development objectives.

In the developing countries, shifts in perspective regarding the population issues facing them are manifold. One elemental reason is that, during the 1970s and early 1980s, more and more reliable basic population data were gathered and analyzed throughout the world. This increased and more comprehensive data collection, largely supported by UNFPA, was most critical in Africa, where many countries had never had a census and thus had little or no information on the size, structure and growth trends of their populations. While there are still gaps in the understanding of population data, knowledge of countries' demographic situations has increased enormously since 1974.

A related development has been the increase in the developing countries in the number of trained demographers and other social scientists skilled in the analysis of population and development interrelationships. This has been due in no small part to the programmes of the United Nations regional and interregional demographic training and research centres. Researchers at the centres, and at many other institutions, have also greatly contributed to our knowledge of how population variables influence and are influenced by other socio-economic variables, and have thus helped to show where policy interventions may be possible and most effective.

Perhaps most important has been the experiences of developing countries themselves with population programmes. As certain countries—mostly in Asia where population problems first reached a manifestly critical state—demonstrated that population was indeed a programmable sector of development amenable to policy measures, other countries with similar perceptions of their population situations began to initiate and adapt programmes of their own.

Thus, since 1974, many governments have gathered more reliable information on their population situations, have developed more skilled manpower to analyze this information and its relation to development objectives and to devise appropriate population policies, and have witnessed the successful implementation of population programmes. When added to the information, education and substantive research activities of the United Nations and other institutions, all these have enabled the development of better integrated population policies and more effective programmes to date. With this in mind, it is clear that the commitment of the developing countries to the solution of their population problems has never been higher than it is now, on the eve of the International Conference on Population.

As a reflection of this increased attention, the international community has given a prominent place to population measures in the International Development Strategy for the Third United Nations Development Decade. There was a call for all countries to "continue to integrate their population measures and programmes into their social and economic goals and strategies". They are also encouraged "within the framework of national demographic policies to take the measures they deem necessary concerning fertility levels in full respect of the right of parents to determine in a free, informed and responsible manner the number and spacing of their children". In support of these measures, "the international community will increase the level of population assistance". In addition, many of the recent sectoral instruments and plans adopted by the international community call for explicit consideration of various population factors in their respective spheres of development activity.

It is among the successes in the population field since the 1974 Conference, particularly in light of the current global economic difficulties that countries have faced and are facing, that population policy-making has now become institutionalized in almost all developing countries. That Conference encouraged countries to treat population policies as an integral part of development planning. Today, ten years later, many of the developing countries have population units within their ministries, mostly in planning or in health. They have considered population factors of such critical importance to the success of their development plans that, as a consequence, their national budgetary allocations in support of their own population programmes have steadily and substantially increased since 1974.

These developments in the population field have had a decisive impact on the deliberations of the governing bodies of UNFPA. UNFPA's Governing Council sets the directions of UNFPA's resource allocations. For instance, in the setting of priorities for allocations, the Governing Council decided in 1981 that assistance to family planning programmes should be considered UNFPA's first priority. This responds to requests of governments representing 80 per cent of the population of the developing regions. This decision was made with due consideration to the economic and demographic indicators prevailing in the developing countries but without sacrificing or neglecting the importance of other allocation categories such as communication and education, basic data collection and population dynamics to which the corresponding priorities were given at the same time. It is as a result of this process of free discussion of global needs and perceptions particular to the United Nations system that UNFPA's enunciated policies continue to be responsive and sensitive to the shifts in policies of countries and at the same time remain universally relevant.

United Nations deliberative bodies are also the main forums in which broader population concerns and new emphases on accepted policies emerge to be considered globally. The problem of aging populations, as an example, has recently come to the forefront of attention of policy-makers in both developed and developing countries. As one result of the significant decline in fertility in the developing countries over the past two decades as well as a rise in life expectancy, shifts in the structure of population will undoubtedly occur in them two or three generations hence which will have economic and social consequences in such areas as housing, employment, provision of social services and education. If developing countries are to adopt policies in anticipation of major shifts in their population structures, the experience of the developed countries, which had fertility declines much earlier and are now feeling the impact of a large proportion of the elderly within their populations, is important for developing countries to consider.

Migration, both international and rural-urban, has also recently become a serious concern of the global community. Its scale has increased in recent years. The problems of international migration arise from three factors: many migrants from developing to developed countries are temporary workers; a sizeable proportion of international population movement is accounted for by refugee movements; and finally, the number of illegal or undocumented migrants is growing. Poverty, unemployment, underemployment and landlessness in rural areas and sometimes development policies themselves have combined to push rural migrants to urban centres in search of better lives. This migration, added to the natural population growth in the cities, has led to the outstripping of urban infrastructures and increasing difficulties in providing adequate water, health services, education and employment. Inevitably, under such conditions, social tensions can intensify and affect internal stability.

Many of the population-related issues have been discussed extensively in the United Nations in the past decade but their relevance to population as such needs further elaboration in 1984. Such issues as the role of the family; the role and status of women, their education and employment; the interrelationships that exist among resources, environment, population and development; and institution-building in developing countries will continue to concern countries even beyond the Mexico Conference.

For an appreciation of the dynamic factors involved in these issues, a clear recognition of the time element is essential. Population policies are statements of goals in population accompanied by a set of programmes elaborated to achieve them. In order to achieve the desired population goals, policies and programmes have to be viewed in at least two time perspectives: the long-term and the short-term. A long-term view of population foresees a moving equilibrium of population and development factors with a corresponding global population stability. A short-term perspective may necessitate a reduction of fertility and a lowering of the rate of population growth as in most Asian countries today, so that population stability can eventually be achieved.

These population issues which will be discussed at the 1984 International Conference on Population will have to be related to the core policies of UNFPA. These core policies on family planning, communication and education, basic data collection and population dynamics stand at present as an integrated, holistic set of policies. They were formulated on the basis of a global consensus, taking into account the varying national views on population and the different cultural, religious and ideological perspectives. They are, in addition, supported by the population policies and programmes adopted and implemented by the developing countries in the past fifteen years and put into effect nationally. In conceptualizing the core policies on the basis of the assisted programmes, UNFPA has learned four valuable approaches:

- *The need for rationality in programming solutions.* The present concern with high population growth rates in developing countries and the successes of current fertility reduction programmes have been primarily due to the effective application of the knowledge gained in the health and social sciences. The solutions to these problems cannot be undertaken on an *ad hoc* basis or in an erratic or isolated manner. They must be rationally programmed to be comprehensive, effective and particularly sustained.

- *A different time perspective.* Population programmes require a much longer time perspective than most other development programmes. Population programmes cannot be implemented or completed in four, five or even ten years. They require a generation or more to take effect.

- *The uniqueness of each country.* Individual countries perceive their population problems differently from others. Each country in its own historical stage has different political, economic, social and cultural conditions. A number of population problems may emerge and converge at different times, requiring action particular to the specific setting. Within the global goals set by the World Population Plan of Action, each government, therefore, must be allowed to make its own decisions, based on its own unique situation, on what it considers best for its own people. The aim of all assisted programmes should be to help countries achieve self-reliance in population matters, including technical training in the administration and management of population programmes, building the institutional capability for research and analysis, ensuring technical co-operation between and among developing countries in both technical assistance and the procurement of supplies and equipment and encouraging innovative approaches in dealing with various aspects of population problems.

- *Perceptions of population problems keep changing as we gain more knowledge and experience.* In the 1950s, demographers and other specialists perceived the problems primarily as questions of morbidity and mortality. The 1960s was the decade that brought about a shift in emphasis to fertility factors in population growth. The 1970s brought a growing awareness of the need to regard population as an integral factor in the entire process of development. In the 1980s, increasing attention has been accorded to the problems of urban growth, migration and aging. Policy-makers must be constantly aware both of the continuity and the changes occurring in the field and be ready to modify policies and programmes when the realities demand it.

Due to different circumstances, the pace of population programming varies. For instance, most African countries view population today with the outlook that prevailed in major Asian countries more than a decade ago. The relatively high population growth rates in African countries have only recently become matters of concern to many governments of the region and in many of these countries efforts are presently under way to strengthen and extend health services to include family planning. It stands to reason that in discerning the changing emphases of population policies in the forthcoming discussions at the 1984 Conference and thereafter, policies must be reconciled with new or different perspectives. The recommendations will alter, modify, add or omit some aspects of particular policies but are expected not to detract from the integral exercise of making policy revisions a coherent part of the global consensus.

From the beginning, UNFPA has initiated activities aimed at increasing the awareness of population issues among policy-makers, parliamentarians, academics, non-governmental organizations and the media by making available a part of its assistance to support global as well as regional and national population information, education and communication projects. These have included:

Since 1978, the issuance of a *State of World Population Report* to describe the global population situation annually and population developments of relevance to countries; initiatives geared towards various decision-making levels of government such as the *International Conference of Parliamentarians on Population and Development* in 1979, the first Conference of its kind under United Nations auspicies which was later followed by similar regional conferences in Africa, Asia and Latin America in 1980-1982; the *International Conference on Population and the Urban Future* in 1980 for the mayors of cities projected to have populations of five million or more in the year 2000; cosponsorship of the *International Conference on Family Planning in the 1980s* in 1981 for family planning programme managers and experts throughout the world; the Fund's financial support to the *World Assembly on Aging* in 1982 for focussing attention on the problems of the aging in the world community; and the establishment by the General Assembly in 1981 of the *United Nations Population Award*, the first global award of its kind and the only United Nations award to date, intended to give worldwide recognition to individuals or institutions that have made the most outstanding contribution to the awareness of population questions or to their solutions.

These initiatives were in addition to the regular seminars, study groups, conferences of ministers, officials, experts and laymen; publications of UNFPA, the United Nations agencies and academic institutions; public discussions and appearances by officers of the United Nations and worldwide reports by UNFPA carried by various media organizations.

To carry out its tasks successfully, UNFPA must have adequate resources to meet the growing demands for population assistance from developing countries. In the past five years resources for population assistance have increasingly fallen short of demand. One of the acknowledged limiting factors to this flow is the escalating rate of expenditures for armaments in national budgets.

Today global armaments expenditures have reached the incredible level of over $600 billion a year. This is over $1.6 billion a day. The total amount of contributions to population assistance through the UNFPA in the past 15 years is a little more than $1 billion—about 15 hours of armaments expenditure at current levels. Similarly, the total annual volume of international population assistance today is a mere $490 million or .000816 of the armaments expenditures for the same period. Recent events indicate that the limited resources for developmental and humanitarian programmes may be diverted into still higher military appropriations. It requires little understanding to realize that massive military expenditures are unlikely to solve the root problems of man. In this nuclear age, preparation for war has become even more questionable as a means towards peace and stability.

Unfortunately, there is a lack of awareness among policymakers of the links between population and global stability, and the role which population plays in shaping political behaviour. While population factors by themselves do not necessarily cause conflict, in combination with other economic, political and social factors, they can intensify it. For instance, the critical struggle for scarce resources is very often intensified by the numbers of people involved—a common characteristic of conflicts. Population policies and programmes by looking towards a moderation of population growth and a rational spatial distribution of population are, in this sense, humane efforts to reduce imbalances and disparities that lead to these crises. Therefore, in the future, would not a tiny shift of resources from armaments to population assistance be one of the effective ways for fostering peace and stability within and between nations?

It is with these thoughts in mind that the population issues in the succeeding chapters should be examined.

Chapter II

FERTILITY, STATUS OF WOMEN AND THE FAMILY

INTRODUCTION

The World Population Plan of Action underscores the importance of the fundamental right of individuals and couples to decide freely and responsibly the number and spacing of their children. It also calls upon countries to help individuals and couples in achieving their desired fertility goals by encouraging appropriate education as well as the means of achieving them.

The findings of the World Fertility Survey in 40 developing countries indicate that in a majority of countries surveyed there is a discrepency between national averages in actual fertility and in desired fertility. For instance, the total marital fertility rate varied between 4.8 and 10.7 and the mean number of desired children ranged between 3.0 and 8.6. Moreover, in 26 of the 40 countries, the mean desired fertility was less than 5 children per woman. Furthermore, a large proportion of couples who did not want any additional children did not practice any method of contraception. Also, the desired number of children is much higher in developing countries than in developed countries.

According to projections of the United Nations, the global birth rate during the 1980-1985 period is estimated at 27.3 per 1000. The corresponding rates for developed and developing countries are 15.5 and 31.2 respectively. During the past decade, there has been a perceptible decline in fertility. The global birth rate declined by 17 per cent during this period. The main contributor to this global decline is the reduction in fertility in developing countries within which the birth rate declined by 19 per cent.

The World Population Plan of Action recommended that not only unwanted pregnancies need to be prevented, but also that involuntary sterility be eliminated. The abnormally high prevalence of sterility and sub-fecundity in several countries of Africa south of the Sahara and in other parts of the world is not only a personal tragedy to many couples, but is also a socio-demographic problem. While there is no clear agreement on either their definition or prevalence, it is estimated that roughly up to 5 per cent of all couples are infertile because of complex physiological reasons and, due to additional social and biological factors, the prevalence of involuntary infertility may be as high as 30 per cent or even higher in some communities. Experience indicates that much of the excess infertility could be preventable if these additional factors could be identified by biomedical research.

While the decline in the birth rate has also reduced the annual rate of global population growth from 2.03 per cent during the period 1970-1975 to 1.67 per cent during the period 1980-1985, the annual increment to world population is projected to increase from 78 million in the 1980s to 89 million by the end of this century. Moreover, 90 per cent of this projected growth is expected to occur in the developing regions.

The key to population stabilization is family size. Stabilization of population will become a reality only when the average size of completed families in the developing countries declines to a level comparable to that currently in the developed countries, which is less than two children per woman.

While a larger number of countries consider their national fertility level high and would like to reduce it, a number of other countries consider higher rates of fertility desirable. For instance, in the United Nations Fifth Population Inquiry conducted in 1982, 46.7 per cent of the developed countries responding indicated that higher rates of fertility were desirable and the remaining 53.3 per cent of the countries responding indicated that their fertility level was considered satisfactory.

By contrast, 64 per cent of 53 developing countries express-ing a view on the subject matter indicated that their national level of fertility was high and only 8 per cent considered it low with the remaining 28 per cent considering it satisfactory. Further-more, 85.3 per cent of those viewing their fertility rate to be high are in favour of policies to reduce it. It should be noted that almost 80 per cent of the total population of developing countries reside in countries which consider their levels of fertility too high while only about 3 per cent live in developing countries which would like their fertility rates increased.

The role of fertility regulation in modifying population growth is increasingly recognized in a number of developing countries. Some 20 developing countries (11 in Asia and the Pacific, 5 in Africa and 4 in Latin America and the Caribbean) have identi-fied quantitative targets to reduce fertility either in the total fer-tility rate or in the crude birth rate. Seven countries have set the year 2000 as the date to achieve their fertility goals and a few of them aim at attaining replacement level.

The results of the World Fertility Survey and Fifth Popula-tion Inquiry indicate that in a majority of countries individuals and couples desire smaller families and the Government of these countries consider their national levels of fertility as too high. This points to the need of increasing access to family planning services including those of natural family planning. The Inquiry shows that, as of 1982, access to such services is permitted in 71 of the 73 developing countries participating in the Inquiry. In 58 of those countries (80 per cent), the governments were either directly or indirectly supporting provision of these services.

The range of contraceptive practice in family planning serv-ices varies considerably, from a virtual absence of practice in a large number of African countries to an estimated 71 per cent of currently married women in Singapore. A simple average of current practice among 51 countries for which data are available is about 32 per cent.

The access and utilization of family planning services depend on a number of factors, among which are: the quality of the serv-ice and its follow-up; availability of different methods and free-dom in their selection; outreach capacity of service coverage; adequacy of supplies and effective management. Over-all, the delivery of these services has not been completely satisfactory in most developing countries that have family planning programmes especially because a large proportion of the population is rural, illiterate and poor.

To improve access to, and delivery of, family planning services, several developing countries have initiated complementary programmes including the provision of incentives and disincentives for individual acceptors; the appointment of motivators and health workers; extensive educational, communication and information campaigns; special population projects for youth and increased involvement of non-governmental organizations, community and women's groups such as mothers' clubs and women's co-operatives. Some governments have set operational targets for family planning projects to measure acceptability and extension of services.

The World Population Plan of Action draws attention to the status of women and invites countries to improve all aspects of women's lives including education, employment, and political participation, as well as their domestic and maternal roles. Experience has shown that in the context of population policy, the educational attainment level and labour force participation of women are particularly important.

There is increasing attention given by developing countries to the role and functions of the family and its effects in such decisions as to when to marry, when and how many children to have, whether to work, where to work, who is to take care of the young and the aged. In the past decade, the family has undergone a transformation—it has become smaller, more diverse and independent of extended kin relationships. While most childbearing and childrearing occur mainly within the institution of the family, recent figures suggest that globally as many as 80 million children are virtually without families. Moreover, it is not clear whether marital unions are becoming more stable or less so in the developing countries since examples of both directions of change can be found.

In countries that have policies to reduce fertility, increasing support has been given to programmes that aim to reduce infant, child and maternal mortality; improve maternal and child health; expand family life and sex education; and delay the age of marriage and family formation. These programmes have been considered important determinants for fertility decline. Their importance can be appreciated if one considers the projected global increase in the number of women and youth by the end of the century. The number of women of reproductive age is projected to increase from 777 million in 1980 to 1,258 million in 2000; and the youth from 657 million to 888 million.

Present technological limitations in fertility regulation methods call for increased investment in the continuing search for a safe, reversible, economical and acceptable contraceptive. The present methods while generally satisfactory and widely accepted are not free from reports of ill effects in a small number of users. The support given by governments for bio-medical research is inadequate compared to the needs of research institutions.

It is estimated that perhaps there are presently 500 million couples in the developing countries who are in immediate need of family planning, including natural family planning information and services. While there has been a steady increase in absolute allocations to national family planning programmes, such allocations are only a small proportion of total national budgets. Among the 14 countries for which data are available, for instance, it varies between 0.04 per cent in Thailand to 3.1 per cent in Bangladesh. International assistance to population activities as a whole amounted to $490 million in 1981. Population assistance as a proportion of all development assistance has declined during the 1974-1983 period. It has been estimated that in 1981 per capita population assistance in real terms was only about 83 per cent of what it was in 1979. Though the International Conference on Family Planning in the 1980s (Jakarta, April 1981) called for an increase from an estimated $1 billion to $3 billion annually in overall national and international expenditures for population and family planning programmes, this goal remains unfulfilled.

UNFPA has expended some $441 million in family planning assistance during the period 1969-1983, representing 45 per cent of total UNFPA assistance during this period. Service delivery programmes have accounted for 69 per cent of this total, followed by assistance to training (15 per cent); support communication (9 per cent); and research (7 per cent), including both social and bio-medical research. UNFPA has extended assistance in family planning to 123 countries and territories, who have requested such assistance as part of policies relating both to population growth and to health goals. Directly-funded women's projects by UNFPA

during this period of time totalled about $14.0 million; this figure
does not include projects which have a women's component in
them.

EXCERPTS FROM STATEMENTS

On the matter of fertility transition . . .

• The decline in fertility in many developing countries has been hailed
as the beginning of the third wave of fertility transitions in the world.
The first took place in Western Europe and North America in the 19th
century; the second in Eastern and Southern Europe and Japan after 1945, when fertility rates turned sharply downwards. This downward trend in birth rates marks the end of an unchanging pattern
which has existed for centuries, since sharply rising population growth
rates have been a fact throughout the modern historical era. . . . (15
January 1980)

• While an over-all decline in fertility has been evident for some time,
the reasons for this deceleration are still not fully understood. It
appears that high levels of economic development and industrialization which accompanied the fertility decline in the developed countries are not always necessary for such a decline in the developing
countries. . . .
   The historical experience of developed countries indicates that fertility declines come about only after reductions in mortality have
occurred. Moreover, where the over-all mortality rate has come down
but the rate of infant mortality has not declined proportionately, we
cannot expect so great a reduction in the fertility rate. (28 August
1979)

• Fertility decline is dependent on a host of social, economic and cultural factors which influence a couple's decision about family formation and ideal family size. Reduction of disparities in income and
wealth, the opportunities offered for women to move from traditional occupations to newer occupations, number of years of schooling,
access to public health and medical care, population education aimed
at helping people to make their decisions on the number of children
they wish to have and the availability of the best means to act on
those decisions—all these contribute to a decline in birth rates. (13
June 1983)

• Unemployment and underemployment are among the key socio-
economic problems that have a bearing on fertility. . . . Unemployment has a direct bearing on population growth rates, since women

find it difficult to enter the work force and men are unable to find dignity in their work and security for the future. (10 May 1979)

• Changes can be achieved only if development programmes ensure equality of access to health care facilities and education to everyone in the society, eliminate forms of malnutrition, and reduce social and economic inequality prevailing in the society. (19 June 1979)

• In addition to family planning, factors such as education of women, greater participation of women in non-traditional roles of economic activity, greater access to health care and the subsequent decline in infant and child death rates have all been found to influence the level of birth rates and have played a part in their decline. Given the multiplicity of the factors involved and the complex nature of the interrelationship, it is not possible to isolate the contribution of each of these factors to the decline in birth rates. One should not in these matters pose a question and answer in terms of either/or because life is, after all, based on the balancing of a number of forces. . . .

An improvement in the quality of life is considered essential in bringing about this decline in birth rates in the developing countries. It appears that the most important policy measures which can improve the quality of life are education, especially education of women, and the development of a more accessible health care system leading to a decline in infant and child mortality rates. Data from the World Fertility Survey and from other sources indicate that the number of children born to a married woman declines directly with the level of her education.

The provision of access to and better utilization of health care systems will lead to a decline in infant and child mortality rates, assuring a greater survival rate for children which, in turn, also will result in a decline in birth rates. Herein lies one important population paradox: the higher the mortality rates, the higher the birth rates, which in turn continue to perpetuate higher mortality rates and so on. On the other hand, a lowering of the death rates eventually will result in a lowering of birth rates also. An examination of different developing countries indicates that the levels of social and economic development vary considerably, which are reflected in the uneven changes in the birth rates. . . . (15 January 1980).

• While the causes for the reversal of trends in birth rates are still being debated among population experts, there is no doubt that the spread of family planning, adequate population information and services, education and greater participation of women in non-traditional economic activities, greater access to health care and the subsequent decline in infant mortality have all been found to influence the level of birth rates. (21 July 1980)

- The spread of family planning is an important factor in reducing birth rates. The large-scale acceptance of family planning itself, however, is closely related to an improvement in the living conditions of the people. (27 October 1981)

On the matter of family planning in fertility transition . . .

- . . . decisions affecting population are made not by governments but by millions of individual men and women. In population work, we have discovered that, whatever the technology employed, the most effective programme is one which reaches men and women directly, through the channels they know and understand. Traditional cultures will accept new practices such as modern family planning, if they can be adapted to prevailing values.

  This understanding, which was perhaps first made a reality in population activities, is central to the world in which we live and to the world of the future. From a perception that birth rates must be reduced if society is to survive in any recognizably human way, we have reached a practical approach which recognizes the individuality of our fellow human beings and the importance of individual decisions to our world. (3 May 1981)

- The success of family planning in bringing down the birth rates and harmonizing population growth with the rate of economic growth depends directly upon a country's social and economic development. Measures to spread the practice of family planning can be effective only when a population is prepared for the concept of "conscious parenthood" by social, economic and cultural development. . . . (29 September 1982)

- It has been UNFPA's experience that if the policy adopted is in tune with the needs and aspirations of the people, and if it is promoted in a manner which is in accordance with religious belief and sensitive to cultural values, there need be no hesitation on the part of governments or local administrations in promoting, advising on and supplying the means of voluntary fertility control. (2 December 1982)

- What is new at this time is the recognition that for fertility rates to fall, it is necessary to create the social conditions in which family planning is a real option. The programme thus becomes an integral part of the social development plan. This is important for all countries now struggling to reduce their population growth rates. . . . We should not underestimate the importance of child-spacing to the health of both mothers and children, a factor which makes family planning services an important element of public health policies in addition to their direct effects on birth rates.

China provides an outstanding example of a country which has lowered its birth rate significantly by attention both to the variables which affect fertility decline and to the direct establishment and implementation of family planning services. Indonesia is another example where the decline is accelerating. In both cases, the programmes have succeeded because they have developed novel methods of effective delivery suitable to their own population sizes and local conditions. (2 October 1982)

• The gaps of unmet needs in family planning are two-pronged: between knowledge of a method of fertility regulation and its use and between the desire to curtail reproduction and use of family planning. A major finding with important implications for those of us active in family planning assistance is the large number of currently married, fecund women who do not want more children. In some developing countries the figure is as high as 60 per cent of such women. (7 July 1980)

• Due consideration must be given to factors that may increase the effectiveness and outreach of fertility regulation programmes such as community-based delivery services, greater involvement of women in population programmes, and the exploration of traditional methods and "natural" family planning. (5 January 1983)

• . . . it is important to give priority to the management of family planning programmes. The technology of family planning has improved remarkably in the last twenty years. But . . . there is much more to successful family planning programmes than technology. Programmes must be managed more efficiently and effectively. We must, therefore, endeavour to improve further our organizational and managerial capabilities to reach those couples who, as the World Fertility Survey indicated, are still in need of family planning services. . . .

Our gains and successes thus far have required . . . the flexibility to adapt programmes to a variety of different local mixes of leadership, communication methods, facilities and attitudes. But dynamism and ability to innovate, as we have realized, are not enough. We have to be consistently sensitive to individual feelings and beliefs in addition. Let us be reminded at this point that increasing the scope of our work will require the positive decisions of millions of couples and continuous respect for individual values.

. . . there must be adequate resources for family planning programmes. The developing countries have adequately demonstrated in the past ten years that, with the proper amount of external assistance and an increasing amount of investment on their part in population programmes, they have been able to moderate population growth. The present need to provide adequate food, clothing and shelter for the 4.4 billion inhabitants on this planet underlies many of the structural difficulties the global economy is now facing. The projected addition of 2 billion more people by the turn of the century demands that, compared to other areas of international assistance, population programmes must be of the highest priority. External assistance is vital in specific areas to make national programmes more effective especially now that many of the developing countries have acquired the necessary conceptual, institutional and human resources to implement them comprehensively and effectively. (27 April 1981)

• Experience in population activities over the years has shown us the importance of the impact of new technologies. Modern family planning has made an enormous difference to the lives of men and women all over the world, in the poorest countries as well as the richest, and has played its part in reducing the rate of population growth, for the world's benefit. . . . (3 May 1981)

• There is also a need for better contraceptives than those existing today. Biomedical research on contraceptives suffers from the lack of adequate funding. (28 August 1979)

• Research efforts should be intensified to promote both the adaptation of contraceptive technology to the needs of developing countries and the development of new methods. (18 June 1979)

• Although . . . the field of population is much broader than family planning, family planning is nonetheless essential to assist families in achieving the number and spacing of children that they desire. Thus, close to fifty per cent of all UNFPA funds have been allocated to this important area. In addition to providing support to existing country programmes, the Fund has also made particular efforts at the country, regional and global levels to improve the delivery of services through new approaches. Attention is being directed to primary health care, community-based programmes, and integrated health and family planning programmes. . . . (29 September 1982)

On the matter of the human rights aspects of family planning . . .

• It was a cornerstone of the World Population Plan of Action that men and women have the right freely and responsibly to decide the number and spacing of their children and the right to the information, education and means to do so. It is a principle which demands respect from the practical and the moral standpoint.

By stating this principle, the Plan of Action did not intend to deny governments a part in the population process. On the contrary, it acknowledges governments' responsibility to provide people with the means to make effective decisions on family size. Government interventions to improve health standards, education, employment opportunities and the status of women have considerable effects on decisions about family size and migration. It is equally clear that where these responsibilities are neglected or cannot be fulfilled, the result is damaging both to individual lives and to prospects for balanced development. (17 June 1983)

- The individual right to develop must be based on the fundamental tenet underlying all human rights—the freedom of choice. This is the reason why the World Population Plan of Action provides, above all else, the right of all couples and individuals to decide freely and responsibly the number and spacing of their children and assumes that in the workings of all population policies and programmes whether they are on family planning, migration, urbanization or others, this fundamental tenet is observed.

The United Nations since its founding has always encouraged, supported and protected the observance of human rights universally. The people of this region—the Caribbean—are fortunate, indeed, that their legal systems have been unrelenting in these guarantees but for this protection to continue the following key concepts must be applied in the observance:

1. All human rights and fundamental freedoms are indivisible and interdependent;
2. These rights must be examined not just from the standpoint of the individual country's condition but globally with a view to setting up international standards;
3. The need to incorporate into domestic law the various provisions of human rights already existing in international law and the more complete and rigorous implementation of rights already existing in domestic law; and
4. The recognition that concomitant to these rights are duties that pertain to the community and the necessity to ensure their application to those most vulnerable in the community such as migrants, women, the aged and the disadvantaged.

All material progress and modernizing efforts will come to naught if in the end the fruits of these labours are not meaningful and satisfying to the individual. Each human being must be given all the opportunity to develop his own potential from birth—this is the right to develop. The three factors of population, economic development and human rights must be taken together, in the effort to promote the well-being of both man and society. (26 November 1983)

- It was never in the vision of the signers of the United Nations Charter to achieve peace through the increase of mortality rates. On the contrary, countries have been encouraged where consistent with their policies and within the framework of the Universal Declaration of Human Rights, to moderate fertility rates in the most humane manner possible. (11 June 1982)

- Although the World Population Plan of Action stated that "all couples and individuals have the basic right to decide freely and responsibly the number and spacing of their children and to have the information, education and means to do so", we are a far cry from seeing this recommendation implemented. It is estimated that more than two-thirds of women of childbearing age lack access to modern contraceptive methods. It should be a goal for the 1980s to make this basic human right a reality. (18 June 1979)

On the matter of population and the role and status of women . . .

- An . . . important issue that has . . . come to the fore concerns the role and status of women in society. It is impossible to think of any aspect of life—involving the local community, the nation or the world as a whole—in which women do not have a role to play. If the goals of development are to be achieved and the full promise of the future to be realized, then women must be able to participate fully, equally and responsibly in the tasks that lie ahead. Population and development programmes should enable women to broaden the choices which affect their personal lives and economic activities, and provide them with increasing access to decision-making processes. (21 July 1980)

- The World Population Plan of Action adopted in Bucharest in 1974 and the World Plan of Action adopted at the Mexico World Conference of the International Women's Year in 1975 had one common goal—the full integration of women in the development process. If development is to be considered as total human development rather than just economic growth, then the integration of women should be taken to mean involvement of women in all aspects of the development process. This is indeed the view that has increasingly motivated UNFPA in providing support for projects relating to women, population and development. (15 July 1980)

- The important role of women has been primarily performed within the structure of the family and this includes more than just the satisfaction of the reproductive and biological needs of the individual. The care and education of children, the provision for their emotional security through human understanding and love has been provided by women essentially within the family—an institutional function which has not wholly been replaced by others. The view and understanding of the function of the family within each culture determines to a large extent the form of participation of women in other social and economic activities. In developed countries, as an instance, where economic opportunities have opened up for women to work outside the home, a woman's view of her role in the family determines the time she will spend with her children to give them warmth, guidance, and affection. (22 November 1983)

- The interrelationship between labour and demography of a country also affects the status of women in the society and the success of its programmes to liberate women from their traditional roles. An improvement in the status of women, by providing employment opportunities for them outside of traditional sectors, is considered important also for a decline in fertility rates. There are wide variations in the female participation rates not only between the various regions of the world but even between different income groups within a country itself. When labour participation rates and unemployment are already high among the male labour force, it may prove even more difficult to create a large-scale employment programme for women. It is needless to say that a failure to generate female employment for improving their status will adversely affect not only the fertility level but also the welfare of women and children in our society. (7 December 1981)

- Any discussion on the role of women in population and development cannot be fully understood without discussing the family as an institution, nuclear or extended. (22 November 1983)

- A number of studies have indicated that the level of education, particularly female education, is a determining factor in fertility decline. Studies based on the data collected by the World Fertility Survey . . . reveal that women who had worked at some time since marriage had fewer children compared to those who had never worked. (2 October 1982)

- Special consideration needs to be given to legislation raising the age at marriage as well as measures which would broaden the scope of education and vocational training for girls and to increasing employment opportunities for women. (28 August 1979)

- UNFPA is continuing to strengthen and accelerate its efforts to support population activities which will help women in developing countries expand their opportunities to contribute to their full integration and partnership in development-related programmes. (18 June 1979)

- There are several basic principles that have guided the conceptualization and implementation of the programmes we support. Such programmes, though population-related, should fit within the framework of the over-all development needs and requirements of the country. They should enable women to broaden the choices in their personal lives and economic activities; and finally they should provide them with increasing access to decision-making processes and resources.

  The UNFPA has always accepted the importance of the role of women in population activities. Women constitute 50 per cent of the world population and their full and equal participation in these activities will have a tremendously beneficial impact on the well-being of the entire human race. We realize, however, that women today play a limited role in many national communities, and that if this role is to be strengthened and expanded, we need to focus on eliminating discrimination and removing obstacles to their education, training, employment and career advancement. The examples of Sri Lanka and Kerala (India) show that as these barriers and obstacles are removed and women brought into the mainstream of national life, there is a distinct improvement in the content and pace of development and in the quality of life of the entire community.

  What have all these UNFPA-supported women-related projects accomplished? They have helped to broaden the options available to women in carrying out their reproductive and productive roles; they have promoted their increasing involvement in decision-making at all levels; and they have assisted women, both as individuals and groups, to build up effective contacts and networks within and across national boundaries. (15 July 1980)

On the matter of the family as an institution . . .

- The World Population Plan of Action sees the family as the cornerstone of society. A better understanding and elaboration of the family as an institution, its dynamics and its relationship to fertility, will be required. . . . (5 January 1983)

- Population growth impinges on the family at many points. It is the father and mother who are frustrated in their desire to give a decent life to their children and it is the child who does not get an education if there is pressure on family resources. It is the older children of the family who seek employment in vain, if the unemployment rate goes as high as 30 per cent or more. It is the whole family that does not get basic medical care and other hygienic services where poverty is accentuated by population increase.

In the developing countries, where population growth is more rapid, changes are occurring in the size and structure of the families that demand our attention when we view the family as an institution and an agent of cultural change. Current United Nations figures indicate that the average size of the family, as measured by the number of persons cohabiting in a single household, is slightly above four persons throughout the world—three in the developed and five in the developing countries.

Urbanization and increasing income are causing more single parents to form their own households. In the urban areas of Latin America and the Caribbean one out of five households is now headed by a woman . . . . Declining mortality has made it possible for families to raise most children to maturity, thus providing longer periods of emotional nurturing and personal growth. Universal progress in education and greater diversity in employment opportunities opens different perspectives in the commitment towards the preservation of the family.

Increasing life expectancy has increased the numbers of the elderly and raises again the role of the family in the care of the aged. And for the young and the adolescent, the family and the home are still the best sources of stability and guidance for the habits and attitudes of a lifetime ahead.

These demographic and other social factors continue to transform the family, but, at the same time, underline the continuing importance of the family as a primary determinant of the survival of the children and the fundamental agent of socialization for the generations to come. Most population programmes stress the reproductive functions of the family and rightly so, in the light of the conditions in the developing countries. It would be beneficial . . . , where an attempt is made to focus both on the role of women and the importance of the family as an institution, to transcend this view and examine the assertion of the World Population Plan of Action that the family is the "basic unit of society". This can underline its role as transmitter and harmonizer of personal and social values for the balanced development of the individual within the communities in which they live. The family must be looked upon not just as an institution that affects fertility but as an institution that fosters and harmonizes values and makes decisions on the size of the family consonant with the dignity and freedom of the human person . . . . (22 November 1983)

- In many areas of the developing world, as in the developed world, a trend towards smaller families has become evident and, ignoring minor temporary fluctuations, there is no reason to expect a reversal of this trend in the foreseeable future. (31 October 1979)

On the matter of family size . . .

- Our concern is with the family as much as with the state, and our concern that families should be properly planned according to social and economic circumstances reflects our belief in the importance of the happiness of the individual. We have, therefore, taken no particular view of family size and have instead tried to make sure that decisions are made freely by the parents and that every possible approach to happier, healthier families is explored. This includes research into natural family planning methods as well as programmes which determine motivation towards family planning, such as education, the status of women and of course the health of both mothers and children. (6 September 1981)

- The values which underlie all our societies depend for their survival on recognition of the importance of the individual, whether as worker, parent or child. It is now universally accepted that family size may affect individual development and that there is a fundamental right to choose the size and spacing of the family . . . .

  Awareness is spreading among parents that the future depends on more than the number of children in the family. Parents are concerned about giving their children the very best of which they are capable; more and more are realizing that increasing the size of the family may decrease the quality of what is available for each child. (2 December 1982)

ISSUES FOR THE FUTURE: FERTILITY, STATUS OF WOMEN AND THE FAMILY

In the further implementation of the World Population Plan of Action in the areas of fertility and the family, attention may be given to the following programmatic issues:

- The importance of the fundamental right of all couples and individuals to decide freely and responsibly the number and spacing of their children as the guiding principle in all population policies and programmes affecting fertility and the family;

- The designing of family planning programmes that take into account cultural values and the social conditions;

- The need, because of the global awareness and increased concern of developing countries with the consequences of high fertility rates, for access to all effective and safe methods of family planning, including natural family planning; and for family planning education and effective delivery of services, particularly in the rural areas, with as much community and non-governmental organization involvement as possible in countries that have family planning programmes;

- The requirement of adequate family life and sex education for adolescents in accordance with the prevailing cultural values in each country;

- The need for social and operational research to ensure that the perspectives of users of contraceptives are taken into account in order to increase the acceptability and effectiveness of family planning programmes;

- The necessity for increased resources for biomedical research in human reproduction to improve the safety and effectiveness of existing family planning methods and to respond to the problems of infertility and sub-fertility;

- The observance of internationally recognized human rights in the development and implementation of incentives and disincentives in family planning and in the implementation of family planning programmes;

- The improvement of the status of women and their full integration in society on an equal basis with men and attention to the significance of the mean age of marriage and the delay in the beginning of childbearing in population policies and programmes;

- The role of the family as the basic unit of society and the primary socializing institution and transmitter of social norms in addition to its relation to fertility; and within the institution, the active involvement of men in all areas of family responsibility;

- The more comprehensive access of all couples and individuals to the necessary education, information and services about population policies and programmes within the demographic goals of countries;

- The setting of quantitative targets for fertility levels and operational targets for implementing family planning programmes in countries that have such programmes;

- The urgent need for increased resources committed to population programmes in countries in order to respond to unmet needs especially in family planning services; and the role of international population assistance agencies, particularly the United Nations Fund for Population Activities, in support of national population programmes.

Chapter III

MORBIDITY AND MORTALITY

INTRODUCTION

A reduction in mortality and an increase in life expectancy of a population are objectives shared by all nations. Mortality rate is generally a good indicator of the level of socio-economic development of a country and of the degree of access to health care by its population. Differences in mortality levels between regions within countries and between different groups of populations constitute a basis on which to institute special health, population and development programmes designed to eliminate such differences.

A refined measure of mortality, which is not influenced by age distribution, is life expectancy at birth. For the world as a whole, life expectancy rose from 45.8 years during the period 1950-1955 to 58.9 years during the period 1980-1985. Though life expectancy in developing countries rose at a higher annual rate, there is still a wide discrepancy between developed and developing countries. Life expectancy at birth in the developed countries is estimated at 73.0 years during the period 1980-1985, whereas in the developing countries it is estimated at 56.6 for the same period.

Life expectancy in the developed countries is not only longer than in developing countries, it does not, in fact, vary much among countries within this group. There is considerable variation, on the other hand, between and among developing countries and regions.

Although average life expectancy in the developed countries reached unprecedented high levels in 1980, four of the 23 countries expressing a view on this matter in response to the United Nations Fifth Population Inquiry still considered their levels unacceptable under their prevailing economic and social circumstances.

On the other hand, among the 77 developing countries responding to the Fifth Inquiry, 56 countries or about 73 per cent considered their level of life expectancy unacceptable even in their prevailing economic and social circumstances. By far, the region with the largest number of countries viewing their mortality levels as unacceptable (31 out of 36) is Africa, followed by Asia and the Pacific, Latin America and the Caribbean, and the Middle East and Mediterranean.

In 1974, the World Population Plan of Action specified precise targets for life expectancy. The Plan called for a minimum life expectancy at birth of 50 years by 1985 for countries with the highest mortality levels, and an increase in average life expectancy to 62 years by 1985 and to 74 by the end of the century for the world as a whole.

Ten years later, it is clear that these targets have not been met. The goal of life expectancy of at least 62 years by 1985 has fallen short of the target by 5 years. Indeed there are still 40 countries—30 in Africa and 10 in South and West Asia—in which life expectancy at birth continues to be less than 50 years.

One of the targets of the World Population Plan of Action specified that "countries with the highest mortality levels should aim by 1985 to have . . . an infant mortality rate of less than 120 per thousand live births" (paragraph 23).

Unfortunately, while infant mortality rates have dropped in virtually all regions of the developing world, the goal set forth in the Plan of Action has not yet been met in all countries with the highest mortality levels.

In fact, the disparity in the average level of infant mortality rates between developed and developing countries is extremely wide—17.0 infant deaths per 1000 live births in developed countries as opposed to 92.0 infant deaths per l000 live births in developing countries. While infant mortality is expected to decline from 133.0 to 110.0 in Africa during the period l974-l984 and from 124.0 to 103.0 in South and West Asia during the same period, the Plan of Action goal will remain unfulfilled in some 26 countries in Africa and Asia.

In association with high mortality, the developing countries also exhibit wide mortality differentials across rural-urban residence, socio-economic groups and the various age-sex categories. Recognizing this as an important problem in social equity, many countries have identified special target groups in their health and development plans. According to the findings of the Fifth Population Inquiry, for instance, among the 77 countries expressing a view on this subject matter, 65 per cent had identified infants, 44 per cent identified children under five years of age, 30 per cent identified mothers, 16 per cent identified rural population and 13 per cent identified low income and other underprivileged groups as special targets for mortality reduction.

The key to a better understanding of the determinants of this high mortality and its wide differentials, which could lead to the formulation of policies and programmes to reduce them, is the pattern in the causes of death. Unfortunately, accurate data on this matter are generally unavailable. However, it is clear that a large majority of deaths in these countries is due to infectious, parasitic and respiratory diseases, the underlying causes of which are generally malnutrition, unhealthy sanitary conditions and contaminated water. The problem of malnutrition, while being common to all ages and both sexes because of pervasive poverty, is particularly acute among children and mothers. Estimates indicate that about one-half of non-pregnant and nearly two-thirds of pregnant women in developing countries (excluding China) suffer from nutritional anaemia.

The problem of malnutrition among infants, children and mothers becomes compounded when accompanied by frequent childbearing and short birth intervals. Studies have shown that those approaches that incorporate elements of nutrition, family planning and a fostering of breastfeeding practices have helped to improve infant, child and maternal health. Additionally, when integrated programmes of maternal/child health and family planning have been undertaken along with other socio-economic and health strategies, there has been a reduction of infant, child and maternal mortality, as well as a decline in fertility.

The World Population Plan of Action recommended that specific interventions designed to reduce mortality and morbidity should be integrated within a comprehensive development strategy and supplemented by a wide range of mutually supporting social policy measures. The various interventions used thus far include: immunization schemes, nutritional efforts, birth-spacing and other maternal and child health activities, environmental health programmes, disease prevention and control strategies, advocacy of healthier lifestyles and increased availability of curative medical technology and general social and economic development.

It is clear that the health sector alone cannot solve all the problems of morbidity and mortality. Progress in this area calls for well co-ordinated, better-managed and locally-adapted programmes. Experience has also shown that active participation of the community and the realization by individuals that premature death and ill health can be overcome have led to better programme success.

The willingness of the developing countries to undertake specific activities to reduce mortality and morbidity as evidenced by the responses to the Fifth Population Inquiry helps to identify strategies and appropriate health technologies to solve their problems. In this regard, an integrated multisectoral health care approach with the full participation of the community and the family needs to be further strengthened.

While the health problems and determinants of mortality in the developed countries are different from those of developing countries, there is a growing consensus that many of the most serious health problems in the developed countries could perhaps be reduced by changes in personal health practices and lifestyles.

One of the most crucial elements in the success of activities aimed at improving health and reducing mortality, particularly infant and child mortality, appears to be the level of education of mothers. Strong differentials exist by educational level of the mother in the utilization of health care, in the practice of family planning, in the physical and mental development of children and in community development. In view of the fact that a majority of women over 15 years of age in the developing countries—53.3 per cent—are not literate, it is extremely important to foster mass education programmes for women and girls.

Improvement of health is an important activity in developing countries. While health expenditures as a percentage of central government expenditures vary between 0.7 per cent and 8.1 per cent, it is estimated that approximately $75 billion annually is spent by the public sector and by private individuals on health care in the developing countries. Additionally, external assistance to family planning, water supply, sanitation and nutrition is estimated at about $1.1 billion. While this amount appears to be considerable, it is generally agreed that there is an urgent need to modify the pattern of health expenditure and to devote a larger share of national budgets to the health sector. Since the health problems of developing countries at the present time are characterized more by infectious, parasitic and respiratory disease, a shift towards supporting activities related to primary health care and simple health technologies and a shift away from sophisticated, hospital-based health care are considered important.

UNFPA assistance to programmes relating to mortality and health reflects its particular institutional perspective on mortality, that is, basically as regards its mutual relationships with patterns of fertility. Thus, much of UNFPA support for family planning service delivery, as well as support communication and training is integrated into maternal and child health care programmes, which often also include components of nutrition, immunization and health education. Facilitating this integrated approach, recipients of training in family planning delivery are often nurse/midwives or traditional birth attendants.

EXCERPTS FROM STATEMENTS

On the matter of mortality . . .

- A large number of developing countries still suffer from widespread infectious and parasitic diseases, poor health and malnutrition which result in high rates of infant mortality and lower life expectancy. These conditions have adversely affected the productivity of the working population. (28 August 1979)

- Apart from avoiding countless personal tragedies and the needless waste of human life, lowering infant mortality has a long-term effect on birth rates. Low rates of maternal mortality are an equally essential basic aim of population and development programmes. In both cases, spacing childbirth has a beneficial effect, allowing children the care they need in early life and permitting mothers to recover fully from the effects of pregnancy and birth. (20 September 1982)

- There is, of course, a clear and substantial link between malnutrition, childhood disease and infant and child mortality. Nutrition programmes can go some way towards increasing the resistance of children to disease, but here again studies show that the mother's level of education and her contribution to family income may have a crucial effect on the nutritional status of her children.

  For the health and well-being of the entire community, public health measures such as clean water and sanitation are, of course, essential. When these are combined with improved access to medical care, infant and child mortality rates decline rapidly. Maternal mortality rates also improve under these conditions. We should not underestimate the importance of child-spacing to the health of both mothers and children, a factor which makes family planning services an important element of public health policies in addition to their direct effects on birth rates. (2 October 1982)

- There are well-established links between patterns of health and population growth. In most of the countries for which there are reliable figures, a fall in birth rates follows a decline in rates of mortality. It is particularly important to reduce infant mortality both as an end in itself and because, according to the evidence of the World Fertility Survey, the loss of a child shortens the interval between births. The result in many cases is a larger family.

  Loss of their children and frequent pregnancies seriously damage the health and lives of mothers. Life expectancy among women of child-bearing age in developing countries is significantly less than that of men. The hazards of childbirth account for much of the difference.

  The circumstances in which a child is born help determine its future. In some developing countries, deaths before the age of five account for as much as half of total mortality. A high proportion of these deaths are the result of infectious or parasitic diseases, which thrive in unsanitary and overcrowded living conditions, the inevitable accompaniments of poverty. Disease is made more dangerous by malnutrition, which increases vulnerability and decreases the ability to recover and is typically found among the very poor.

  A considerable improvement can be made by spreading awareness of the causes of disease and helping to eliminate them. It has been shown that the children of uneducated mothers, in other words those least likely to know about the importance of nutrition and hygiene, are twice as likely to die in infancy as the children of literate mothers.

  The chances of survival of a child born within two years of an older sibling are far worse than those born after an interval of four years or more. Child-spacing by the use of contraceptives or other means is a vital part of infant and maternal health programmes.

In those countries which have registered the most rapid declines in infant mortality, their success has been accompanied by a drastic reduction in parasitic and infectious diseases, by improvements in maternal and infant resistance to disease through adequate diet and by the introduction of child-spacing through modern family planning methods. (26 September 1983)

On the matter of health . . .

- The most important single element in bringing down mortality is access to health care. The poor, and especially the rural poor, have less access to health services and are more susceptible to disease than the better-off or urban residents. Lasting improvement in mortality rates demands a structure for the prevention and cure of disease which reaches every section of society, and particularly the rural areas where the vast majority of the developing world's people live.

  Over the long run, the cost of health networks is one of the most effective investments a country can make. (26 September 1983)

- The cost of health networks, including population services, initially appears high, because it entails setting up training systems, with the physical and personnel inputs which this demands, and extensive supervision once training is complete. But investment in human resources has definite advantages, both because the resources are largely found within national borders and because it is a double investment—first, in improving the quality of the services supplied, and secondly, in broadening the range of skills available among the population as a whole. (31 May 1983)

- In the present and likely future atmosphere of limited resources and hard choices, developing countries' governments and those who work with them have a responsibility to make the most effective use of the resources available. Better health and lower mortality have a high claim to consideration as development priorities, both for themselves and for their beneficial effects on many other aspects of development. Not least among these is population growth. (26 September 1983)

- Investment in human resources is, over the long run, one of the most effective a country can make, but returns are found over the long term rather than the short term. We are finding in health, as we have found in family planning, that we should not seek short cuts; the steady building of an effective health service is part of the process of building the nation's capacity for development. (31 May 1983)

ISSUES FOR THE FUTURE:
MORBIDITY AND MORTALITY

In the further implementation of the World Population Plan of Action in the areas of mortality, morbidity and health policy, attention may be given to the following programmatic issues:

- The setting of more realistic targets for lowering infant and maternal mortality and increasing life expectancy rates in view of the failure of many developing countries to attain the targets set by the World Population Plan of Action;

- The sustained and vigorous efforts by governments to reduce mortality levels and differentials in countries and to improve the health of all sectors of the population through policies and programmes designed to encourage individuals and families to assume greater responsibility for their health; improvement of management and coordination of the work of all health-related agencies and increased involvement of the community and non-governmental organizations in the planning, implementation and evaluation of health programmes;

- The reduction of maternal morbidity and mortality through improved perinatal care and nutritional programmes for mothers and an increased role for family planning as a basic health measure in all maternal and child health programmes;

- The importance of breast-feeding and its effects on increasing birth intervals and its nutritional benefits to infants;

- The priority in primary health care programmes of maternal and child health programmes including birth spacing and the appropriate health technologies within them to reduce maternal and infant mortality and increase child survival, especially in developing countries;

- The need for preventive action programmes to reduce premature deaths of adults through excessive consumption of tobacco, alcohol and other drugs and the need for information on the effects of these substances on the health of individuals;

- The relationship between the level of education of women and the survival and health of children and the importance of mass education programmes for women and girls in countries where illiteracy is high;

- The need for increased resource allocations to health programmes to eliminate inequalities in access to health care and social services particularly in rural areas, and the role of international population assistance in support of national health programmes intended to reduce mortality and morbidity levels of the population.

Chapter IV

POPULATION DISTRIBUTION, INTERNAL AND INTERNATIONAL MIGRATION

INTRODUCTION

Population distribution has emerged as an important concern in many developing countries since the 1974 World Population Conference. There are many reasons for this concern, but the critical ones are the high rates of population growth, slow economic growth rates, wide interregional disparities in income and levels of living, differences in the degree of exploitation of natural resources and adverse effects on the environment. Because of these factors, the spatial distribution of population in a number of developing countries is generating forces which conflict with optimal patterns of development and the equitable distribution of the benefits of such development. Though regional planning is an important discipline in itself, the full integration of population distribution policies with regional planning has yet to take place. Of the 109 countries responding to the United Nations Fifth Population Inquiry, 77 countries desired changes in their population distribution, of which 64 were developing countries.

In 1950, 29 per cent of the world population lived in urban areas; the corresponding figures for the developed and developing countries were 53 per cent and 17 per cent. By 1980, 41 per cent of the world population lived in urban areas, and the corresponding figures for the developed and developing countries were 71 per cent and 31 per cent. These percentages, however, conceal some important structural changes that have occurred during this period. In 1950, urban dwellers constituted 444 million in the developed countries compared to only 287 million in the developing countries, whereas by 1980, over 1 billion persons were urban dwellers in the developing countries compared to slightly over 800 million in the developed countries. This shift in the proportions of urban population was naturally the result of differential urban growth rates of population in the developing and developed countries. Since 1950, average annual urban growth rates of population have remained much higher in the developing countries than in the developed countries. In addition, the disparities between the growth rates have widened over time even though the annual average growth rates have declined. The average annual urban growth rate in the developing countries during the period 1950-1960 was slightly less than twice the corresponding growth rate for the developed countries, but for the period 1980-1985, it was nearly three times that and by the year 2000, the annual average urban growth rate in the developing countries is projected to be nearly four times the urban growth rate in the developed countries. By the year 2000, the urban population in the developing countries will outnumber those in the developed countries by a ratio of 2 to 1 which implies that over 2 billion persons will be living in urban areas of the developing countries compared to 1 billion for the developed countries. Thus, in the year 2000, half of the world population will be living in urban areas; while in the case of developed countries four-fifths will be dwelling in urban areas, the percentage for the developing countries will be about 44 per cent.

These trends in urbanization by themselves provide formidable challenges to the developing countries, but they are in addition compounded by the growth of primate cities and metropolitan centres. In 1950, there were seven metropolitan cities with populations exceeding 5 million each, with Greater Buenos Aires and Shanghai the only such cities in developing countries. At present, there are 29 such metropolitan cities, 19 of which are in developing countries. The projections indicate that there may be 59 agglomerations by the end of the century with 47 of them in the developing countries. This has naturally aroused the concern of many governments. According to the United Nations Fifth Population Inquiry, 55 governments (of which 47 are developing country governments) perceive the rate of growth of the largest metropolitan areas in their countries to be too high and 47 governments desired to decrease in-migration to such areas.

Population distribution policies can be successful if one understands the basic factors underlying such autonomous movements of population and then develop appropriate measures to modify these trends. In developing such policies, it is essential to compare the private costs and benefits against the social costs and benefits. In many countries, natural increase accounts for more than one-half of urban growth, the rest being accounted for by in-migration, especially from rural areas. A number of factors lie behind the rural migration in the developing countries, the principal cause being the rate of population growth itself. Land is the principal source of livelihood in the rural areas, and it has become scarce, resulting in smaller plots of ownership and the growth of landless agricultural labourers. Most rural migrants from the lowest income groups often fail to secure productive employment in the urban areas, but they still find that they are better off than before by remaining a part of the informal labour sector in the urban areas. Rural areas lack not only sufficient means for income-producing avenues but also many public services such as educational and health facilities.

The success of population distribution policies, therefore, will depend on the extent of its integration with the over-all development policy and especially with the strategy of rural development. If rural development programmes are designed to increase the welfare of the masses of rural people, it will ultimately succeed in encouraging the population to remain in rural areas and stem the flow of people to metropolitan centres.

Excessive movement of population towards the metropolitan centres can be curbed only if alternative urban centres are developed. It is important to devise employment programmes and social schemes to attract persons to medium and small towns. Similarly, special development schemes will need to be devised to resettle people in sparsely populated areas.

At the international level, the questions on population distribution are concerned with three important aspects: (1) the nature and volume of international migration; (2) protection of human rights of migrants and (3) refugee questions.

The 1970s saw important changes in the migration flows between countries. Several European countries which had promoted immigration of workers to offset their labour shortages virtually stopped the inflow of migrant workers. On the other hand, migration to oil-rich Middle Eastern countries rose substantially during the period. Also, during the same period, the traditional immigration countries such as Canada, Australia, and New Zealand, altered their immigration policies to achieve a better balance between their labour requirements and economic conditions. As regards permanent settlers, with the exception of the United States, the intake of migrants has been reduced in all the main immigration countries since 1975 and the tendency is either towards stabilization or decline in the total numbers. Most of the permanent migrants originate in developing countries and the movement has become a "north-south" movement.

Labour migration, on the other hand, constitutes the major component of international migration since the Second World War. In Europe, nearly three-fourths of the 6.6 million foreign workers in 1973 came from outside the European Economic Community. Since 1973-1974, there have been extreme reductions in certain traditional flows of workers and in a few European countries some repatriation of foreign workers has taken place.

The Middle East is another area where the pattern of international migration has drastically changed. During the 1950s and 1960s, long-term or permanent inter-Arab migration was dominant. Since the beginning of the 1970s, however, in-migration of temporary workers from outside of the Arab region has assumed great importance. Expatriate workers constitute nearly a third of the total work force in the eight major oil-exporting countries of the region.

However, the tightening of the opportunities open for migration and the lack of employment opportunities in developing countries has resulted in an unprecedented rise in undocumented migration. The Intergovernmental Committee for Migration estimates that there are between four and five million undocumented migrants in North America. For Latin America, estimates vary from two to three million, in Europe, perhaps a million and a half. In the Middle East, there may be between 350,000 and 500,000. Africa and Asia may have between them more than one million undocumented migrants. Thus, it is a problem faced by every continent, and is not confined to developed countries alone.

The total numbers involved in international migration, both documented and undocumented, form a significant proportion of the work force in a number of recipient countries and this has become an area of active policy concern. Illegal migration will probably form a greater proportion of future international migration flows as more restrictions are placed on intercountry migration. Therefore, it is important to consider illegal movements as a type of labour migration and to agree on an international code of conduct with respect to the rights and obligations of individuals and countries and incorporate measures to protect the human rights of migrants.

A third aspect of international migration is the movement of refugees across national borders. Since the First World War, more than half of all international migration has been accounted for by refugee movements. At the beginning of 1981, the number of refugees was estimated at nearly 14 million; in Africa alone, refugees probably number 6 million. Refugee movements in recent times have often been the result of political changes and often involve large numbers of ethnically and culturally homogeneous groups. They are often illiterate and unskilled rural people who lack the means of starting their own economic life in a new setting. International assistance can only be of a temporary nature and unless recipient countries develop programmes to integrate them into their own economies, they are bound to remain on the periphery.

Finally, the success of population distribution policies depends on the ability to integrate them with other population and development policies and programmes, as envisaged in the Rome Declaration on the Urban Future. For this purpose, the Rome Declaration has specifically pointed out three elements:

1. the formulation of comprehensive national population policies;

2. policies for balanced development, and

3. policies for the improvement of urban areas.

National population policies should specify national and subnational goals on population growth rates, levels of fertility and mortality rates and on rural-urban distribution of population. Policies for balanced development should aim to develop a balanced pattern of urban settlements, i.e., small, intermediate and large cities, reduction of disparities between rural and urban areas and provision of access to all social services in rural areas. Finally, policies for the improvement of urban areas should develop special programmes for the vulnerable groups of the urban sector and provide access to urban social services for these groups.

As part of continuing efforts to increase awareness of the causes and consequences of population phenomena, and to facilitate the exchange of experience in dealing with these issues, in 1980 UNFPA sponsored the International Conference on Population and the Urban Future in Rome, Italy. The Conference was attended by mayors, administrators, and planners from 41 cities whose populations are projected to be 5 million or more by the year 2000, as well as by national planners from the 31 countries where those cities are located.

Also in the field of population distribution and migration, UNFPA has funded a number of studies, as for instance those being undertaken in Indonesia, Malaysia, the Philippines and Thailand under the auspices of the Association of South East Asian Nations. This policy-oriented research is concerned with rural development and population distribution. Pakistan has received UNFPA support to investigate migration, urbanization and development in that country, while Senegal is utilizing the results of UNFPA-supported research on labour force migration in its development planning activities.

EXCERPTS FROM STATEMENTS

On the matter of migration . . .

• Measures to influence and direct migratory movements and to improve population distribution to conform with economic opportunities should be supported. This is an area of great concern to many countries but little attention has been given so far to develop effective policies and programmes that take into account local conditions and motivations for such population movements. (18 June 1979)

• The spatial distribution of population is becoming a matter of increasing concern to many countries. Such phenomena as rural overpopulation in relation to the available agricultural land, urban sprawls, open unemployment in the cities and underemployment in the countryside are manifestations of unbalanced population distribution and unfulfilled expectations. There are equally problematical issues in international labour migration and the plight of the refugees. How, therefore, can the underlying causes of these problems which are rooted in the economic and social structures of society, be remedied? And how can countries initiate action towards a more balanced redistribution of population within their national boundaries? (28 August 1979)

- In the past few years, more and more countries have indicated a special interest in the field of population distribution. . . . They are increasingly concerned with the redistribution of population in a planned manner, particularly from congested urban areas to rural areas for more balanced spatial distribution of human resources. . . . Although international migration has benefitted a number of countries, especially in South Asia, by providing valuable foreign exchange in the form of foreign remittances, it should be remembered that most of this migration is of a temporary nature. Migration of this kind raises a number of issues which need international agreements and solutions. At the same time, it is essential to protect the human rights of such immigrants. When such migrants return to their homeland, they may face problems of resettlement. In the next decades, these problems will undoubtedly become very important. (19 May 1980)

- There is a further concern in Africa about the problems of the spatial distribution of population on this continent. The problems of refugees and the question of how to deal with them are issues of population distribution which encompass rural-urban migration, unbalanced distribution of population in relation to available resources, unemployment, underemployment and excessive growth of urban centres. While this is not particularly serious, it is best at this time to look at their consequences for the future. (6 July 1981)

- Our agenda for the future may include, as appropriate . . . research on the social and economic consequences of rural-to-urban migration and the implications for the older population of such migration. . . . (27 July 1982)

- Countries which wish to develop policies on voluntary migration should be assisted in order to enable them to bring about a balanced population distribution. (31 October 1979)

- Taken altogether, the vast and largely uncounted flows of people across national borders amount to one of the most important changes in the population scene in the last decade. Unfortunate recent cases, where workers were welcomed by labour-shortage countries in times of expansion, only to be rejected abruptly when foreign labour was no longer needed, warn of an international problem in the making. The time has come, not only for systematic research into the volume and the nature of migration, voluntary and involuntary, but for some form of international agreement which will protect both the territorial and economic integrity of sovereign states and the human rights of individual migrants and their families. (21 March 1983)

- The influx of immigrants, short- and long-term, legal and illegal, creates particular problems for industrialized countries. Most immigrants come from the developing world, and while there is an increasing flow to the oil-producing developing countries, most go to the industrialized. Some go for settlement, but a growing number intend to stay for a short time, until they have saved or sent home enough to return. These workers tend not to become part of the social fabric of their host country and sometimes their position and that of the host country become unduly difficult as a result.

    A significant minority of immigrants have no proper documents. Many of them make a valuable contribution to the economic life of their host country, but remain in a twilight zone out of the sight of censuses and registration, and consequently of policy-makers. Social programmes cannot include them, and their contribution to the tax base remains unrealized. Nevertheless, they have rights and responsibilities. Equally, host country governments have responsibilities as well as rights regarding those within their borders, whether legally or illegally. Sending countries too have international obligations and a say in the future of their nationals. (6 October 1983)

- Little effective research has yet been done into the effects of this sort of migration either on the sending or on the receiving countries. As the flow of people and money increases, better understanding will become essential. (20 September 1982)

- Another type of migration which has become an international issue is the problem of refugees from various countries. Large-scale migration of population for political reasons is becoming commonplace in the world today, and there is an increasing need for mechanisms to take care of their problems. Many countries to which refugees first flee are unable to handle them. This is fast becoming an important international population issue and its solution will require the assistance of many international and national agencies. (19 May 1980)

- It will be of prime importance to discuss these issues and to arrive at an international convention protecting the rights of individuals while safeguarding the interests of governments and establishing the responsibilities of both host and sending countries. (6 October 1983)

On the matter of urbanization . . .

• The greatest impact of population growth between now and 2000 will be reflected in the growth of urbanization, created not only by the natural increase in urban population but largely contributed to by massive migrations of population to these areas in search of employment. The projected rates of growth of cities indicate that some are likely to reach proportions which are totally unfamiliar to town planners. There is not only an explosion of population in these areas but at the same time they are also experiencing an implosion. The city centres are unable to handle such large numbers of people and urban facilities are on the verge of collapse in some of these urban areas. In fact, the problems created by the failure of the transportation systems, the cost of housing and higher wage costs are leading to a relocation of offices and firms away from such city centres, which will in turn only increase the difficulties already faced by such areas. (15 January 1980)

• The limited opportunity for employment and for earning one's living in the poor rural areas has resulted in massive movements of population to large metropolitan areas and urban centres in these countries. Such movements are stimulated by the fact that most of the investments being undertaken in these countries are largely confined to such urban areas and, therefore, are fuelled by expectations of securing employment and income. . . .

 In the past, in a number of instances, urbanization was considered the handmaiden of industrialization, and this enabled industries to reap the benefits of economies of scale. But, at present, urbanization in many developing countries is a movement by itself, unaccompanied by industrialization and is already resulting in the proliferation of slums and shanty towns and in diseconomies rather than economies of scale. This has led to a major increase in anti-social activities and to making our cities insecure, both for life and property. (13 May 1980)

• The growth of urbanization in the less developed countries reflects as much the lack of rural development as the growth of industry and employment in the urban sector. Thus, the problems of urban future and metropolitan growth in the less developed countries cannot be divorced from the issues of total development of the country. (19 May 1980)

• In most countries, cities enjoy some measure of autonomy and planners have been able to fashion and implement policies and programmes within national constraints and within over-all national planning. Demographic factors continuously affect and shape the nature and characteristics of cities. But planners have no control over the growth, size and distribution of population between rural and urban areas within their own countries. Therefore, an appreciation of the demographic process in operation within cities and of its relationship with regional and national population trends will help to understand some of the problems that need to be faced as a result of rapid urbanization. . . .

This expected growth of urban population in the less developed countries not only reflects the natural increase in urban population but also significant migrations of population in search of employment to these areas. The process of urbanization now taking place in the less developed countries partly represents a new phenomenon compared to the earlier phase of growth of cities. The movement of population to the cities in the less developed countries is a result of a "push" factor as well as a "pull" factor. The nature and composition of this migration has intensified such problems as the proliferation of slums in many cities of the less developed countries. (1 September 1980)

- Most of the migrants to the cities are adult male labourers and the pressure on employment generation, therefore, is much greater. It is also worth noting that both the financial and social costs of generating a unit of employment in the urban areas are often several times larger than the comparable costs of generating a unit of employment in the rural sector. (7 December 1981)

- It is widely recognized now that national policies and programmes especially geared to the managing of problems of crowded cities and which reverse the flow of population, not by compulsion but by developing "growth poles", are a necessity to deal with these problems of metropolitan growth. The development of underpopulated regions by providing social overhead facilities such as education, health, transportation, housing, water, irrigation and, above all, employment opportunities to attract settlers is becoming an important policy instrument to divert the influx from the metropolitan centres. However, this policy has failed to "take off" due to the high cost of investment involved. (15 January 1980)

- Part of the migration to cities is caused by the lack of social services and living opportunities in rural areas. The establishment of health, educational and recreational facilities in the rural areas and measures to reduce the disparities in income and levels of living between the two areas are important ingredients of policies devised to stem the tide of urbanization. This ongoing process is the product of industrialization, economic development and technological changes in agriculture, transportation and communication systems. But effective population and development policies can make this process orderly, less expensive and harmonious with the process of total societal development. These policies may even enable the reversal of some earlier trends in urbanization to take place by promoting the growth of smaller cities, the development of satellite towns to reduce population pressures on super cities and the development of rural areas which may promote some movement of population back from cities to rural areas. . . .

The problem of urbanization is but one aspect of the problem of population redistribution. Populations tend to move to areas where resources and jobs seem to be available. Therefore, national policy can play an important role in reducing the growth of cities by encouraging a policy of decentralized investment, and the geographical redistribution of employment opportunities, so that excessive concentrations of population can be avoided.

The implications of managing cities of such giant size will indeed be staggering when we consider the impact on demand for urban services and resources by such unprecedentedly large numbers of people. It has been estimated that during the next two decades over 600 million people will be added to the labour force in the less developed countries alone, and most of these will be flocking to the cities in search of jobs. Urban unemployment is already a serious problem in many cities today, as we know, and a further increase will intensify the problems of poverty.

The consequences of the interrelationships between population growth and the urban environment have received considerable attention in recent years. Pollution and degradation of the environment are closely related to concentration of industries, high density of automobiles and congested living conditions. While some measures have been in operation to monitor and reduce levels of pollution in the metropolitan areas of the more developed countries, few such measures have been initiated in the cities of the less developed countries.

In the past, the process of urbanization was stimulated by the availability of low-cost energy. However, the soaring cost of energy in recent years has made living in urban areas not only more expensive but has also increased the social burdens of supporting the growing large populations in the cities. Any national policy to optimize energy utilization should consider the energy costs involved in alternative urbanization policies.

Demographic factors appear to be the crucial determinants of the future course of urbanization. However, despite increasing recognition of these factors, the integration of population issues with over-all development policy by taking into account their impact on urbanization is still very inadequate. There is an urgent need to incorporate systematically these factors into urban planning and programming. But, such programming is hampered primarily by the inadequacy of relevant demographic data, especially in the less developed countries. It is also true that most city governments are not adequately staffed with the experts needed to collect, analyze and incorporate such demographic data into the urban planning process.

The Fund's own analysis of the demographic aspects of urbanization and their implications for the urban future makes it clear that these questions cannot be divorced from either regional or national policies or from issues of population and development. As we know, cities are particularly vulnerable to the vicissitudes of economic prosperity or crisis in any nation. They are the mirror image of successes or frustrations of national development, and their problems represent in microcosm the larger problems of the nation itself. (1 September 1980)

- The projected increases in population as a whole and in urban numbers in particular are not inevitable. We are learning something about the dynamics of societies in a phase of rapid growth. . . . Purposeful interventions have helped to bring down death rates. Experience in many countries shows that there may be equally effective interventions to bring down birth rates and influence the rate and direction of population movements.

  One such intervention is the redirection of urban growth, either to the countryside or to smaller cities. Our societies, though they may be powered by the cities, draw much of their strength from the land. The creation of secure and productive sources of income for rural populations, and the establishment of a network of services and support systems in the rural areas, can help to relieve pressure on the cities, and thus reduce the risk of breakdown of economic and political systems. The development of smaller urban centres has in many cases not only stimulated rural sector activity but simultaneously established alternatives for urban development. (2 December 1982)

- Research has shown that the movement to the cities is not a once-for-all permanent shift on the part of the migrants. Depending on the circumstances of the country, movements may be seasonal or dependent on age, marital status or economic conditions. In some developing countries, a form of "rural urbanization" is taking place, where village dwellers commute daily or weekly to work in the city. While the resident population of the city centre remains roughly the same, that of the semi-urban area around it increases dramatically.

There is a discernible movement towards development of the medium city, which in the view of some planners and economists can stimulate development of both urban and rural areas. While large enough to create the vital interactions which make urban centres the powerhouses of development, the medium city does not draw off skilled and educated people from the rural areas for permanent settlement, but rather supplies them with the inputs which will help the development of agriculture and rural-based industry. (21 March 1983)

- It is true that the problems of rapid urbanization have also generated a number of political issues, but these are often specific to each country, and therefore are best discussed in national forums. There is further an urgency to anticipate and design measures to cope with the emerging urban problems of the year 2000. Otherwise the sheer magnitude of these problems is likely to overwhelm us all, leading to inaction and the eventual breakdown of cities themselves. If we judiciously use our faculties of foresight and take steps to begin dealing with these problems, it may still be possible to steer the cities on a course of harmonious development. (1 September 1980)

- The Rome Declaration, adopted by the International Conference on Population and the Urban Future by consensus, emphasizes the close interrelationship between metropolitan planning and management on the one hand and national planning on the other. In order to meet the twin objectives of "managed population growth and planned urbanization", the Declaration calls for the formulation of comprehensive national population policies by all countries by 1985, policies for balanced rural-urban development, and policies for improvement of urban areas. (3 October 1980)

ISSUES FOR THE FUTURE: POPULATION DISTRIBUTION, INTERNAL AND INTERNATIONAL MIGRATION

In the further implementation of the World Population Plan of Action in the areas of population distribution and migration, attention may be given to the following programmatic issues:

- The need in formulating comprehensive policies on population distribution to take these elements into account: costs and benefits to individuals, families, communities, regions and the country as a whole; various forms of population mobility; beneficial and adverse consequences of spatial distribution—these considerations should aim at achieving broader societal goals such as improving the quality of life;

- The integration of a coherent urbanization policy within the over-all development plans of countries which should consider the current high levels of migration to primate cities; the development of medium-sized centres; effective interdependence between urban and rural areas, and the use of incentives rather than migration controls;

- The orientation of rural development programmes more to rural productivity and development goals rather than just population retention; and increased assistance, information and community support for rural migrants in receiving areas, especially for the disadvantaged groups;

- The observance of human rights in all measures in international migration aimed at the reduction of illegal entry, stay or employment of international migrants, and other regulatory and control arrangements by adherence to the guidelines set forth in the international conventions;

- The adherence to provisions of international instruments in the special case of refugees and the orientation of national programmes towards the prevention of the causes of the increasing refugee movements;

- The respect for basic human rights and fundamental freedoms of individuals in international migration policies; the consideration of the well-being of migrants with the receiving country's economic and social needs; the equal treatment of migrants and their families with that enjoyed by nationals in the receiving countries; the normalization of the family life of migrants and the increased information and education of migrants concerning their rights and obligations, and economic opportunities;

- The formulation and implementation of comprehensive population distribution and migration programmes integrated sectorally with development and population plans as the Conference on Population and the Urban Future has recommended by 1985; and the commitment of increased resources by governments in support of these programmes, and the contribution that can be made by international assistance.

Chapter V

POPULATION GROWTH AND STRUCTURE

INTRODUCTION

The total population of the world is projected to increase from 4.7 billion in 1984 to 6.1 billion by the year 2000. If the present downward trend in fertility continues, it is projected to stabilize at 10.2 billion by the end of the next century. The annual world population growth rate declined from a high of 1.96 per cent during the period 1960-1965 to 1.67 per cent during the period 1980-1985 and is projected to fall to 1.52 per cent by the year 2000.

While the global population growth rate is declining, population structure is undergoing some major changes brought about by the declines in fertility and mortality rates. During the past decade, the global birth rate declined by 17 per cent and for the developing countries the decline was 19 per cent. The countries which experienced the largest declines in birth rates during this period, exceeding 15 per cent, contain about two-thirds of the total population of the developing countries. The average annual birth rate for the developing countries declined from 45.4 per 1000 population during 1950-1955 to 31.2 per 1000 during 1980-1985.

There has also been a dramatic decline in mortality rates. The average annual death rate for the world as a whole declined from 19.7 per 1000 population during the period 1950-1955 to 10.6 per 1000 during 1980-1985. The decline is even greater when the developing countries alone are considered—from 24.4 per 1000 during the period 1950-1955 to 11.0 per 1000 during 1980-1985.

One of the important demographic consequences—with socio-economic implications—of these changes in the demographic parameters is the aging of population. The current estimate of "older" population, that is, 60 years and over, in the developed countries, is about 185 million or over 15.8 per cent of the total population. While only 6.3 per cent of the population of developing countries is in this age group, the absolute number of older persons is already higher—230 million—in this group of countries. Between 1985 and the year 2000, the developing countries are expected to experience a 57 per cent increase in the number of older persons in their population as against only a 26 per cent increase in the developed countries. This rise in the absolute size of the older population indicates a predictable increase in the need for medical, housing, economic and social services for the elderly in both developed and developing regions.

In the analysis of the interrelationships between population, resources, environment and development, it is important to bear in mind all these shifts in the global demographic profile. While an understanding of these interrelationships is vital for the economic management of global resources and for the protection of the environment, it should be remembered that population is central to these relationships: population trends not only affect these other factors but are also modified by them.

At the conceptual level, integration of population with development must be seen as a most crucial issue in order that population can be treated as endogenously related to other variables in development planning. This will help to pave the way for the implementation of policies and programmes which can influence not only the magnitude of various demographic parameters affecting population growth and its structure but also the welfare of various segments of the population. For instance, programmes to raise standards of nutrition and education will inevitably contribute to the welfare of children.

The integration of population with development is also crucial in dealing with another problem arising from population growth and changes in population structure, namely, the large increase in the numbers of youth who will be entering the labour force. Projections of the International Labour Organisation of the annual average growth rate of the labour force indicate that, while in the developed countries this figure is projected to decline from 1.28 per cent during the period 1970-1975 to 0.58 per cent by 1990-1995, in the case of developing countries it is projected to increase from 1.97 per cent to 2.23 per cent during the same period. As a consequence, the total labour force is projected to rise from 1.1 billion in 1975 to 1.9 billion by the year 2000. While the net addition to the labour force in the developed countries will be 100 million during the same period, from 500 million to 600 million, the net addition to labour force in the developing countries by the year 2000 will exceed the present total labour force of the developed. The question of how these countries will generate enough employment to absorb this net addition to the labour force demands great attention.

A direct consequence of the lack of employment opportunities in the developing countries is the growth in the number of poor persons, those who lack adequate nutrition and other minimum essentials. If the present economic trends persist, it is estimated that the numbers of persons living in absolute poverty may rise from about 600 million in the mid-1970s to over 800 million by the end of this decade.

In assessing the interrelationships between population, resources and the environment, it is important to differentiate the effects on the environment resulting from over-exploitation of natural resources arising from the pressure of population growth in the developing countries, and from high levels of per capita consumption in the developed countries. Population growth and increase in per capita income continuously generate increasing demand for a variety of goods and services. This increasing demand for cereals, fishery products, forestry products, minerals, water and energy has, in many cases, resulted in the over-exploitation of natural resources and consequent deforestation, soil erosion, losses in agricultural productivity and a general deterioration of the environment.

The relationship between land and population, through the linkages between food and employment, plays a critical role in the quality of life and of the environment. A study by the Food and Agriculture Organization of 90 developing countries indicates that 46 per cent of the population lived in countries where arable land per capita was already the lowest. This raises serious questions about the ability to raise future food output through an expansion of cultivated areas. At the same time, due to environmental degradation, the quality of arable land is rapidly deteriorating through such processes as desertification, deforestation, salinization and waterlogging. If the present trends in desertification continue unchecked, an amount of land twice as large as the current desert area of 792 million hectares could be converted into desert by the year 2000.

A primary concern of the interrelationships is "carrying capacity", that is, how many people can be supported by the global ecological system, and at what level. Carrying capacity is a dynamic concept, the parameters of which change as discoveries are made, new technologies are developed and are put into practice, and as techniques of resource management are improved. However, many new discoveries, technologies and techniques cannot be made operational without first incurring substantial investments in research and development.

The relationship between food and population in the developing countries is emerging as a crisis of monumental proportions affecting their development programmes. If past trends in food and population growth rates continue, FAO estimates that the net import requirements of cereals would rise from 52.5 million metric tons during the period 1978-1979 to 165 million metric tons in the year 2000. A joint FAO/UNFPA study of potential land supporting capacity found that all regions except southwest Asia could meet the food needs of their populations in the year 2000, assuming intermediate levels of inputs, improved varieties of crops and unrestricted movement of potential surpluses within each region. However, when food movements are assumed only within and not between countries, it was found that with low levels of inputs 65 developing countries would have between them in the year 2000 a population of 441 million in excess of their ability to provide food from their domestic supply. Of this "excess" population, 55 per cent would be in Africa. The imbalance between food and population growth implies continuing widespread malnourishment, poverty, high mortality rates and shortened lifespans.

The solutions to the issues raised by the interrelationships between population, resources, environment and development lie in prudent management. These interrelations are products of the interactions between demand and supply factors. Demand is the combined effect of population growth and changes in its structure and per capita income growth. The supply factors are determined by land and its quality, availability of natural resources, the state of technology and potential future discoveries. A lasting solution to these problems will therefore look at both sides of the equation and pay equal attention to measures to curb the growth of demand, and to ways to economize in the use of resources through careful management.

UNFPA has financed action programmes as well as training and research activities concerning population growth and structure and their implications for the environment and development. Such assistance spans the various categories of UNFPA assistance. For instance, many of the family planning programmes to which UNFPA has provided support have been undertaken by countries with a view to modifying population growth trends. Population education programmes often include components designed to sensitize audiences to the impact of population growth on development, natural resources and the environment. On the global level, UNFPA has assisted activities related to population aging through, for example, support for the 1982 United Nations World Assembly on Aging, and for Opera Pia International, a non-governmental organization active in promoting the consideration of aging as a component of national population and development planning.

Research supported by UNFPA related to the interrelationships of population growth, environment and development includes the joint UNFPA/Food and Agriculture Organization study of *Land Resources for Populations of the Future*, as well as research undertaken by the International Labour Organisation on the interactions of population trends, employment and socio-economic development, and on the interrelationships of population, labour and poverty. In addition, UNFPA has continued to provide support to the United Nations Population Division to carry out research such as that on the role of population factors in socio-economic progress in developing countries, and on the relationships between development and fertility decline in those countries.

EXCERPTS FROM STATEMENTS

On the matter of population structure . . .

- With the decline in fertility in an increasing number of developing countries, population structures will rapidly change. The problems of an aging population will have to be faced. This will be a topic of growing concern to many developing countries in the coming decade. Programmes have to be designed to meet this challenge. (18 June 1979)

- In developing countries, the large proportion of those under fifteen years old in the total population has profound implications for governments and institutions initiating and implementing policies on fertility trends, employment, industrialization, education and housing and the resources which need to be mobilized to meet this change. In developed countries and, increasingly, developing countries alike, the growing numbers of those people beyond sixty-five years of age are also beginning to make their influence felt on policy needs. This increase in the proportion of the aged will require shifts in resources to welfare systems tailored to the needs of this population group and will have evident effects on the residential and labour-force mobility. (28 August 1979)

- The growth of population in the Third World, still reflecting largely the success of efforts at lowering mortality rates, has altered not only the magnitude of the population problem but also the shape and character of these problems. Most of the population in the Third World is now constituted by children and young people. Nearly 40 per cent of the total population of the Third World is now below the age of 30. At the prevailing birth rates, nearly 125 million children are born every year. The particular age structure of the population obviously has important implications for development strategies. The growth in numbers of children will raise the demand for a variety of goods and services, such as infant food, maternal and child health care, and school facilities. As these children grow older, they will enter the labour force, thus raising the level of resources required for creating additional jobs. As they get married, the demand for housing, transportation and a host of other services will also rise.

     The high proportion of persons below the age of 15 in these Third World countries will lead to a swelling of the labour force in the next two decades, and it is estimated that new entrants seeking employment will exceed 600 million. (13 May 1980)

- The increase in the number of the aged of the world's population both in developed and developing countries points to the need for national policies and institutional responses to a problem which was not anticipated until the early seventies. It is important to realize that while the proportion of the total population over 65 years of age may be small—representing only 5.6 per cent of the world population in 1975 and forecast to be 6.3 per cent in the year 2000—the aggregate number of people over 65 years of age is sizeable. In 1975 it stood at 226 million but this figure is expected to be 391 million by the year 2000—almost double. The impact of these numbers will fall most heavily on the less developed countries. It is projected that the less developed world will have 227 million people over 65 years—60 per cent of the world's total.

  This trend, combined with the increasing proportion of youth as a percentage of the total population, should be of concern to all of us. Thus, it is necessary to begin studying these structural changes in population at all levels so that appropriate policies, institutions, training facilities and programmes may be developed to deal effectively with the problems caused by increased longevity and the alteration of the age structure of populations. (19 May 1980)

- The UNFPA because of the provisions of the World Population Plan of Action and because of its special responsibility for keeping aware of changes in the population structure has taken an increasing interest in these matters. (16 June 1980)

- Population dynamics has produced contrasting structures of population in the developing and developed countries. While it has moved overwhelmingly in favour of a younger population in the developing countries, the decline in fertility to near-replacement levels and the lengthening of the life span to over 70 years are resulting in an increasing proportion of older persons in the developed countries. (21 July 1980)

- If the less developed countries are feeling the strain now, what will be their position in twenty or thirty years time, when their predominantly young populations are themselves parents? Population growth carries its own inertia. Stability follows only after a lapse of time. This means that action—or the lack of it—now, will have its effect in the next generation. (3 May 1981)

On the matter of the aging . . .

- We live in an aging world. More people than ever before are surviving to old age. We think of this as mostly a phenomenon of the industrialized countries, as indeed it is. One person in ten in the industrialized world is over 65 and in some countries the proportion is twice that figure.

But aging is becoming a feature of the less developed countries also. . . . In the world as a whole, the number of older people has nearly doubled since 1950, and half of them live in the less developed countries.

This is a remarkable change. Instead of human life being measured in a handful of years, we are approaching the psalmist's span of three score years and ten, and in many parts of the world have already reached it. The diseases which shortened the lives of our forebears and of many in our generation are on the retreat. (6 September 1981)

• While the progressive aging of societies is neither an unexpected, unforeseen event nor a random incident, its scale of occurrence, its implications for global and national responses, its outcome for the social and economic institutions in societies and its long-term consequences for the pattern of human life are all basic issues assuming new relevance and they need to be better understood for the formulation of national population policies and programmes. . . .

Issues in aging refer both to humanitarian and developmental aspects. They relate either to the improvement of the personal situation of the elderly individuals, or to strengthening of the family ties and a renewed role for the family or a host of public and private programmes that would better integrate the elderly and their contributions into over-all development.

The effects of aging of population at the individual level bring into focus issues related to the provision of physical, economic and social services to the elderly. Besides the need to ensure an adequate and regular post-retirement income, access to basic health care services, and exposure to proper health and nutritional education, it is also necessary to include homes for the aged, personal care services at home for those with physical disabilities, social support in alternative living situations, counselling, and social or leisure-time services and activities.

The aging of population also has implications for the role and functions of the institution of the family. Throughout the world, families are becoming smaller, structurally more diverse, and independent of extended kin relationships. Some of the responsibilities for providing income and social security to the elderly have shifted from families to governments. It is important in this shift to achieve a positive, active, and developmentally-oriented view of the aging. The elderly must be considered an important and necessary element in the development process at all levels within a society and they must be given opportunities for self-expression in a variety of roles in the community and the economy.

Conditions of work, standards of living of the population, and availability of health care are each important factors contributing to longevity. All these factors are part and parcel of the development process and while development alone will not lead to an increase in the number of the aged in the total population, it alters the nature of the "aging" problem in these countries because of the structural changes in their economies.

The economic status of the elderly is largely determined by their income, individual roles and family situation. The sources of income for the elderly of the developed countries include pensions, social security and social insurance. Similarly, the elderly's economic role is influenced by their health, perception of retirement, and nature and availability of employment. The public debate in the past decade or two in the developed countries on the status of the elderly has mainly arisen from a concern for their economic well-being. This has led to the development of special provisions in the social security system to supplement the incomes of the elderly who were very poor and other policy measures to help retain the elderly within the labour force.

The issue of economic status of the elderly in developing countries is even more complex and is modified by additional factors such as the nature and structure of their underdeveloped economies, the differential patterns of residence in rural and urban areas and forms of family support. There is an enormous sectoral variation among the elderly of the developing countries. In the "modern" organized sectors of the economy, provisions for some form of old age pensions exist, but there are few income sources for the elderly among agricultural labourers and those belonging to the urban poor. From a welfare point of view, their needs are the greatest, but few mechanisms to supplement their incomes have been developed so far in these countries.

A survey of social security programmes around the world indicates that there exists some form of public pension or social insurance in the organized sectors of about 75 developing countries. While there is a large variation among them in both the extent of coverage and the percentage of their GNP spent on such programmes, the issues that confront them in an expansion of such programmes on a wider scale are similar. They include, for instance, an institutional capacity to undertake demographic and economic projections for the future, the estimation of functions relating to the relative emphasis on the public pension system vis-à-vis family support, the determination of the rapidity of spreading the coverage to the entire population, and an adequate understanding of the nature and extent of appropriate benefits to the participants in the programme. Social security planning has to be a far-sighted and technically sophisticated activity and in this connection, there is an urgent need to catalogue existing systems, disseminate technical information, interpret available data and most importantly, continue research on the development of promising strategies.

The macro-economic implications hinge on the crucial question of how an aging population will affect the rate of economic growth of a country. This assumes some significance because aging can affect the level of productivity, consumption patterns, savings behaviour and consequently the quantum and pattern of investment. (24 November 1982)

• In our experience, the countries most capable of handling population issues successfully have the ability, first, to perceive the issue in conceptual terms, then to programme its practical implications. And having developed a response, they must be capable of making resources available to put projects into operation. Behind each stage of the process lies the necessity for political will, the desire to effect and adapt to change.

These capabilities are needed in regard to the aging as in other aspects of development. Some countries are already looking forward to a time when there will be considerably more older people than there are now, and in a greater proportion to the whole population, and these countries are making their preparations now to care for their aging population. Typically, they will have a social structure which recognizes the value of the older person and permits senior citizens to make a contribution to the community. They have an economic structure which caters to the needs and the abilities of older people, either through extended family networks or, as in the case of industrial countries, through social security, living and working facilities for older people, and so on.

These countries bear the responsibility for helping their aging population, either by financial or technical assistance. It is part of the function of concerned international agencies to point out that responsibility whenever necessary and to help transform perceptions into effective action.

Another group of countries has the conceptual capability and possibly even the resources but is reluctant or unable to act effectively. In this case our role is to urge the necessity for action, not for the sake of these nations alone, but for the sake of those others on whom the effects of their actions will fall and for those who need assistance, technical or financial.

A third group of countries badly needs assistance of all kinds in evolving and acting upon policies for the future. Our task here is to channel to them whatever assistance may be necessary, and to try to ensure that assistance is available when, where and in the kinds and quantities it is needed. . . . (6 September 1981)

- The role of concerned international agencies is, therefore, not confined to aid-giving in the traditional sense, but rather to act as concerned collaborators between the governments and peoples of those countries needing assistance and those who can give it, and as transmitters of ideas and as arousers of concern. In common with nearly all voluntary funds of the United Nations, UNFPA finds itself constrained today, by the consequences of global inflation, exchange rate fluctuations and general economic uncertainty. We have been asked to limit ourselves to the most urgent needs of the countries which we serve in order to use our resources to the best effect. Still, we have a mandate to fulfill, and with the approval of our Governing Council and within our means, we will continue to fulfill our responsibilities to the aged. Our agenda for the future may include, as appropriate:
    1. *basic data collection.* Continuing the work already done in the collection, analysis and projection of data on the aged in our technical assistance programme in regard to censuses, sample surveys and methodology and projection techniques;
    2. *research.* Continuing research on the implications of a country's changing age structure for labour supply and for social services; research on the social and economic consequences of rural-to-urban migration and the implications for the older population of such migration; research on measures to maximize the contributions of the elderly to socio-economic development and intercountry research on changes in age structure and their implications for economic and social development. . . .
    3. *support communication.* UNFPA will continue its support communication activities in countries and institutions with added emphasis on the problems of aging and may include dissemination of research findings and training methodologies, information on legislative policies as well as other governmental policy and programme information.
    4. *collaboration with concerned institutions.* Continuing our support for international and national institutions concerned with the needs of the elderly in the areas of family life, education and spiritual work. Our collaboration with organizations reflects our concern not only with the scientific aspects of aging but also its humanistic dimensions. . . .

5. *policy consultations.* Continuing the Fund's collaborative efforts for purposes of policy information to countries and institutions with centres for the study of the elderly. . . .

To shape a more satisfying future we have to acknowledge the interdependence and creativity of all people, both young and old. We have come to the present because of the labour and sacrifice of those who gave their best in their youthful and middle years. It is our reciprocal obligation to the aged to make each of their remaining years more meaningful and more fulfilling. (27 July 1982)

On the matter of environment, resources, population . . .

- Irreparable damage is being done to natural resources and the environmental balance in the struggle to survive. The result of this is internal and international tension as social, economic and political stresses increase. (3 May 1981)

- From Malthus to the Club of Rome, the notion of numbers of people has been linked to food or resources. The lessons of these studies are to make us conscious of the interrelationship between people and resources. Today, we look upon our goal as one of ensuring that there are adequate resources for our numbers so that the quality of life improves and the individual is assured the opportunity to develop his potential fully. (26 April 1979)

- The lack of integration of population programmes with the process of development has been responsible for the lack of appreciation of its linkages with natural resources and environment. This, while leading to an over-emphasis on the implications of alternative development strategies on monetary resources, has almost neglected its impact on the demand for natural resources and its consequences on the environment. It is also necessary to point out that the impact of population change and development on resources and environment is quite different for the developing and developed countries. While poverty is essentially the cause of deterioration in the human and natural environment in the developing countries, the environmental deterioration in the developed countries is caused primarily by their affluence.

  The pressure of population and the increase in poverty are forcing the developing countries to exploit their natural resources to an extent which is producing not only severe environmental problems but is eroding their future production potential. The excessive reliance on chemical fertilizers to increase agricultural and food production, the overgrazing of pasture lands, accelerated felling of trees to meet fuel requirements, the phenomenon of over-urbanization, the faster depletion of non-renewable resources, among others, are all factors which have relevance for the future development of the developing countries. These factors will lead to a deterioration in natural soil conditions which will reduce future output from the land, to the emergence of semi-arid zones or deserts and to a deterioration of urban living conditions as a result of the inability to provide for housing, education and health facilities to keep pace with urbanization. Solutions to these problems can be found only if we link population programmes with development strategies by which it will be possible to integrate an optimal resource-use pattern with the quality of the environment.

Society must be made aware that unbridled growth of its population puts severe strains on the use of material and natural resources, the supplies of which are not unlimited over time. While the formulation of the "limits to growth" thesis may not have mathematical precision, it contains valid propositions which cannot be ignored in any future development strategy of the world economy. (19 June 1979)

- We are tending globally towards a more holistic view of development with its emphasis on relating environmental factors to programmes. Population growth and development patterns not only affect the demand for resources but also generate environmental changes which will have repercussions on the future carrying capacity of the earth. At the global level, it is not only necessary to take into account the resources required to feed, clothe and shelter a growing population but also the type of technology which will make this possible without worsening the environment. It is, indeed, proper to ask at this point how far population and development plans are consistent with the prudent use of resources, and do not bring about the degradation of our environment. (28 August 1979)

- As we look towards the years ahead, broader conceptualizations and better integration of factors are needed in thinking about development. The recent energy crises that have afflicted both developed and developing countries have called our attention to the limits of our use of non-renewable resources. The extensive deforestation in many developing countries that has caused soil erosion, change in weather conditions, and a decrease in the productivity of the soil to produce food has alarmed us about the carrying capacity of our environment. And the excessive and unnecessary consumption of goods and services within and among countries now demands the reconsideration of our familiar life-styles. Planning the future of countries must not only relate at this stage development factors with population but must equally accentuate the relationships of these two factors with the use of resources, the environment and the values that should govern the life-styles of the citizens.

Development in its broadest integration demands the consciousness of limits to enable individuals to act without degrading themselves and their environment and so prevent further individual or national growth. This ethic of restraint is linked to a respect for the value of all life, especially human life, its authentic fulfillment and the true meaning of happiness. Material goods alone, however necessary, cannot achieve this, nor can they be sought unless people themselves adopt attitudes which enable them to restrain excessive desires that ultimately lead to environmental degradation. (29 August 1979)

• A question relating to population-resource balance which we cannot overlook is whether the carrying capacity of the earth will suffice to meet the needs of a greatly increased world population at a hoped-for higher economic standard. While carrying capacity is not fixed but can be a dynamic variable, such improvement can take place only by adopting appropriate development strategies, including technology, and by sound management of resources. In the long run, resources are not given but determined by human activity. (21 July 1980)

• In the developed world, where each person born will consume 20 to 40 times more in his or her lifetime than a person born in a developing country, the drive to fulfill continuously rising material aspirations will have a major impact on the environment, on the possibilities for meeting the most basic needs for the poor majority in the developing world and on the struggle for more just economic relationships within and between nations. In this context it is worth remembering that population growth is a problem only when resources cannot meet the needs of people, and that by definition, it is as much a problem of regulating the use of resources as it is of regulating births. (12 July 1980)

• Action aimed at stabilizing the level of world population in accordance with the availability of world resources is but one aspect of the equitable distribution of the benefits of world development, although an important one. (13 May 1980)

• There seems to be a multiplier effect in tensions produced by the stresses on the international community which seep down to the smallest units of society. The signs were there three years ago, but many did not heed the warnings. Today no country in the world can go it alone. The world has become interdependent as never before.

From our experience in dealing with the problems in the developing countries, it appears that the key factors contributing to this situation are the depletion of natural resources, the deterioration of the environment we live in, and rapid population growth. These three factors are likely to be the most critical problem areas for the world in the decades ahead with rapid population growth the most important of these three.

Population growth continuously generates an increasing demand for a variety of goods and services. Most of these goods, such as food grains, fishery products, wood, minerals, water and energy are the results of the exploitation of natural resources. For instance, a levelling off of global grain output and total fish catch in recent years with population steadily rising has already upset the population-food balance.

A change in the supply situation of a natural resource can have far-reaching consequences for the global economy as illustrated by the effects of a rise in the price of petroleum, a basic source of energy. It has led to an over-all rise in prices and has intensified the search for, and research in, alternative sources of energy. It has necessitated the restructuring of productive processes, shifting from high-energy technologies to low-energy technologies with consequent changes in location of industries, employment, income distribution and in patterns of consumption.

Because of the search for alternative energy solutions, some nations in the industrial world are considering greater use of nuclear energy and are willing to take the attendant risks to the environment. These risks possibly include levels of radiation, and those associated with the dumping of nuclear waste. It will necessitate constant monitoring of the levels of permissible radiation, and even contingency plans for the swift movements of populations in the event of an unforeseen nuclear hazard.

The pressure of population resulting in more intensive use of natural resources has led to deforestation, soil erosion, losses in agricultural productivity, deterioration of the environment and massive movements of population from rural to urban areas. Therefore, the developing countries are increasingly concerned about internal tensions of a more uncontrollable nature in the future. (20 December 1980)

• The consequences of the interrelationships between population growth and the urban environment have received considerable attention in recent years. Pollution and degradation of the environment are closely related to concentration of industries, high density of automobiles and congested living conditions. While some measures have been in operation to monitor and reduce levels of pollution in the metropolitan areas of the more developed countries, few such measures have been initiated in the cities of the less developed countries. (1 September 1980)

- The question of integration is particularly important when we consider the interrelationship of population, natural resources and the environment. All planning, all our thoughts and dreams for the future, are based on the assumption that development activities will not irrevocably upset the balance of the ecosystem which sustains us. In order to justify this assumption, positive steps are needed to protect the environment. . . .

  Irreparable damage becomes a real possibility unless ways can be found to meet the needs of growing populations for water, food, fuel and building materials. We are working towards a better understanding of the effects not only of population growth, but of industrial and agricultural development, and of the eventual costs and benefits of taking steps against environmental damage. (20 September 1982)

- The International Development Strategy for the Third United Nations Development Decade, adopted by the General Assembly in December 1980, as well as other reviews, studies and strategies, have . . . identified population, along with resources and environment, as three vitally important areas of concern to mankind in the remaining years of this century and beyond. (29 September 1982)

On the matter of poverty, employment and population . . .

- How the increase in global population in the 1980s and beyond will affect the global future and the whole range of international relationships can be assessed only by understanding that most of this increase would take place in the areas which have already experienced the largest increases in population between 1950 and 1980, the poorest regions of the world. A likely consequence of this will be a further increase in the numbers of the poor, a worsening of the depth of deprivation and a further widening of the international disparity in incomes.

  The existence of poverty and the problems of development are not new, but what population growth in the past three decades has done and will continue to do in the future, is to make these problems more intractable by changing their scale. For example, while world grain output doubled between 1950 and 1978, per capita output increased by only one-third during the same period. The facts are not very different for health care, education or employment opportunities in the developing countries. Given these facts, there is no reason to believe that the "world population problem" has been solved, even though fertility rates have begun to decline. (21 July 1980)

- At present, the poor are more susceptible to disease and have less access to health services. Rural populations are at greater risk than urban residents. One of the most important passages in the World Population Plan of Action recognizes these inequalities and it is a goal of the Plan to reduce them. It should be clearly stated once again . . . that in the quest for better health, lower mortality, slower population growth and over-all development, a vital element is equal access to the benefits of development. (31 May 1983)

- One of the factors in the increase in the number of the poor is the growth of the number of unemployed and underemployed. . . . The availability of arable land in many countries is limited and there is growing landlessness. This has resulted in a growing landless agricultural labour surplus and unemployment in the rural areas. (27 October 1981)

- Unemployment has a direct bearing on population growth rates, since women find it difficult to enter the work force and men are unable to find dignity in their work and security for the future. Employment opportunities also affect the distribution of population throughout a country. It is also directly related to the structures of society since high technology and capital intensive development, often supported by foreign investments, do not generate the needed number of jobs to meet the demand. And unemployment appears to increase as measures against inflation become more stringent. (10 May 1979)

- While the total world population is expected to increase from 4.3 billion in 1980 to 6.2 billion by 2000, the total labour force is projected to increase from 1.8 billion to 2.6 billion during the same period.

- The ILO projections of annual growth rate of labour force indicate that, while in the more developed countries, it is projected to decline from 1.28 per cent during 1970-1975 to 0.58 per cent by 1990-1995, in the case of developing countries, it is projected to increase from 1.97 per cent to 2.23 per cent during the same period. As a consequence, the total labour force in the developing countries will increase from 1.1 billion in 1975 to 1.9 billion by the year 2000, whereas the change will only be from 0.5 billion to 0.6 billion in the case of the developed countries. Thus the net addition itself to the labour force in developing countries between 1975 and 2000 would exceed the total labour force of the developed countries in the year 2000. (7 December 1981)

- In fact, if the people in the developing countries are to better their living conditions, the number of jobs to be created will have to exceed the additions to the labour force to take into account the backlog of the unemployed and underemployed. These facts will require a rethinking of the modes of employment creation and in promoting appropriate technology. (15 January 1980)

- The extent of the deterioration in levels of living in the Third World countries will, therefore, depend not only on levels of production of cereals, fish and other sources of protein but also on the opportunities to obtain employment. . . . The high proportion of persons below the age of 15 in these countries will lead to a swelling of the labour force in the next two decades, and it is estimated that new entrants seeking employment in developing countries will exceed 600 million. The countries of the Third World presently lack both the resources and the knowledge of the strategies which could deal with this emerging employment crunch. (13 May 1980)

- Within a given socio-economic framework, the demographic configurations largely determine the supply of labour. The stage and pace of development, on the other hand, determine the demand for labour and show how a society utilizes its manpower. Any imbalance between population growth and the pace of development translates itself into a disequilibrium between the supply of and demand for labour. In a developing economy, it is reflected in the differences in the labour force participation rates of the various segments of population, the direction and extent of internal and external migration, and in the proportions of unemployed and underemployed in the labour force. In a highly developed economy, the imbalance between the supply of and demand for labour is corrected partly by controlling the volume of immigrant labour and by substituting machines for labour in various production activities.

   The unprecedented growth in the labour force during the past thirty years in the developing countries has generated a number of serious economic problems. Agriculture has been the mainstay of employment and livelihood in these countries, but as the pressure of population rises, the scope to absorb large numbers within agriculture is becoming severely restricted. Even though the proportion of labour force in agriculture has declined from 80 per cent in 1950 to about 65 per cent by 1970 and the trend is still continuing in the same direction, the actual numbers of persons dependent per hectare of cultivated land continue to rise and it is adversely affecting the living conditions of people in the rural areas. The problems of unemployment and underemployment have become acute though their extent is not fully brought out by the surveys of labour force and unemployment. In the densely populated regions of Asia, the numbers of landless labourers who form the most vulnerable group in the rural sector have also been growing at an alarming rate. One wonders how these countries will be able to generate enough employment not only for the currently unemployed but also for the numbers that will be added to their labour force between now and the year 2000. . . .

The problems, the needs, and the consequences of a growing urban labour force are quite different from those of rural labour force. . . . Both the financial and social costs of generating a unit of employment in the urban areas are often several times larger than the comparable costs of generating a unit of employment in the rural sector.

The interrelationship between labour and demography of a country also affects the status of women in the society and the success of its programmes to liberate women from their traditional roles. An improvement in the status of women, by providing employment opportunities for them outside of traditional sectors, is considered important also for a decline in fertility rates. There are wide variations in the female participation rates not only between the various regions of the world but even between different income groups within a country itself. When the labour force participation rate and unemployment are already high among the male labour force, it may prove even more difficult to create a large-scale employment programme for women. It is needless to say that a failure to generate female employment for improving their status will adversely affect not only the fertility level but also the welfare of women and children. . . .

A global view of labour and demography would be incomplete without mention of international migration. Historically, migration has been a minor part of the mechanism by which imbalances in the labour market were corrected, but its importance is increasing as communications improve. Migration of labour from Europe in the 19th century was important to the development of the New World. More recently, Western Europe has depended on migrants from developing countries to meet part of its labour requirements. Now it is the turn of the oil-rich to draw on the supply. Though migrants form a tiny fraction of the total population, their experience and their earnings are important to several developing countries which are suppliers of labour. Policies aimed at eliminating imbalances in the labour market will be fruitful only if they are undertaken within a long-term perspective. . . .

Though models are of limited use, they still provide some insights into the workings of economic and demographic variables under different policy stimuli and initial assumptions. . . . For the success of

employment and development programmes, we should first know of
the magnitudes of the different variables at different time periods;
secondly, we should perceive the objectives to be attained at the end
of the time-frame; and thirdly, we should adopt strategies and policies and act on them. (7 December 1981)

On the matter of food and population . . .

• The growth of world population and its regional distribution between
  1930 and 1975 has already brought about a major transformation in
  the world food economy. While world grain output nearly doubled between 1950 and 1975, per capita grain production increased by only
  one-third during the same period. Regions which were net exporters
  of grain during the 1930s have become net importers of grain in the
  1970s, partly reflecting those changes. Food has become such an important item in the world that its possession is considered important
  as an instrument of foreign policy. Given the constraints imposed by
  a paucity of investible resources for increasing the growth of grain
  production in a number of countries, this role of food is likely to gain
  even more importance by the year 2000. (15 January 1980)

• In a number of developing countries, there has already been a marked
  deterioration in the balance between food output and the size of population. . . . Most of the countries of Africa have population growth
  rates exceeding 3 per cent per annum and they are also experiencing
  the most severe imbalance between food output and population. Estimates of the Food and Agriculture Organization indicate that per
  capita food output in Africa declined at an annual rate of 1.3 per cent
  during the period 1970-1977. It appears that there has been no improvement in these conditions since then. The severity of these conditions can be fully gauged only if we also realize that most countries
  of Africa have the lowest per capita incomes among the countries of
  the Third World.
      The emergence of these imbalances cannot be blamed on an increase
  in fertility rates but, on the contrary, it has been brought about mainly
  by a greater decline in mortality rates compared to declines in fertility rates. However, the situation is not confined to countries in Africa alone, and similar imbalances between availability of food and the
  size of population are emerging elsewhere in the Third World. In the
  1980s, the growth of the Third World population may lead to further
  deterioration in these conditions. (13 May 1980)

• . . . the information exists to show us how to produce enough food
  for a growing globe. This has been shown in practice over the last

three decades as food production, except in cases of war or natural disaster, has kept pace with population growth. In theory, this process could go on—if the effects on the natural environment could be correctly forecast and disruption minimized. The environment, as we are rapidly discovering, has limits to its resilience, but if our technical ability continues to improve we may mitigate many of the worst effects of our demands upon it, and turn others into positive assets. (3 May 1981)

• The first question confronting us is carrying capacity. How will we provide for the population of the future? Taking the world as a whole, this may seem possible, but how is the geographical distribution of food production to be made to follow the geographical distribution of population? Will the inputs and technology available to the developing countries be sufficient for them to meet their food requirements? Can agriculture in developing countries become as productive as it is in the developed countries? We already have the technology to achieve this, but can the changes be made without adverse environmental effects?

On the other hand, if feeding the world's population is to depend on international transfer of food, how is a foolproof system to be developed? What mechanisms and agreements will be needed so that political considerations do not enter the transaction? (25 April 1983)

ISSUES FOR THE FUTURE:
POPULATION GROWTH AND STRUCTURE

In the further implementation of the World Population Plan of Action in the area of population growth and structure, attention may be given to the following programmatic issues:

• The concern with the age distribution of the population especially for the needs of the children and the youth and the integration of specific programmes for their welfare with the development plans of countries;

• The implications of the changing age structure of the population particularly that of the aging and its effect on the over-all development of the countries in the provision of social and health services and the consideration of the active contribution of older people in the economic and social life of their communities;

• The constant awareness of the interrelationship between population, resources, environment and development and the rational use of resources for a balanced growth as population increases in order to prevent environmental degradation.

Chapter VI

PROMOTION OF KNOWLEDGE AND IMPLEMENTATION OF POLICIES AND PROGRAMMES

INTRODUCTION

Population policies and programmes can be more effective if they are firmly grounded in demographic and related statistics and take into account the basic relationships between population variables and other socio-economic factors. In fact, demographic statistics constitute the basic data on which the whole edifice of socio-economic planning is erected. The size of the population, the age structure, fertility and mortality rates, and the rate of growth of population constitute some of the basic information needed for determining the sectoral allocation of resources and their growth rates. The World Population Plan of Action pointed out three means of obtaining statistics: (1) the population census, (2) the civil registration system, and (3) sample surveys, in particular the World Fertility Survey. In all these areas, significant achievements can be cited as having occurred since the 1974 World Population Conference.

During the period 1975-1984, the World Population and Housing Census Decade, 192 countries and territories, comprising about 95 per cent of the world's population, have completed or plan to complete a census of their population. Two notable achievements in population censuses since the adoption of the Plan of Action were the completion of national censuses covering virtually the entire African continent and the 1982 population census of China. During the period 1975-1982, 34 countries in Africa had completed their censuses—in many their first comprehensive population censuses—and another 13 countries plan to complete censuses by the end of 1984. The African and China censuses received substantial financial and technical support from UNFPA and other United Nations agencies and organizations.

A national civil registration system provides, on a continuing basis, such information as data on births, deaths, and marriages, and can serve as a vital component of the monitoring of trends in fertility and mortality and the impact of family planning programmes on them. Due to various factors such as low levels of literacy, and the lack of ready access to registration centres, civil registration system coverage is far from satisfactory in many developing countries. To overcome these difficulties, a number of countries, such as India, have instituted sample registration surveys.

The World Fertility Survey was established in 1972 with the objective of assisting countries in acquiring scientific information on fertility and its regulation, including levels and differentials; in strengthening the ability of the countries to carry out fertility surveys; and for ensuring internationally comparable fertility data. Some 42 developing countries and 20 developed countries participated in this programme. As a result, a wealth of data has been collected for undertaking extensive research in the fields of fertility, family planning, and infant mortality at the national and international levels.

Another area of population statistics vital for developing population policies is migration statistics. At present, migration statistics suffer from a lack of uniformity in concepts, definitions and classifications. The United Nations system has been striving to correct these deficiencies and to develop uniform data and reporting systems.

The collection and accumulation of demographic statistics by itself would be of limited use unless they formed a basis for research and analysis to improve understanding of the causal relationships between population and other variables and thus aid in developing appropriate policies and programmes. The World Population Plan of Action has pointed out areas for high priority research particularly relevant to the formulation, evaluation and implementation of the population policies consistent with full respect for human rights. Broadly, they cover various aspects of integration of population with development, the family cycle in relation to development, determinants of levels and trends in fertility, the status of women, aspects of child and infant mortality, internal and international migration, population modelling and simulation, and the interrelationships between population, resources, environment and development. The progress of research in those areas since the 1974 World Population Conference is uneven. While significant gains have been achieved in the understanding of factors affecting fertility and its determinants and, to a large extent, in the understanding of the relationships between mortality and health care, research in the areas of migration, status of women, and the family cycle have only just begun. Similarly, the lack of firm research findings on the different aspects of the relationship between population and other development variables is one of the major obstacles to complete integration of population with development planning.

With reference to the establishment of national research institutions, according to the United Nations Fifth Population Inquiry, 55 per cent of those developing countries which responded by mid-1983 reported that they had a research institution which provided information on various aspects of population and development.

The collection of basic population data, the development of analytical research and the implementation of population policies and programmes presuppose the availability of an adequate supply of trained manpower. The developing countries have become acutely aware of the shortage of trained personnel. A number of institutions have thus been established to relieve this shortage in developing countries with international assistance. The most notable of these are the United Nations-sponsored regional and interregional demographic training and research institutions.

Trends in demographic parameters are influenced by human attitudes towards childbearing, marriage and family relationships. Therefore, it has been realized that people's better understanding of the impact of population on socio-economic well-being is a prerequisite for the success of population policies and programmes. Thus, population information, education and communication have assumed great importance as integral parts of population programmes.

Population information and education programmes include the introduction of population issues in school curricula and the use of mass media and community workers to spread population information. A large volume of literature on action programmes in those areas has been produced under the auspices of national and international organizations.

The ultimate objective of the collection of basic data, research and analysis and the training of manpower in the population field is the complete integration of population with development planning. It is believed that such integration will not only have a beneficial impact on population trends, but will also result in an increase in the general welfare of the population.

A basic aim of UNFPA assistance is to enable countries to become self-reliant in the integration of their population policies and programmes with the development planning process. Training, as well as country-specific research, are thus important elements of programmes in each of the UNFPA categories of assistance. Total assistance to training activities during 1969-1983 amounted to $223.9 million, including assistance to demographic training and research centres, training of local practitioners, nurse/midwives and traditional birth attendants in family planning service delivery, training of census enumerators, and others.

UNFPA assistance in the field of basic data collection for the period 1969-1983 totalled $163 million (about 16.5 per cent of total UNFPA assistance), of which approximately 73 per cent has supported national population censuses, with the remainder allocated for demographic surveys, and civil registration and vital statistics systems. Among the activities UNFPA has funded in this sector, the African Census Project, undertaken between 1970 and 1977, provided support to 22 African countries, including 18 countries which had never before had a complete census enumeration. UNFPA was the chief source of external assistance for the 1982 population census in China, in the amount of about $12 million, that country's first modern, electronically tabulated census, which involved the enumeration of nearly one-quarter of the earth's people.

UNFPA assistance to population information, education and communication, absorbing about 12 per cent of the total UNFPA programme from 1969 to 1983, has amounted to $114 million. Action programmes in this growing area include in-school and out-of-school population education; the introduction of population information and education into such settings as the industrial work place and training programmes for agricultural extension agents; and communication support through various media for family planning or census activities.

Through a variety of modalities, UNFPA has assisted countries in all developing regions in their efforts to institutionalize the consideration of population factors in the development planning process. This assistance includes support for the establishment of "population units", most often within national ministries of planning or health, and other assistance to enhance the utilization of population data in the formulation of population and development policies and programmes, including the evaluation of population policies and programmes.

EXCERPTS FROM STATEMENTS

On the matter of countries achieving self-reliance . . .

• It has always been the objective of the UNFPA in the field of international co-operation to promote countries' self-reliance. UNFPA believes in international partnership with governments for the attainment of development and population goals. This is one of the reasons why it is so important that understanding of the relationship of population and development reaches people in their homes and in the communities in which they live. Their participation in the process of reaching these goals is essential to the success of any such enterprise.

Undoubtedly, social communication will play a vital role in this strategy, and this will continue to be a challenge to all those who are now preparing themselves to work in the field of communications.

To get the message through the right medium to all citizens of the country, that population consciousness is as important for the individual as it is for the viability of the economy, is a continuing task in the years ahead. (18 August 1981)

• At the national level, countries are becoming more and more self-reliant in policy formulation, planning and the implementation of population programmes. In order to increase national capacity to undertake various programme activities, it will be necessary to give increased attention in developing countries to the training of local staff and facilitate the setting up of population units in the ministries concerned with population and development. (31 October 1981)

- We know that most of the resources needed to meet the problems of development already exist within countries; and these resources have been mobilized in population as in other fields of development. In the current atmosphere of financial constraint and uncertainty, it becomes all the more important that national resources be used to their fullest extent. It is part of the task of concerned international organizations and individuals to advise, encourage and promote self-help wherever possible, at all levels and in co-operation with the efforts of governments and international groups. It is in this way that we shall be able to render the greatest possible service to development and to humanity, which is the reason for development and its greatest resource. (6 September 1981)

- During the past twelve years of the Fund's operations, we have succeeded in promoting awareness of population problems and in securing the commitment of developing countries to population programmes as vital components of economic and social development. The most tangible result of this awareness and commitment is the present conceptual and operational capability of countries to implement and execute population programmes within their economic development plans. Moreover, these programmes have been implemented with increasing allocations of national resources in accord with the view that countries must increasingly become self-reliant. (2 October 1981)

On the matter of basic data collection and analysis . . .

Population data constitutes the basic input on which the whole edifice of the planning structure is erected. Even at the simplest level, the size of the population and the rates of growth constitute important elements for determining the targets of growth of different sectors of the economy.

Just as working out alternative scenarios for different assumptions regarding the rate of investment on targets in per capita income, it is possible to work out similar alternative models incorporating different assumptions regarding the likely changes in fertility or other demographic variables. (19 June 1979)

- . . . there is a continuous need to strengthen the data base as well as the various types of governmental and community machinery for planning, promoting and co-ordinating population activities with development policies and programmes in developing countries, particularly at the local level. To what extent can we encourage governments to focus and act on this aspect of population work? (28 August 1979)

- Considerable progress was made during the 1970s to improve the quality and the magnitude of demographic data required for planning and policy-making in developing countries. However, reliable population data are still seriously lacking in many countries. Continuing attention will have to be paid to meet this need through improved census operations, strengthened vital statistics registration and developing sample surveys and other statistical data collection systems. (31 October 1979)

- In the past, the integration of population with development planning has been hampered by a paucity of detailed data on a number of demographic variables. Since the Bucharest World Population Conference, the United Nations, population institutions and countries have now made available more reliable population data for development planning, model building and policy formulation. The experiences of the developing countries in population programming and implementation provide valuable insights in the execution of any development programme. (13 June 1983)

- It is only with a proper scientific assessment of demographic trends and their relationships with other socio-economic phenomena, based on accurate statistics, that action-oriented population programmes can be developed, sustained and strengthened. (29 September 1982)

- What is needed now are techniques of processing population information and merging it with data in other areas to produce a rounded picture of the development process. (20 September 1982)

- The new information technologies have been applied directly to gathering and analyzing population data, so that more is now known than ever before about the size, structure and movement of populations. This information has been used to seek the causes of population growth and movement and to forecast its effects; this in turn has helped to shape government policy. (3 May 1981)

- Tremendous advances have been made in the accumulation of data, methods of analysis, demographic theory and understanding population phenomena in general. The enormous progress achieved in our understanding of human fertility through the findings of the World Fertility Survey, is a case in point.

  Thanks to the painstaking work of demographers in all parts of the world, we are now able to identify and understand the many dimensions of population issues related to growth, fertility, mortality, migration, distribution and composition.

Developments in methodology have been equally important in collecting demographic data, in making estimates with limited information, in undertaking projections, and such tools as regression analysis and model life tables.

Substantial progress has also been made on theory. The various attempts to synthesize demographic with social and economic variables and the continuing refinements of the theory of demographic transition are indications of the increasing comprehensiveness of the discipline.

The emergence of demography as a scientific basis for policy decisions was made possible by the extensive research undertaken during the past few decades. . . .

The ability to collect, store and process information for analysis has, of course, been enhanced by recent advances in modern electronics. Not only is the aggregate store of information vastly increased but also the ability to compare and analyze, creating new categories which can themselves be compared and analyzed. Possibilities and connections hitherto unthought of or thought impossible are revealing themselves every day.

As we look forward, we realize that the society of the twenty-first century will be characterized by a flood of data on every aspect of life—an information society. Our ability to collect, store and process information has grown exponentially, far more rapidly than the capacity for synthesis and interpretation. The wise use of the enormous and growing quantities of information available now and becoming available to us calls for concentration on the development of techniques and methodologies to avoid what might be called information overload. Procedures for selecting data for relevance, quality, adequacy and accuracy are of great importance.

There is no doubt that demographers are able to make better long-term projections than at any time in the past. While their projections currently extend well beyond a century and a half, their substantive interpretation needs to be considerably improved.

For instance, the projected population of the world in the year 2140 is 10.5 billion. While this information is important in itself, a series of significant questions related to the relationships between population and human needs have to be answered. Apart from indicating the quantitative and qualitative needs of such a population for health, employment, food, and shelter, it will be necessary to think about the cultural and ecological adjustments that would be necessary to maintain a relatively stable social order for vastly increased numbers of people.

We can already build into demographic analyses the effect of social and economic variables such as health status or income levels on a population. We can analyze and compare the data from a dozen different sectors at many different levels of social organization, and reach conclusions which have profound importance for communities and countries.

In the future it seems entirely possible that we shall be able, if it is desired, to build in other more complex, less easily quantifiable variables such as biological and environmental interactions. Population numbers are assuming new relevance as concern increases for the effect of population growth on the environment and the resource base.

It would obviously be impossible for a single discipline to study and provide answers to all the complex issues related to human welfare. It is clear that the demographer of the next century will have to work in very close collaboration with scientists of many other disciplines if he is to give meaning to his numbers.

The changing role of demography will also demand greatest attention to maintaining scientific objectivity. We should constantly be on our guard against the use of science in the service of political bias or polemical viewpoints. In the long-term the survival of demography as an applied science may hinge upon the capacity of its practitioners to maintain their objectivity.

We see in the work of demographers both points of leverage and points of stress. While high technology in the form of electronic information systems will greatly help their work, demographers of the twenty-first century will be expected to possess both vision and adaptability. In the end it will be the creativity of the human mind which will shape the future. (9 December 1981)

On the matter of research and training . . .

• It is important to note the emergence of scientific research on population issues. . . . It is only with a proper scientific assessment of demographic trends and their relationships with other socio-economic phenomena, based on accurate statistics, that action-oriented population programmes can be developed, sustained and strengthened. . . .

While action cannot always await the findings of research, there is a continuous need to learn more about the dynamics of population change so that countries will be in a better position to plan programmes and policies. Adequate solutions to population problems can emanate only from adequate demographic analysis and population studies. (29 September 1982)

- Universities can play a significant role in developing a successful population programme. First, the universities have a traditional role, which is to collect and analyze population data to work out their implications, possible future directions and the necessary policy prescriptions. Demographic research should form an integral part of university research. The universities can also play a new role. Most programmes that fail do so because of inadequate institutional support and lack of management skills. Building of institutional infrastructure is a time-consuming process. Universities can lead research on existing structures and suggest how they can be modified or expanded so as to undertake the management of coherent programmes. (2 October 1982)

- It would be tragic indeed if, as has so often happened with many survey results, the data obtained were not utilized, studied, evaluated and applied in the formulation and implementation of population and development policies. (7 July 1980)

- Neither the collection of basic data nor any other field of population activities can be satisfactorily undertaken without the necessary trained personnel. Our aim here should be the self-reliance of countries. . . . (10 May 1979)

- The success of all of these programmes requires well-trained personnel at the national and sub-national level. And the UNFPA has invested considerable sums in assisting the nations of the developing world to become self-reliant in their population activities. At the regional and also at the national levels, training programmes for nurse/midwives, educational planners, development specialists and others have been undertaken, pointing to that day some time in the future when the developing nations will need only financial support to meet their population needs and to achieve their demographic transition. (29 September 1982)

- The experience gained in running country programmes has been buttressed by UNFPA-supported intercountry activities which have helped in the design of national projects and in the development of methodologies for training and for materials design and testing. They have also assisted training facilities and related technical support. Without this support, many national projects would not exist, and the quality of others would be inferior. (7 March 1983)

On the matter of population education and communication . . .

• Everyone is an actor on the population stage. At one time or another, we all make what could be called "population decisions"—to leave or stay in the place where we were born, to marry or stay single, to have or not to have children, to give birth in a hospital or at home, to send our children to school or put them to work. Although they may be conditioned by public policy, we do not usually think of them as "population decisions", because they are in the end private, not public.

Yet the results of all these private decisions amount to major changes in the size and structure of a population—national rates of growth, of urbanization, of age distribution, of infant or maternal morbidity and mortality. It is the task of government to translate those results into public policy, and perhaps to attempt to change them. But because trends in population are the result of individual decisions, change can only be effected by changing the basis on which decisions are made.

Population education is part of the process. It has been established that a higher level of literacy in a society goes along with lower fertility. . . .

Beyond the mere ability to read and write, learners acquire through the education system a variety of information which may affect their "population decisions". They may learn about world or national population growth, about cultures other than their own, about health, nutrition and hygiene. They may learn about their own bodily functions, about sexuality, pregnancy and birth. These various elements have come to be known as "population education".

Effectively, population education defines itself in practice. Broadly, we might describe it, first, as being intended to develop awareness and understanding of the causes and effects of population growth and movement. Secondly, it is intended to assist learners in their roles as population actors and to help them evaluate the consequences of particular actions. An important part of the content of a population education programme comes from related areas of study—human sexuality, social and economic change, ecology, family and social structures, for example. The precise mix and the emphasis given to each part reflect local perceptions and sensibilities. . . .

The thread of population education thus runs through many other forms of education, helping learners to understand the relationship of population to the different aspects of development and to assess the impact of their individual decisions on their society. This in itself

is one of the goals of development—the formation of minds trained
to think clearly about the present and the future. . . .

The goal of population education is to equip the learner to analyze
and make decisions about issues of population growth and movement;
the decisions will be the learner's own. It must be a process of investigation and analysis, using such data as are available—with, if possible, some indication of how data can be evaluated—and with a
critical eye on the values which lie behind assumptions about population.

This may sound like a very ambitious target—but the world in
which our children are growing up is changing faster than at any previous stage of its history, and particularly fast in the developing countries in which most population growth is taking place. The challenge
to the population educator—as to all educators now—is to help the
young adapt to the changes taking place around them, for which traditional values do not necessarily provide a sure guide, and to help them
learn how they may take a hand in shaping their own destiny.

Common to all aspects of population education is the intention to
bring about change—and this is what perhaps marks off population
education from the disciplines with which it is connected. Population
education is by its origins and in practice a tool of public policy. . . .

Since population education in the developing world began as a
response to concern about rapid population growth, it is sometimes
assumed that its relevance is limited to countries where growth is
perceived as a problem. But, as we have seen, population education
is not a prescriptive programme dealing only with a limited range of
population scenarios. It is perhaps worth remembering that the concept first saw the light of day in the industrial countries, in response
to declining growth rates. Today, population education is appropriate in both developed and developing countries, in those whose governments feel a need for larger populations as well as in those in which
it is desired to decrease the rate of growth or retard the pace of rural-
urban migration. It may help to confront the problems posed by
declining rural populations, high infant mortality or extreme poverty.
By increasing awareness and understanding of the factors involved
in population change, it can contribute to the perception as well as
to the solution of population problems of whatever kind, at national
or local levels.

There are differences in the way in which population education is
approached at different stages of development and in different parts
of the world, but these are principally differences of emphasis. In practice, the approach depends on national and local perceptions. In Asia,
for example, where many governments consider rapid population

growth an obstacle to development, population education programmes are designed with an eye to influencing fertility. Cultural sensibilities have prevented direct instruction about such subjects as human sexuality in many Asian countries, but this reluctance is gradually disappearing as population becomes an acceptable topic for public discussion.

By contrast, many African and Latin American countries emphasize the personal and family implications of population change, especially in the early stages of the programme. Projects may therefore be labelled "family life education" though their content has evolved to include population dynamics and the environment, as in Mexico or Paraguay. African approaches usually emphasize cultural diversity, education for development, environmental issues and family life or sex education. The change from a sectoral description to the general term "population education" is largely a matter of timing. Growing awareness gradually brings acceptance.

Continued expansion of interest in and commitment to population education can be expected in the future. Present programmes will be further developed and refined in teacher training, including pre-service, in-service refresher training courses, use of "distance" teaching methods, and continuing monitoring and evaluation, so that content and structure may be reinforced and modified. (7 March 1983)

• Effective communication by population institutions . . . has resulted in the development of awareness of the importance of population issues and in the understanding of population as an important variable capable of development planning. Face-to-face communication in communities by men and women known by different names—the community worker, the health promoter, the agricultural agent, or the literacy worker—has resulted in a widespread change of attitudes and behaviour on the part of many couples in all regions of the world on family planning.

Communication has played a vital role in efforts and commitment of governments and of national institutions towards the reduction of mortality and the achievement of a more balanced population distribution.

In the process of development of awareness of the importance of population in development planning, communication has always been a two-way process on the part of governments and UNFPA. If we have been successful in our efforts it has been because we have listened to governments and we have been receptive to their needs and aspirations. Furthermore, the work of the Fund has always been characterized by an adherence to each country's view and policies on population. In this sense, programmes have been genuine dialogues with the people through their national governments and local institutions. (18 August 1981)

• The importance of the communications media in awakening interest and satisfying the need for information in the population field cannot be over-emphasized. . . . Without a keen awareness on the part of the public of the importance of the population question and the possibility of its solution, there can be no tangible success. . . . (19 September 1983)

• . . . even considering the documented declining fertility, it is not the time to relax our efforts. Information and services have to be made more readily available to those who desire to control their fertility. Our work is far from done. More than ever before, we need to make a greater effort to assist countries in their population programmes. (7 July 1980)

On the matter of integration of population policies with development planning . . .

• In the past, the solution most often proposed to deal with population problems was largely framed in partial terms. Thus, the pre-eminent emphasis suggested by many on family planning activities, almost to the exclusion of other programmes. This, from the very beginning, was never a view shared by UNFPA. However, what many . . . scholars and scientists had been urging during this period, with subdued voices, drowned out by others, is now being heard and understood with greater clarity and a greater sense of urgency: partial solutions do not solve problems and may, in fact, exacerbate them. What is needed is to seek solutions that see all of the parts in their total context. As this realization obtained greater currency, two trends could be observed which are important to our understanding of the population and development interrelations: The thinking about development has had to abandon some of its familiar assumptions and certitudes while the conceptualization of population issues has broadened.

With respect to development thinking, the 1970s saw the emergence of a healthy agnosticism concerning the indirect, so-called "trickle down" approach to development which characterized so much of programme activities in the preceding decades. Doubts have been raised concerning the relevance of neo-classical and Keynesian economics to Third World development. Preoccupation with aggregate economic growth and industrialization has diminished. In its place there has arisen a greater awareness of the need to look at the structure of societies, and the way these affect people. There is greater concern about matters of absolute poverty, about the values of social orders which are conducive to and even connive at inequality in the distribution of income, goods, services and opportunities, and in problems of high and rising rates of unemployment.

From this has arisen a search for a development strategy which focusses attention on more specific areas of human need—such as water, health, education, sanitation—as a means of achieving a more abstract concept such as an improvement in the quality of life.

Concomitant with this is an attempt to channel resources to particular groups in society, those in greatest need. It focusses not only on the unemployed and the underemployed, but also on those most poor and destitute, the so-called unemployable.

While, by the end of the decade the issue of the nature and processes of development was undergoing some fundamental rethinking, the conceptualization of the field of population was showing greater maturity and sophistication. The dominant perception of population programmes as being synonymous with family planning was giving way to a new realization of the breadth and complexity of the issues and the ways in which they might be met. In addition to focussing largely on growth and, as a result, fertility, attention is increasingly being directed to matters of mortality, internal and international migration and the spatial distribution of population. Furthermore, there is greater sensitivity to the range of population issues and their perceptions, and to the need to look beyond the global, and even the national, level to sub-groups within the society. From this broadened understanding it was not difficult to conclude that just as there is no single definition of a population problem, there is similarly no single or partial solution to the problems, no matter how defined. It is within this context that attention is being directed to the linkages between population and development planning. . . .

The issue of population . . . is one which has an influence on all the inputs of development planning and which, in turn, is influenced by the thrust of those plans. Yet it would be wrong to regard it as a vague and amorphous factor lurking in the background; just as with health or education, population is susceptible to being treated in a programmatic way as the Fund has proved in its programmes of assistance. And . . . population programmes, whether designed for an increase or a decrease in the birth rate, are as worthy of their own place in a country's over-all plan as what one might term the more "traditional" sectors. It is true that the effects of such plans have to be seen in a long-term perspective—indeed, some programmes may take a generation to make their impact—but it is equally important to realize that population is a programmatic factor in the creation of development plans.

In the late 1950s and 1960s, the "solution" proposed by some, and I use the word advisedly, was to limit population growth. But clearly that was too simple, as well as unrealistic, because of the synergistic relationship between the problem and the solution.

Now we are less quick to offer or accept such solutions. What we seek is a process—which for want of a better term we call the linkage of population and development planning—which will help us to grapple intellectually, conceptually and programmatically with the issues.

This involves among other things greater disaggregation in the data in order to understand the differential processes at work in a society. It also entails more attention to population movements and distribution.

At the next level it implies the search for an understanding of the mutual impact of population and development processes and programmes. In the past, as noted earlier, the focus was on the effects of population growth on the achievement of development goals. We must continue on this search but with greater sophistication, while we devote additional attention to the other influences which population can exert on development planning. . . .

From this deepened understanding, we hope that we will all be able to develop more sensitive and suitable population policies which are integrated into development policies and programmes. These policies, which might be called "second generation population policies" to differentiate them from those policies that concentrated on only one aspect of the subject, should be more responsive to meeting the needs of people in the last years of the twentieth century, as well as those of generations to come. . . .

The challenge facing us is to be able to relate more coherently population variables to the over-all development planning of countries and use the implications of population studies to improve the analysis which forms the basis of such plans. We must never underestimate the importance of basic material—the demographic and other population-related statistics without which the scientific core of the input to the over-all development policies of a country is missing.

Neither the collection of basic data nor any other field of population activities can be satisfactorily undertaken without the necessary trained personnel. Our aim here should be the self-reliance of countries so that they can undertake their own demographic research and statistical analysis.

The collection of population data and the provision of trained personnel for such crucial work must, however, be complemented by both the knowledge whereby such information can be incorporated into development planning and the focal point at which such a merging of information can take place. . . . Such knowledge, it hardly needs saying, must go hand in hand with the institutions which are ultimately designed to translate the results of such research into implementable plans.

Four related activities—the provision of adequate population data, the development of human resources through training programmes, the establishment of institutions for relating such data to the formulation and implementation of policies, and the research into the nature of the relationship between population information and development planning—are all vital for the integration of population and development policies. (10 May 1979)

• If the Fifties was the decade in which the "population problem" was perceived and studied by demographers, primarily as questions of morbidity and mortality, the Sixties the decade that brought about a shift in emphasis to the fertility factors in population growth, the Seventies the decade of growing awareness of the need to regard population as an important and integral factor in the entire process of development, then it is clear that the Eighties should be the decade in which population will be embodied in development policies, programmes and strategies resulting in effective realization of major population objectives. . . .

It is vitally important to assure that all the various population elements including fertility, mortality, population growth, structure and spatial distribution are perceived as what they are—important variables that act on and are acted upon by governments and by the international community to improve the well-being and quality of life of mankind. (18 June 1979)

• Population data constitute the basic input on which the whole edifice of the planning structure is erected. Even at the simplest level, the size of the population and the rates of growth constitute important elements for determining the targets of growth of different sectors of the economy. However, the treatment given to population in national and international development strategies differs quite considerably from the treatment given to a number of other economic and social variables. While many of these variables are considered endogenous to the process of development, population is often treated as an exogenous factor. This is largely due to the fact that economists whose thinking dominates the field of development lack a coherent theory of population within their discipline and hence consider population growth as not so amenable to control as some other economic variables.

The tendency to treat population as an exogenous factor was further reinforced by a development strategy, adopted especially in the 1950s and 1960s, which emphasized investment in industry to accelerate development and targetted only for an aggregate growth in per capita income without specifying any conditions on the distribution of income. International development assistance programmes and the global development strategy also provided further support and impetus to this approach. With hindsight, one is able to point out now that this approach has failed to take into account a number of interrelationships among population growth, resource use, environmental deterioration and the process of development. The emphasis on investment in industry in the development strategy and the neglect of many other aspects of development, while populations have been growing, have not solved the problems in the developing countries. . . .

In fact, UNFPA, from its very beginnings, never considered population programming as an investment for fertility control alone or as an end in itself but always considered it as one of the elements of the development strategy depending upon the special needs and circumstances prevailing in a particular country. . . .

The integration of population programmes with specific aspects of the development strategy can lead not only to an increase in general welfare but can also have a beneficial impact on population trends.

The integration of population programmes with the development strategy will be possible only if population is treated as a separate sector just like any other sector in the planning process. It is true that in a number of countries financial provisions for population programmes are separately indicated in their development plans, but this is not tantamount to treating population as an endogenous sector within development planning. It is true that high rates of population growth may not be the most pressing problem in every country. In some countries, as a matter of fact, low fertility may be a problem, while in other countries birth rates, though high, may be considered quite satisfactory, taking into account the variety and quality of natural resources they possess in relation to the size of their populations. But even those countries will require reliable basic population data for decision-making at various levels in planning for their economies. In some countries, spatial maldistribution of the population may be the most important problem. All such problems of population dynamics can be recognized and studied only if population is treated as a programmable sector within planning.

Just as working out alternative scenarios for different assumptions regarding the rate of investment or targets in per capita income, it is possible to work out similar alternative models incorporating different assumptions regarding the likely changes in fertility or other demographic variables.

It is important to recognize that such assumed changes in demographic variables are not merely the result of autonomous changes in them but are also induced by further investment in population activities as well as in socio-economic programmes. When this relationship is understood, it also becomes clear why expenditure incurred on population programmes deserves to be treated like investment in any other productive field.

Fertility rates have been found to decline with declines in mortality rates, especially infant and child mortality, with rising educational levels, improvement in the social and occupational status of women and reduction in inequality in the distribution of income and wealth. These changes can be achieved only if development programmes ensure equality of access to health care facilities and education to everyone in the society, eliminate forms of malnutrition, and reduce social and economic inequality prevailing in the society.

The implementation of a programme which takes into account the relationships mentioned above obviously will call for changes in the strategies of development which have been followed till now. The basic objectives of development policy may have to shift from the achievement of targetted rates of per capita income to the enhancement of the general welfare of the population. For this purpose, the pattern of investment will also need to be altered. Larger amounts of investment may have to be made in non-commodity production sectors, such as health care, education, and others. Institutional and economic reforms should also form an integral part of the new strategy. . . .

If population programmes are integrated with the development strategy, we need no longer consider the rate of growth as exogenously given. In order to integrate population with development strategies, a long-term perspective is necessary. This is so because population changes are essentially phenomena brought about by inter-generational shifts in demographic variables and as such the time-frame must be extended, to cover the lifetime of a generation at least. This is probably another reason why population has not been incorporated as an endogenous variable in earlier strategies. Until now, development planning has been confined to shorter time horizons within which population changes appear to be inconsequential. But, when we extend the time horizon to a long-term perspective, it can be seen that this is not so. But, the achievement of this long-term objective is possible only if we incorporate investment in the population sector

in the short-run plans, taking into consideration its long-run returns.
. . . (19 June 1979)

• It is important . . . to recognize that population is a distinctly
programmable sector within national development plans and global
development strategies, including the International Development
Strategy for the Third Development Decade. . . . At both the national and international levels, efforts to improve equity, social justice
and the quality of life of mankind must continue to take into account
the essential relationships that exist between population and development. (31 October 1979)

• The United Nations has always considered population variables to
be an integral part of the total development process. Interrelationships are both sources of stress and points of leverage. If some
problems are addressed and not others, interrelationships can act as
constraints that impede the effectiveness of policy measures. (21 July
1980)

• Broadly speaking, we can attribute the success of governmental population programmes to several factors: first and foremost, the perceptions of the governments of the developing countries of their
population problems have undergone a dramatic change in the past
15 to 20 years. In the early 1950s there was only one country, India,
which had recognized the importance of a population policy. By now,
the governments of almost all countries in the world have understood
its significant role in relation not only to development but also to
resources and to environment. This change in the attitude to population issues is the result of painstaking and patient work on the part
of a number of individuals including academics, public administrators, social workers and others; the institutional groundwork built
up by private and voluntary agencies, both national and international; and the actions initiated by the governments themselves. During
the past two decades, many of these individuals and agencies have
provided the intellectual basis for the conceptualization of population issues and thus helped governments to incorporate population
as an important area amenable to programming like any other development activity.

   This conceptualization has been based on the findings of a number of empirical studies on the relationships between population and
various socio-economic factors and on the experiences gained in the
process of implementation of population programmes themselves.
Population now appears to be an area of development where technical factors have been successfully integrated with socio-economic and
cultural variables both in drawing up and in implementing
programmes. . . .

This integration of population with development has resulted ultimately in evolving a comprehensive view of population, one that is no longer confined to issues of fertility and mortality rates and their levels, but which also incorporates other important questions such as the status of women, population behaviour, and population redistribution. This expansion of issues under population is in large part an outcome of the experience gained in implementing concrete programmes in different parts of the world and the problems encountered during this process. Indeed, consciousness of the importance of population and the conceptualization of population issues and the translation of these issues into workable programmes as integral parts of the development process should be considered the hallmark of our achievement in the past 15 years.

The second factor which has contributed to the success of governmental population programmes is the adaptation of techniques of implementation which have already proved useful in other areas of development activity. The exchange of experiences of various sectors and the integration of population programmes with these sectoral programmes have helped considerably in improving the results of national projects. For instance, the implementation of population programmes in Mexico is guided by the National Population Council which is composed of eight ministers and represents such important social sectors as health, education, and housing . . . agriculture, finance and planning. The integration of population programmes with important socio-economic sectors is reflected in significant declines in fertility rates in Mexico. The Mexican population growth has fallen from 3.3 per cent in the early 1960s to 2.5 per cent at present. Emboldened by these results, the Mexican Government has laid down a target for its population growth of 1 per cent per annum by the year 2000. (12 May 1981)

• It was the unprecedented growth in the 1950s and 1960s, coupled with greater knowledge on the part of many governments of developing countries, that led to a growing sense of the urgent need to integrate population factors into development planning. A large number of governments which had previously subscribed to the notion that large populations would not be detrimental to future economic growth, and had viewed population policy interventions as unnecessary or even harmful to development, reversed their position in the 1970s. (8 July 1982A)

• Much progress has been made in dovetailing population and other development programmes, but . . . what is needed now are techniques of processing population information and merging it with data in other areas to produce a rounded picture of the development process. At the policy level the high priority which population issues claim is still not often reflected in the machinery of government. At the practical level, there is still a real need for additional training in managerial skills to carry out integration of programmes on the ground. It should be made clear at all levels that population has a pre-emptive claim on national attention and resources. (20 September 1982)

• Never before has the dynamics of population assumed greater significance than at the present time. It has not only led to a re-examination of traditional explanations for demographic transition, but has also questioned the conventional thinking on the interrelationships between population and development. These elaborations in the fields of demography and economics have profound practical implications for the currently less developed countries. . . .

Let us examine the changing perceptions of the processes of development, of population, and of the linkages between the two. From the mid-1940s until the latter part of the 1960s, development economists were relatively optimistic concerning future possibilities for continued development in the Third World. They perceived development to be a gradual but continuous and cumulative process which could effectively rely on marginal adjustments in its spread among groups within nations, as well as across the boundaries between nations. . . .

In the course of the last three decades, the concept of population and development has been modified considerably. Initially, in the 1950s the concept was that industrialization was the key to development. In the 1960s and 1970s, views on development began to change, emphasizing more and more the provision of basic needs and the quality of life for people in the developing countries. Similarly, at the initial stage of the involvement of the United Nations in population programmes, the drive was to assist countries purely in the field of family planning with the hope that this would result in a diminution of the population growth rate and thus contribute towards improving economic development. So the intimate linkage was defined from the beginning in terms of economic growth rate and population growth rate, or, at the very least, the population growth rate was seen as a factor in hampering the rate of economic growth in developing countries.

Since the adoption of the World Population Plan of Action at Bucharest in 1974, the emphasis has swung to aspects of human welfare, the quality of life, and the humane aspects of economic development. This means that all population programmes, while strategically important in terms of economic development, must be modified so that the individual's potential is given the opportunity to develop fully. In this way, the concept of population programmes aiming at individual development is linked to the total development effort.

The political forum of the Bucharest Conference—the first of its kind—served to direct attention to, and interest in, a broader, less simplistic, more sophisticated view of the mutual interrelationships between population and development factors. The World Population Plan of Action firmly established population as an important element in international strategies to promote development and to improve the quality of life, and set as an important goal the expansion and deepening of the capacity of countries to deal effectively with their national and subnational population problems.

The Bucharest Conference, while clearly recognizing that population policies, and in particular the policies for moderating fertility and population growth alone, could not solve the problems of development, noted that such policies, in conjunction with an intensified development effort, could make a significant contribution to their solution. Population policies were stressed to be an integral part of, but never a substitute for, development policies. Therefore, it was emphasized that policies and programmes designed to influence population trends, composition and distribution should go hand in hand with socio-economic development policies.

In this framework, the approach to population issues becomes much more complex and broader. Rather than looking at population in the aggregate, attention is directed to the components of the population. Population growth, assumed to have been independent of socio-economic development and change, is now seen as intimately and mutually related. . . . The maturation and sophistication of population thinking has put an end to simplistic models of population change. UNFPA, from its inception, has acted upon this broader view of population concerns. . . .

Thus having re-established the linkage, and the need for greater attention to the population and development interface, we find ourselves today standing at a very broad frontier. For, having identified the need to integrate population factors into development planning, we find that there is still much territory to be explored to bring this idea to its full fruition and implementation. (29 September 1982)

• The treatment of population in national and international development strategies, although gaining considerable importance in a number of developing countries, is not yet commensurate with the treatment normally accorded to other social and economic variables—that is, as an endogenous factor in planning. The experience in population programming during the past fifteen years unequivocally indicates that it is as much amenable and related to factors of development as any other economic variable. Since this is so, then it is important to identify those factors which population influences most and incorporate these relationships as essential ingredients of development planning. (13 June 1983)

ISSUES FOR THE FUTURE: PROMOTION OF KNOWLEDGE AND IMPLEMENTATION OF POLICIES AND PROGRAMMES

In the further implementation of the World Population Plan of Action in the area of increasing the knowledge of population and the implementation of population policies and programmes, attention may be given to the following issues:

- The strengthening and improvement of the collection and analysis of population data for further integration within social and economic development plans through better vital registration systems; development of migration statistics; participation in population and housing census programmes; more accurate sample surveys and periodic surveys on fertility, family planning, health, mortality, migration and technical assistance and the safeguarding of individual privacy in these processes;

- The establishment or maintenance of capability for demographic research and the evaluation, analysis and dissemination of collected data in all governments with the co-operation of non-governmental organizations and the scientific and academic community at national, regional and global levels; the emphasis on policy-oriented research;

- The expansion of training programmes in population to ensure an adequate cadre of trained personnel to formulate and manage population policies and programmes and the intensification of population information, education and communication programmes to increase awareness of population issues;

- The attainment of self-reliance by governments in the management of their population programmes through better co-ordination at the national level of international assistance; adoption of effective financial management of programmes and the adequate monitoring and evaluation of programmes for policy-making and programming.

Chapter VII

INTERNATIONAL CO-OPERATION AND THE ROLE OF UNFPA

INTRODUCTION

Of all the global issues that mankind faces today, population is the one area in which expectations for success were the least, but which turned out to be the opposite in a relatively short period of time. International co-operation has been catalytic in this regard. Such co-operation has helped to forge links between local, national and international approaches to population problems, as for instance with the initiatives of national parliamentarians to further communication among themselves at the regional and global level. It has facilitated the exchange of experience and expertise in population programming among countries with similar problems but at different stages in the formulation and implementation of policies. Comparative and co-operative research has led to greater and more refined understanding of the interrelationships among population and development variables. Finally, international assistance has played a vital role both in increasing awareness of the consequences of population trends for national development goals, and in enabling countries to become self-reliant in collecting and analyzing population data, formulating effective policies, and implementing programmes to achieve balanced development.

It was not until the late 1960s that the first United Nations resolution was formulated on extending population assistance to countries in need. This assistance, based on the expressed needs and requests of countries, now flows voluntarily from developed to developing countries. Today, there is hardly a government among Member States of the United Nations which does not have a population policy, even though these nations have different political philosophies, cultures and religions. Programmes for the reduction of fertility, where there is a felt need to do so, have been universally implemented.

The successes that many governments have achieved today resulting in the collective decline of global population growth rates have been partly due to the programmes initiated and maintained with increasing momentum over the past 15 years. In the majority of these programmes, United Nations assistance has played an essential, if not indispensable, role.

UNFPA was created (i) to build up, on an international basis, with the assistance of the competent bodies of the United Nations system, the knowledge and the capacity to respond to national, regional, interregional and global needs in population and family planning; to promote co-ordination in planning and programming, and to co-operate with all concerned; (ii) to promote awareness, both in developed and in developing countries, of the social, economic and environmental implications of national and international population problems, of the human rights aspects of family planning, and of possible strategies to deal with them, in accordance with the plans and priorities of each country; (iii) to extend systematic and sustained assistance to developing countries at their request in dealing with their population problems, such assistance to be afforded in forms and by means requested by the recipient countries and best suited to meet the individual country's needs; and (iv) to play a leading role in the United Nations system in promoting population programmes and to co-ordinate projects supported by UNFPA.

Since becoming operational in 1969, UNFPA has transferred well over one billion dollars to developing countries in the various categories of population assistance, thanks to the unwavering support of many developed countries. Today, more than one-fourth of all international population assistance is channelled through UNFPA, now the largest source of multilateral assistance for population activities.

During this time of rapid expansion in its programme of assistance, the role of UNFPA within the United Nations system has evolved considerably. While continuing its close operational relationship with the United Nations Development Programme, UNFPA was placed by the United Nations General Assembly under the Assembly's authority in 1972 (resolution 3019(XXVII)), and at the same time, without prejudice to the policy functions of the Economic and Social Council, the Assembly decided that the Governing Council of the United Nations Development Programme would be UNFPA's governing body concerned with the financial and administrative policies of the Fund. In 1979, the General Assembly affirmed that UNFPA is a subsidiary body of the Assembly.

Working in co-operation with governments, intergovernmental organizations, agencies and organizations of the United Nations system, and non-governmental organizations, UNFPA, in accordance with its mandate from the Economic and Social Council, has played a leading role in the United Nations system in promoting population programmes and in co-ordinating the assistance it provides. While the role of UNFPA has evolved both *de jure* and *de facto* over the past decade-and-a-half, it is not apparent that the former fully reflects the latter.

From 1969 through 1974, the year in which the World Population Conference was held, UNFPA had disbursed funds for population activities totalling $110 million. For each of the past six years (1979-1984), UNFPA has dispersed more funds annually than was expended during the entire 5-year period from the time UNFPA became operational in 1969 through 1974. This expanded role of UNFPA had not been foreseen, and the present organization of population assistance and activities within the United Nations system may not fully correspond to the tasks given to UNFPA or expected from it. Decisions on policy and programme content are made by a multitude of bodies within the United Nations: the Economic and Social Council and the Governing Council reporting through it to the General Assembly; two functional commissions of the Economic and Social Council; and the regional commissions of the United Nations. Even though such decisions or recommendations are not necessarily addressed to UNFPA, they influence the funding decisions of the Fund and the Governing Council's responsibilities concerning the organization. A rethinking of the United Nations system's organizational approach to decision-making in population matters might be in order, to increase the effectiveness and efficiency of the population and development assistance provided by the system as a whole.

The importance of taking both a global and a long-term view with regard to matters concerning population policies and programmes cannot be overstated. We cannot afford at this point to slacken the support for developing country population programmes aimed towards stabilizing world population. The crucial role of international assistance in this effort has been emphasized by the 1979 International Conference of Parliamentarians on Population and Development in its call for an annual sum of one billion dollars in global population assistance by 1984. To sustain and increase the momentum generated over the past 15 years will require no less than the continued perception of the population problem, and the commitment to its solutions by all countries, as one of the most urgent tasks to be faced through the next century if we are to stabilize population in less than 130 years from now.

EXCERPTS FROM STATEMENTS

On international co-operation in population matters . . .

- The interdependence of the global system has made it necessary, as never before, that an innovative management approach be taken for the solution of global problems. And in the face of shrinking international resources available for assisting developing countries and the growing political and economic tensions, it is necessary to exercise the utmost care in establishing global priorities. In this respect, population certainly deserves one of the highest considerations in view of its critical role in almost every sector of economic, social and political life. (21 July 1980)

- Had fertility levels remained the same as in the 1950s for the rest of the century, the estimated global population in the year 2000 would have been 7.5 billion instead of the United Nations medium variant projection of 6.1 billion. For every dollar of external assistance to population, the recipient countries are themselves spending on the average, two dollars of their own resources to implement the population programmes. Population is, indeed, the one area among the number of serious global issues in which the United Nations response has proven adequate, timely, economical and effective.

Now that the required momentum has been gained and partial successes have been achieved, it is time to sustain this effort consistently and boldly. Effective management demands that investment must be increased in sectors where the objectives are evidently being realized. (11 June 1982)

• The extension and intensification of population programmes have produced an explosion in demand for financial resources, technology and human skills. To supply them will call for an international effort even bigger than we have seen so far.

To take the question of financial resources first. The share of national resources devoted to population has increased absolutely and as a proportion of development budgets. . . . Although international assistance has also increased, countries on the average spend on population four times as much from local revenues as they receive from UNFPA, the biggest multilateral source of international population assistance.

It is clear that additional resources for population programmes will largely come from governments themselves. (20 September 1982)

• While external assistance can perform a supplementary and catalytic role in promoting population programmes, . . . countries will in the end have to rely primarily on their own resources for implementing effective programmes within this concept of self-reliance. Towards this end, let me therefore suggest:

First, all those . . . countries which are in a position to provide external aid should increase their assistance to population programmes to the maximum amount possible within their national budgets;

Second, there should be more co-operation . . . in contraceptive technology research and demographic and policy studies;

Third, larger exchange of experts in population should be promoted by encouraging some of the existing national training institutions . . . to become centres for regional co-operation. (27 October 1981)

• The developing countries themselves have considerably increased their investment in population programmes and during the past ten years have acquired the necessary conceptual and institutional framework to effectively implement them. One should view the significance of external assistance in this context, its catalytic and crucial role in sustaining and raising the momentum of population programmes that we have already set in motion. (12 May 1981)

• There must be adequate resources for family planning programmes. The developing countries have adequately demonstrated in the past

ten years that, with the proper amount of external assistance and an
increasing amount of investment on their part in population
programmes, they have been able to moderate population growth....
External assistance is vital in specific areas to make national
programmes more effective especially now that many of the developing countries have acquired the necessary conceptual and institutional
and human resources to implement them comprehensively and effectively. We must, therefore, strive collectively to achieve the goal set
by the International Conference of Parliamentarians in 1979 of one
billion dollars of annual population assistance by 1984. This is a
modest amount—unable fully to meet even current demands and
future needs. (27 April 1981)

• While imbalances created by poverty, malnutrition or ill health persist, the social tensions arising out of population pressures will permeate every aspect of life on earth.

For this reason, a renewed international effort to stabilize world
population at the earliest possible time and at the lowest possible level
is imperative. Certainly this was the basic message of the statement
issued by the International Conference on Family Planning in the
1980s, held in Jakarta, Indonesia.... The Conference noted: "There
is an urgent need to increase current expenditure in developing countries from an estimated current $1 billion to approximately $3 billion annually in order to meet population and family planning
programme needs". We are all well aware that improved maternal
and child health services, lower infant mortality, wider access to education, greater opportunities for women, later marriages and reductions in income disparities are all forces which can help to bring about
the "demographic transition" from high to low birth rates. To achieve
this will require continued efforts to integrate population and development planning. It is within our capacity to hasten the demographic
transition in the less developed countries in the remaining two decades
of this century. (12 June 1981)

On the role of UNFPA . . .

• I believe that UNFPA has played an important and catalytic role in
population assistance in the 1970s. I remain confident that this role
can be enlarged and expanded in order to meet the foreseen increases
in both the need and demands for assistance from the developing countries. The success of such an endeavour requires a substantial increase
in our resources. We are conscious, at the same time, that we in
UNFPA have the responsibility to continue responding effectively

and efficiently to the challenges of the decade that lies ahead. (16 June 1980)

- In the course of years, there have been obvious accretions to UNFPA's role in extending population assistance and, as a result, UNFPA's responsibilities have widened beyond that of a strictly funding agency. The Fund has not only played "a leading role in the United Nations system in promoting population programmes", as requested by ECOSOC, it is now playing a co-ordinating role outside the United Nations system by working closely with donor and recipient governments and non-governmental organizations in extending population assistance. More than a quarter of the total global population aid to developing countries is now channelled through the UNFPA annually. Through periodic consultations with population institutions and through an extensive information programme, the UNFPA has established linkages to interested parties beyond the population field. (18 June 1979)

- The maturation and sophistication of population thinking has put an end to simplistic models of population change. The UNFPA, from its inception, has acted upon this broader view of population concerns. (29 September 1982)

- The wide-ranging and serious population issues and problems the world will face in the coming years are a great challenge to UNFPA. Its mandate and resources will make it necessary to concentrate on rather specific goals which it should endeavour to accomplish in the 1980s. Some of these goals or objectives are not necessarily measurable and it might be difficult to identify concrete targets. Moreover, these goals are not to be accomplished by the Fund alone since the attainment of any one of them can easily absorb the Fund's total resources for any given year. Rather, they indicate directions to which the Fund should devote its major attention. The most important goals, not necessarily in the order of priority, are the following:

  —increase awareness and understanding of population problems and issues and to strengthen the commitment of developing and developed countries to deal with them;

  —provide for the formulation and implementation of population policies in accordance with the needs and perceptions of the countries themselves and integration of population aspects into all development planning and programmes;

  —build up the capability of developing countries to design, administer and evaluate population programmes with a view to promoting self-reliance;

—increase access to information and means to attain desired family size and spacing of births in fulfillment of several international instruments and declarations adopted in recent years but far from being realized;

—redouble efforts to improve current contraceptive technology and develop new, more effective and acceptable means;

—reduce infant mortality and specifically to realize the target of bringing the level down to 50 per thousand in developing countries by the end of this decade in accordance with the International Development Strategy;

—promote the full participation of women in all aspects of population-related development programmes; and finally

—address particularly the needs of disadvantaged population groups in all supported population programmes. (2 July 1981)

• In spite of continuing world economic tensions and stresses, the Fund has been able to create a global atmosphere of consensus on the need to evolve population-related development programmes in practically all of the developing countries. (3 October 1980)

• The UNFPA as the largest source of multilateral population assistance must adapt its policies and operations to the foreseeable changing needs of countries. It must consolidate the gains made and maintain the momentum of the programmes that have proven effective in affecting population trends. This will entail redoubled efforts at applying the concepts and goals of the World Population Plan of Action concerning the interrelationships between population and development as well as adopting a broader outlook in the interpretation of the Fund's mandate into its operational guidelines. (31 October 1979)

• As far as we may increase and stretch our assistance, it is still true that UNFPA and the other international agencies cannot supply more than a small proportion of the resources needed for development. We can, however, act as a catalyst in the development of ideas and approaches to development problems and thus through small inputs produce larger results. Our approach to international assistance will concentrate even more than in the past on supporting projects which will develop their own momentum and stimulate the community both by education and example. (20 September 1982)

• The challenges of future population programming are serious and wide-ranging. The mandate of UNFPA and a flexible interpretation of it should permit the United Nations to respond to changing population issues and needs. (29 September 1982)

ISSUES FOR THE FUTURE: INTERNATIONAL CO-OPERATION AND THE ROLE OF UNFPA

In the further implementation of international co-operation and the increasing role of the UNFPA, attention may be given to the following issues:

• The encouragement of technical co-operation between developing countries, between developed and developing countries and between developing countries and bilateral and multilateral organizations; and the exchange of information and experiences between countries particularly on successful programmes and training;

• The need for increased international assistance in population to about $1 billion per annum as recommended by the Colombo Conference of Parliamentarians in 1979;

• The importance of the support for population programmes by all the concerned organizations of the United Nations system and non-governmental organizations; the involvement of all the decision-making levels in the countries including parliamentarians, mass media, academic and scientific communities and city executives in the awareness of the importance of population and in the implementation of programmes;

• The strengthening of the role of the United Nations Fund for Population Activities within the United Nations system to ensure more effective delivery of population assistance; and the rationalization of decision-making regarding population matters within the United Nations.

Chapter VIII

BY THE YEAR 2000 AND BEYOND

The year 2000 marks not only the end of a century but also the end of a millennium. It will be a time when philosophers and historians look back to the past in order to summarize and highlight events that may have an effect on the future. While the thirty-five year effort of governments to work out population policies and programmes is only a short period of time in a millennium, it adds up to more than a third of the past century.

This volume has reflected the process of population policy-making of the United Nations Fund for Population Activities with the developing countries in support of their population programmes in the past decade and a half. These policies were sanctioned and validated, both nationally by the countries themselves and globally by United Nations deliberative bodies and conferences. The text has explained sectorally the demographic situation that has led to these policies, surveyed the policies of UNFPA that have resulted from working with national population programmes and touched upon some of the important areas for probable policy formulation among the issues that will come before the 1984 International Conference on Population relevant to the developing countries.

No one can really predict the future. Human knowledge is tentative and forecasting what will happen an uncertain exercise. Projections not being predictions indicate at most what is likely to happen. They can be fallible as some past errors in demographic projections have illustrated. Nevertheless, scientific methods, by uniting rational thought and empirical facts in a systematic and explicit manner, are the only reliable bases for anticipating what will be the probable developments in the future.

The experience of UNFPA in policy formulation indicates that an effective population policy must have its proper time perspective and must be scientifically-determined in its component elements, normative and applicable at different levels, multisectoral in its emphasis and measurable in its impact and consequences.

A clear recognition of the time element is essential in the appreciation of the dynamic factors that go into policy formulation. The goals of population policies and programmes vary in perspective and in the periods for accomplishing the ends.

It is also necessary if population policies are to become programmable sectors in the development plans of countries that the process of formulating them should be clearly scientific. They should be based upon representative data collected through technically sound methods, dependable analysis of population factors and reliable projections of impact and consequences. The alternative is to rely on intuitive knowledge or emotional reaction to facts, which may be useful in some other human activity but is hardly amenable to rational programming and in the long run is less likely to influence succeeding population events in the direction of desired goals.

Once the policies have been formulated, the manner and execution of programmes among the alternatives that they present depend on the judgement and values of the decision-maker or policy-maker. The lessons derived from UNFPA's experience with developing country programmes indicate that these judgements are more effective if the views of the widest possible sector of society are considered before judgements are made. A wider comprehension of the reasons and substance of population policies guarantees an equally wide participation in their execution.

Population policies are ultimately meant to influence individual behaviour. They are norms intended for groups or individuals at different levels where their prescriptions are acceptable. The population policies embodied in the World Population Plan of Action are norms of the highest generality since they were adopted by global consensus of countries and are intended to be guidelines for policy formulation by all countries. Below these are the regional, national and sub-national policies, each comprehending a set of policies of a more restricted and specific application than the preceding one. At the end of this continuum is the individual, whose decisions and behaviour are the most important of all, for it is the individual who makes the choices on having children and not governments or institutions.

Population policies are intended to be valid for the period of time necessary for leaders to strategically adjust to the changing perceptions and goals of population in countries. Ideally, they are conceived and formulated with the most current and best available demographic and socio-economic data available, as well as with awareness of the research and findings in related studies likely to influence population variables. By the year 2000, for instance, it is possible that the findings and applications of current bio-genetic research on human and plant life will alter our views on fertility, morbidity, mortality and food production.

Population policies also must be periodically reviewed and evaluated—an integral part of policy-making in order to keep policies relevant to changing population and socio-economic conditions. The 1984 International Conference on Population is one such synoptic, global evaluation of what has transpired in the field of population in the last ten years. The suggestions for the further implementation of the World Population Plan of Action will have to be responsive to probable developments in the future. The decision to hold this Conference ten years after the 1974 Conference is appropriate, because a decade is about the shortest adequate period of time in which to discern significant demographic and socio-economic changes. A periodic evaluation of the World Population Plan of Action every ten years can keep its provisions current, meaningful and programmable well beyond this century. For donor countries to population assistance programmes, this has an added significance. It will give them a periodic opportunity to review the population programmes that can be effectively assisted and to examine the consistency of these programmes with the population policies of the recipient countries and the global community.

The fundamental aim of all population policies, the World Population Plan of Action explicitly states, is to respect human life and to improve the levels of living and quality of life of all the people in all countries. Thus, implicit in all the national policies that have so far been adopted by countries and implemented by population programmes is a coherent effort to realize this goal.

An understanding of the evolution of UNFPA policies can be of value in determining how this primary objective has been real-

ized up to now. These policies are, in essence, summaries of the
management and direction of population programmes in developing countries. As such, they indicate the extent and scope to which
these countries have implemented them. The policies are usually more specific than the general language of the World Population Plan of Action and can, therefore, contribute to the
programmatic content of the proposals for further implementation of the Plan.

The linking of all these population policies with the aim of the
World Population Plan of Action requires an acceptable theory.
Throughout the centuries, there has been speculation about the
meaning and significance of human numbers in terms of survival
and welfare. And early in historical records, governments were
showing concern over the related phenomena of births, deaths,
movement and growth of population.

About twenty-five hundred years ago, some Chinese writers
were already proposing governmental action on population matters. What is novel in modern thought on population is the extent and scope of governmental intervention designed to influence
individual demographic behaviour—a concept which started in
India in the 1950s with the policy that population must be a stra-
tegic part of its development plans.

These modes of thinking would not have come about if, as in
previous millenia, nature had taken care of an almost impercept-
ible increase in global population growth rates by maintaining
high birth rates sanctioned by predominant values on fertility
in almost all societies, and high death rates because of the prevalence of infectious diseases, malnutrition and inadequate health
care. It was the rational, scientific advances in medicine and health
care in the last century and a half that caused the rapid deceleration of death rates. With high birth rates still culturally sanctioned, it was unavoidable that global growth rates would increase
so rapidly as to alarm, in the last twenty years, health officials,
social scientists and policy-makers of their exponential consequences. To these were added the additional knowledge from environmental and ecological studies which, at about the same time,
warned that rapid population growth rates can threaten the viability of the environment for humans.

Governmental intervention, because of the comprehensiveness
of its legislative and executive regulations compared to those of

private organizations, was increasingly called for and accepted in the developing countries. What remained in the theoretical consideration of the social programmes intended to correct the harmful effects of unrestrained population growth rates was the question: In whom did the primary responsibility for these social programmes lie? Was it with the individual decisions as Malthus and his adherents contended in the 18th century or was it in the economic and social transformation of societies as Marx and his adherents contended in the 19th century? One of the accomplishments of the World Population Plan of Action was the reconciliation of these two contending viewpoints. The provision that all couples and individuals have the basic right to decide freely and responsibly the number and spacing of their children and the provision that the main responsibility for national population policies and programmes lies with national authorities in interrelating population and development consistent with their national sovereignty and values, harmoniously reconciles these different viewpoints. The responsibility for addressing the problems of population lies in both—in the government for adopting policies and programmes consistent with its sovereign views and the prevailing cultural values and in the individual for making the ultimate decision about the desired number of children.

The World Population Plan of Action further accommodates the views of religions on human procreation by reminding governments that, independently of the realization of economic and social objectives, respect for human life is basic to all countries, and that the family, as the basic unit of society, should be protected. Policies should respect different views on population within countries.

The final binding thought for the year 2000 and beyond is to shape a more satisfying future for the forthcoming generations—to plan and work to bring about a global society that is secure and viable, one in which individuals can develop their full potential, free from capricious inequalities of development and threats of environmental degradation. This should be done without violating the dignity and freedom of the human person and by giving all people the knowledge and the means to bring forth only the children for whom they can provide the fullest opportunities for growth. To make this the fundamental motive of all individuals is to put reason behind human desires. This is a task that calls for a prolonged and sustained education of everyone, in which all these efforts in population in the last fifteen years are indeed but a few short steps in a thousand mile journey.

Chapter IX

THE
MEXICO CITY
CONFERENCE

Opening statement by Rafael M. Salas
Secretary-General of the International Conference on Population
To the International Conference on Population
Mexico City, 6 August 1984.

POPULATION:
THE MEXICO CITY CONFERENCE
AND THE FUTURE

I should like to begin my statement in the language of this country—a tribute to Mexico which honours us today by hosting this International Conference. It is also a homage to the Spanish-speaking countries whose presence binds us beyond their common history and culture.

Ten years have elapsed since Bucharest and it is significant that we should be meeting in what for many years has been known as the New World.

I should like to thank the Government of Mexico for giving us the opportunity for serious reflection on our experiences and the events of the last decade. In particular, we are grateful to His Excellency President Miguel de la Madrid Hurtado, who, with profound understanding and broad vision of the future, encouraged and approved the holding of this Conference.

I should also like to thank all the Mexican institutions that assisted us, especially the National Population Council and the Ministry of Foreign Affairs, which, both in New York and in this historic city, have given us the needed support. Mexico once again by this Conference, demonstrates its recognition of the importance of population as an integral factor in development—a position it has consistently held since 1972.

We are certain that with the same spirit and decisiveness that prevailed in Bucharest ten years ago, this Conference in Mexico City will give the adequate and effective response to the challenges of all the countries that hope for peace.*

Ten years ago I addressed the World Population Conference in Bucharest on behalf of the United Nations Fund for Population Activities. At that time, the Conference's primary concern was the "unprecedented and sustained population growth ... taking place in countries least able to support it". On that occasion I proposed, along with others, that population be taken as an integral factor in the development plans of countries. I envisioned a society of the future as one that would avoid the extremes of both excess and deprivation, with sufficiency for all—to prevent what was apparent—our numbers pressing on the world's known resources as to threaten the viability of our environment.

In the last decade, several important developments have taken place in population: the global population growth rate has declined but the annual increment of absolute numbers continues to grow; our awareness and understanding of population issues have expanded and population concepts have been increasingly refined in the areas of fertility, mortality and morbidity, migration and urbanization and population structure; national population policies and programmes have now been adopted and integrated in development plans by most developing-country members of the United Nations; family planning information and services have become widespread and more effectively implemented in countries that have such policies; technical and managerial training

---

*The paragraphs above translated from the Spanish.

and competence in population programmes have manifestly increased as have the number of government institutions attending to population problems. But the complex and delicate nature of the relationship between population and development—the cardinal conclusion of the World Population Plan of Action—is now, and will continue to be, of critical concern to all countries of the world.

The United Nations involvement in population has been in response to the international community's recognition of the importance of population issues at the national and international levels and of the need to co-ordinate the developing countries' requirements for assistance in population in accordance with their national goals. The guiding principles of the United Nations action in population are: respect for national sovereignty, neutrality in judgement, effectiveness in its policies and innovativeness and flexibility in its approaches to issues.

It is in the spirit of global understanding and co-operation in population that we have come together in this hospitable, beautiful and symbolic City of Mexico, which is now the world's most populous city and is projected to remain so when we enter the new century that is almost upon us. It holds within its environs a microcosm of our concerns for today and our hopes for tomorrow.

We are here to strengthen and sustain the momentum of past efforts; to foresee emerging problems and within our foresight, direct our thoughts and initiate action for the future.

The preservation of human life on earth is the end of all population endeavours. This requires that we understand the dynamics of population and its relations with life-support systems. Human beings continuously adapt themselves to the environment by regulating their own behaviour to match the physical and natural constraints to life. Rapid population growth during the past three decades has led to the renewed perception that an equilibrium between population and the life-support systems has to be achieved.

Population growth

The world population, which stood at 3.99 billion in 1974 reached 4.76 billion by 1984. The annual rate of population growth, however, declined from an estimated 2.03 per cent in 1974 to 1.67 in 1984. Despite the observed decline in the global growth rate, the annual increment to world population has remained almost constant at 78 million throughout the decade, and is expected to increase further to 89 million by 1995-2000.

The United Nations estimates that the world population will continue to grow for another 110 years, although at a progressively slower pace. According to the medium variant, world population will increase to 6.1 billion by the year 2000 and it is projected to stabilize at 10.5 billion by the end of the next century. Ninety-five per cent of this future growth of global population will occur in the developing countries of the world. Sixty per cent of these countries consider their rates of population growth as too high.

The deceleration in the rate of population growth has been a slow process and indications are that unless the current momentum to reduce fertility is maintained, there is a probability that the population growth rate may even increase during the remainder of this century.

Fertility

The global birth rate declined from 32.7 in 1974 to 27.3 in 1984. This implies a 17 per cent decline at the world level and a 19 per cent decline for the developing regions as a whole. The levels of fertility continue to vary substantially among developing countries. Several countries of Asia and Latin America have experienced rapid declines in fertility, while very high fertility rates continue to exist in much of Africa and Western Asia.

On the level of desired fertility, the findings of the World Fertility Survey show that while the national averages in total fertility rate among married women varied between 4.8 and 10.7, the average number of desired children ranged only between 3.0 and 8.6. In the United Nations Fifth Population Inquiry conducted in 1982, nearly two-thirds of developing countries indicated that their national level of fertility is high and desire reductions. Government programmes to reduce fertility are available in countries covering 80 per cent of the population of the developing world. However, the levels of desired fertility in developing countries are still higher than the fertility level necessary to eventually attain population stability—approximately 2.1 children per woman. Near replacement fertility levels have already been achieved in most developed countries.

The continued momentum of population growth in the developing countries will lead to a doubling by the year 2025 in the number of women in the reproductive ages, currently estimated at 873 million. It has been estimated that at present there are roughly 500 million couples who are in need of population education and family planning services.

Mortality and morbidity

In the past decade, there has been a worldwide improvement in health and human longevity. In developed countries, the life expectancy at birth has risen to 73 years. Expectation of life at birth in developing countries has risen from 52.4 years in 1974 to 56.6 years in 1984. But this average has fallen short in developing countries by five years of the World Population Plan of Action target of 62 years. There are at least 40 countries in Africa and Asia where life expectancy at birth continues to be less than 50 years. Of equal concern is the inability of some 26 African and Asian countries to attain the Plan of Action target of reducing infant deaths to 120 or less per 1000 live births by 1984. A large differential exists in the level of infant mortality rate between developed and developing countries—17 per 1000 live births in developed as opposed to 92 per 1000 live births in developing countries.

Migration and urbanization

Population distribution has emerged as an important concern in many developing countries since the 1974 World Population Conference. In the United Nations Fifth Population Inquiry, 77 countries desired changes in their national distribution, of which 64 were developing countries.

The world is becoming more urban. The proportion of urban population has increased from 38.0 to 41.3 per cent since Bucharest, and is expected to reach about 50 per cent at the global level by the year 2000. The dominance of primate cities in the process of urbanization has brought in its train a number of problems which very often outweigh the benefits of urban life to its dwellers.

The increase in the number of metropolitan centres and the concentration of population in those centres have been phenomenal during the past decade. The number of cities of 4 million or more increased during the decade from 28 to 41 at the global level. There was almost a doubling of the number, from 15 to 27, in the developing countries. The number of such cities in the world is projected to rise to 66 by the year 2000.

There have been important changes in the volume, direction and characteristics of international migration flows since the Bucharest Conference. These relate to four important groups who together constitute international migrants: permanent immigrants, labour migrants, undocumented or illegal migrants and refugees. The human rights and welfare aspects of these population movements are of increasing concern today.

Population structure

One significant characteristic of the demographic transition, both in developed and developing countries, is the changing structure of the population. Population aging is most pronounced and has become an issue for public policy in developed countries. On the other hand, young-age dependency and the increase in the size of the labour force continue to be important factors in the population structures of developing countries.

The critical role of women in the achievement of population and development objectives has been increasingly recognized during the past ten years. If their potential contribution is to be fully realized in the forthcoming decades, their equal and active participation in development must be explicitly considered.

Regional variations

One of the significant features of world demography lately is the clearer emergence of intraregional similarities and interregional differences in population issues, reflecting the scale, rapidity, duration and timing of demographic transition.

Fertility and infant mortality are the most important issues in sub-Saharan Africa and in many parts of South Asia. Other parts of Asia have successfully curbed growth but are still facing the question of integrating population and development policies. Urbanization and migration are Latin America's most serious problems, while high growth and heavy in-migration are features of countries of the Middle East. In the developed countries, aging of the population is the most significant demographic feature. The responses to these regional variations differ from one country to another, but all of these demographic events are now taken as part of the development process—a vindication of the Bucharest message.

The World Population Plan of Action

The significant demographic developments I have just outlined are relevant to your examination of the recommendations for the further implementation of the World Population Plan of Action.

Since the consensus of Bucharest, the Plan has served as the fundamental guidepost for the formulation and implementation of population policies and programmes and the basic framework for global co-operation in population among countries. Its fundamental Principles and Objectives have through the decade proven their validity by the comprehensive commitment to population policies and programmes by all the developing countries today.

The Principles and Objectives of the Plan will foreseeably remain valid during this century and beyond and, therefore, are not at issue in this Conference.

Nevertheless, new information on, and perceptions of, the other provisions of the Plan continually emerge from demographic trends that necessitate a periodic review of their significance. National population goals must be systematically reassessed and accomplishments as well as failures of population programmes alternatively measured. This is the task that is ahead of you in the next six days—to examine, determine and agree on global strategies that can complement national population policies and programmes and make the provisions of the World Population Plan of Action a continuously operative and relevant framework for national and international efforts in population.

On the Recommendations

In doing so, let us be reminded of the two basic tenets: the sovereign right of countries to determine their own population policies and programmes and the fundamental right of individuals and couples to decide freely and responsibly the number and spacing of their children. These two principles should underlie your forthcoming discussions and decisions.

In the examination and analysis of the recommendations before this Conference, it would be advisable if the following perspectives developed through the years of work in population are taken into account:

First, to view these policies as a continuum from national to global needs. Individual countries perceive population issues differently from others, each with its own political, economic, social and cultural frame of thought. This uniqueness must be acknowledged and governmental decisions which are territorially sovereign must be respected in their applicability to national needs. However, we live in an era where communication has compressed the world into one community; where national population policies have tangible global repercussions. This Conference, which is the second United Nations effort at a consensus on population issues and which aims for policies of global applicability, exemplifies this continuity. Countries should, therefore, seek consistency between national and global goals and policies;

Second, to take a longer time perspective when examining population policies. All the recommendations before you are addressed to the future. In this Conference we will speak of population stabilization in about 80 to 110 years—a time when most of us living today will not be around. Population policies take effect within a much longer time-frame than any other development or humanitarian programme. Short-term objectives of population programmes take effect in not less than a generation. Countries should, therefore, assume that the recommendations they will examine have this underlying time element;

Third, to be aware of the interrelationships of the specific recommendations. It was the understanding of the delegates in Bucharest that the Plan of Action is to be taken as a whole, before the parts are examined. This Plan is the only synoptic document that embodies policies for global applicability in population. Neither its Principles and Objectives nor the conceptual boundaries of population must be lost sight of. Thus, the proposed recommendations have been put together sectorally with care, consistency and compatibility to the Principles and Objectives of the Plan. Equally important as the number and content of the recommendations, which delegates will address with their national priorities, is the interrelationship. Countries should, therefore, strive for coherence among the recommendations, and between the recommendations and the whole Plan;

Fourth, to be conscious of the changing perceptions of population issues. In the 1950s, demographers and other specialists perceived population primarily as questions of morbidity and mortality. The 1960s was the decade that brought about a shift in emphasis to fertility factors in population growth. The 1970s brought a growing awareness of the need to regard population as an integral factor in the entire process of development. In the 1980s, increasing attention has been accorded to problems of urbanization, migration and aging without abandoning the importance of population growth. In recent years, advances have been made in bio-genetic research on human and plant life that may directly or indirectly affect the views on fertility, morbidity, mortality and food production. Countries should, therefore, be conscious that these recommendations are based primarily on our present state of knowledge and that there is always the possibility of different conclusions emerging from technological advances and innovations; and

Fifth, to be alert to the primacy of the individual and his rights, and the importance of the family as a socializing institution. Population policies are ultimately meant to influence individual behaviour. Starting with India in the 1950s, Governments of developing countries have adopted population policies and programmes as part of their development plans with the declared objective of improving the levels of living and the quality of life of people. Because population policies and programmes were meant to be comprehensively effective, governmental intervention was an unavoidable consequence. But Governments as mediating institutions do not bear or decide on the number of children. It is the individuals and the couples that must make decisions on fertility, which the World Population Plan of Action explicitly states must be made "freely and responsibly".

Fertility decisions are normally made within the family. In addition to its role as an institution that affects fertility, the family fosters and harmonizes personal and social values. It is the "basic unit of society" that assures the balanced development of the individual within the community in which he lives.

Countries in framing these recommendations should be sensitive to the basic right of the individuals and couples to make free and responsible decisions on fertility and the significance of the family in these decisions.

International co-operation

In the last fifteen years, international co-operation in population and population assistance have played a vital role in creating the awareness of the consequences of population trends in national development programmes, facilitated the exchange of experience and expertise in population programmes among countries, multiplied and refined the understanding of population and development factors through comparative and co-operative research in academic institutions and forged the links between local, national, regional and international population policies and programmes.

Of the several global issues that beset mankind today, it is only in population where national effort and international co-operation have had some success in attaining an agreed global objective: the moderation of the global population growth rate. As the documents before you indicate, the global population growth rate has declined. Several countries have demonstrated that national population policies and programmes can indeed be effective in reducing the rates of fertility.

In these efforts, the developing countries have shown increasing self-reliance in the implementation and support of their programmes. Taking the case of the United Nations Fund for Population Activities as an example, for each dollar of assistance that it extends, the developing countries, on the average, are investing four dollars from their own budgetary sources to these activities. All population agencies—multilateral, bilateral, governmental and non-governmental—have played an indispensable part in encouraging and assisting developing countries to implement their national programmes. But, in ten years, requests for assistance from developing countries have progressively exceeded the capacity of the population agencies to meet them.

One factor that has often been overlooked is the link between population and global security and the role which population plays in shaping political behaviour. Although population pressure by itself does not necessarily cause conflict, in combination with other economic, political and social factors, it can be critical; as a struggle for scarce resources very often intensifies with the increased number of people involved. Population policies and programmes by looking towards a moderation of population growth and a rational spatial distribution of population thus represent humane efforts to reduce imbalances and disparities that lead to crises.

Because of the urgency and universality of population issues today, increased international population assistance deserves priority.

The task ahead

Distinguished delegates, you have before you the eighty-five recommendations considered and approved by the Preparatory Committee in two prolonged sessions attended by representatives of more than 100 countries this year. These have been amply discussed, examined and agreed by consensus and are now submitted to you for your final decision.

Only you as representatives of sovereign countries have the right to consider, judge, decide and agree on what is proper for the further implementation of the World Population Plan of Action. Our duty in the Secretariat is to facilitate your consensus on these issues. But before you deliberate on them, I would like to offer a thought on the ultimate goal of our efforts as far as we can perceive it at this time.

Population growth is the critical factor—to be considered in relation to an equally critical factor, the life-support systems of this planet. Population should be viewed in its entirety—as a resource, as a constraint, as a consequence, as a determinant and as an integral element of life.

The nature of population indicates that it is necessary to have both a time horizon and objective goals for effective implementation of population policies and programmes. Knowledge of its time paths is necessary to appreciate its relationships with ecological factors and their implications for a sustainable society. At any point in time, the sustainability of a society is limited by the availability of known resources and their rate of utilization, the levels of technology and the financial, technical and managerial constraints facing different countries. Within these time paths, it is obvious that a few countries may, in the short run, have to increase their population for the optimum utilization of their resources. But all countries should aim for a level of population in balance with its sustainable capacity. In the long term, the balance between population size and sustainability is a moving equilibrium determined by changes in technological progress, resource discoveries and utilization, innovations in social organizations and manifestations of human ingenuity.

Our goal is the stabilization of global population within the shortest period possible before the end of the next century. The combination of rapid population growth, slowly growing incomes and inadequate level of technology continue to widen the disparities in international levels of living and frustrate the efforts of developing countries to improve the quality of life of their people. Even a high growth rate of 5 to 6 per cent in national income of the developing countries between 1985 and 2000 would still leave over 600 million persons below the poverty line. Population stabilization will make it less difficult for the developing countries to improve their levels of living. Voluntary family planning is a vital means in reaching this global goal provided it is in accord with individual human rights, religious beliefs and cultural values. It is essential that population programmes be maintained until the promise of stabilization is within sight.

Only the determined, rational and humane national population policies of countries can bring about a more satisfying future for the forthcoming generations. Governments must plan and work to bring about a global society that is secure and viable, one in which individuals can develop their full potential free from the capricious inequalities of development and threats of environmental degradation. This should be done without violating the dignity and freedom of the human person and by giving all people the knowledge and the means to bring forth only the children for whom they can provide the fullest opportunities for growth. Education should enhance this vision as the motive of all human efforts in population.

We are here not in a mood of confrontation but in a spirit of consensus. We have come to contribute to each other's knowledge, to address our mutual concerns and to look at the future for new opportunities. The answers we seek will not come easily, but they should challenge us as nothing else.

Closing Statement
14 August 1984

Let me at this closing hour, congratulate you, Mr President and distinguished delegates, for the successful conclusion of this International Conference on Population.

This has been the briefest, most economical, least documented, and one of the best attended international conferences sponsored by the United Nations in the past decade. I say, "briefest" because it took the participants only seven working days to conclude their business—United Nations conferences usually take at least two weeks to complete; "most economical" because the total cost of the Conference was only $2.3 million of which only $800,000 came from the regular United Nations budget, compared to the $3.7 million for the World Population Conference in Bucharest; "the least documented" because only 173 pages of documents were needed for the participants to make decisions on the recommendations; and one of the "best attended" because representatives from 147 States were present compared to Bucharest's 136.

This Conference confirms that the principal aim of social, economic and human development, of which population goals and policies are integral parts, is to improve the standard of living and quality of life of the people. In promoting and implementing population policies and programmes, national sovereignty and individual freedom of choice are paramount.

The further implementation of the World Population Plan of Action is now assured through the recommendations you have adopted by consensus. The significance of these recommendations is expressed in the well-written and concise Declaration of Mexico. Both highlight the following topical developments since Bucharest:

- Population growth, high mortality and morbidity, and migration problems continue to be causes of great concern requiring immediate action;

- Governments' increasing involvement in population policies and programmes and increasing efforts on their part to attain self-reliance;

- Governments are requested to make universally available information, education and means to assist couples and individuals to achieve their desired number of children, consistent with human rights, without coercion on the one hand or deprivation on the other. Abortion is not to be promoted as a method of family planning;

- Special attention should be given to maternal and child health services within a primary health care system;

- Integrated urban and rural development strategies should be an essential part of population policies;

- Governments are asked specifically to protect the rights of migrants;

- There are stronger recommendations for protecting the rights and improving the status of women and these have been established as a separate section of the final document;

- Women should have full access to education, training and employment to enable them to achieve personal fulfillment in both familial and socio-economic roles;

- The elderly and youth are given special attention;

- The importance of the United Nations system for the successful execution of population programmes is acknowledged as is the need for strengthening the ability of UNFPA to respond to those needs;

- The importance of non-governmental organizations is recognized in the pursuit of innovative solutions to population problems;

- The provisions of the Plan clearly reflect the need for operational programmes and increased resources to support them.

We are particularly grateful to His Excellency Mr. Miguel de la Madrid Hurtado, President of Mexico, for his personal interest in welcoming us on behalf of the people and Government of Mexico. We are indebted to His Excellency Mr. Manuel Bartlett Diaz, Minister of Interior of Mexico and Head of the delegation of

Mexico, for his statesmanship role as President of this Conference and for his dynamism in leading us to this successful conclusion. We are grateful to Dr. Fred Sai for the skill and impartiality with which he chaired the Main Committee.

On behalf of Mr. Sankar Menon, Deputy Secretary-General and the Secretariat, I would like to take this opportunity to thank all other officials of the Government of Mexico for the extraordinary hospitality they have extended to us.

We are grateful for the contributions to this Conference of the United Nations system, the various inter-governmental organizations, and the non-governmental organizations—

- to the members of the media who have so diligently covered our sessions;

- to all the United Nations departments and units involved in running the Conference, the interpreters, the translators, the secretaries and all of those people who have worked behind the scenes to ensure the smooth running of this Conference;

- to the Mexican Government for all the services it provided in terms of conference facilities, local staff, security, and transportation.

Above all, let me thank each of you, distinguished delegates. The achievements at this Conference were due to your dedication, persistence, forebearance, patience and wisdom in these deliberations.

This Conference has awakened the need for a periodic assessment and review of the World Population Plan of Action and the progress made in population by all countries. As a final parting thought, I would like to suggest that the countries present call for another population Conference ten years hence—in August 1994—to examine the relevance of the decisions made today for the years ahead. As we have learned in the last seven days, population is both a national and global responsibility that must be attended to until global stability and security are in sight.

REFERENCES FOR INTRODUCTIONS
TO CHAPTERS II THROUGH VII

Intergovernmental Committee for Migration. "Worldwide Situation and Problems of Undocumented Migration, and the Role of Planned Migration of Qualified Personnel from Developed to Developing Countries". Paper presented to the Expert Group Meeting on Population Distribution, Migration and Development, Hammamet, Tunisia, 21-25 March 1983.

Lightbourne, Robert and Macdonald, A.L. "Family Size Preferences". *Comparative Studies*, No. 14, November 1982 (London: World Fertility Survey).

Nortman, Dorothy. *Population and Family Planning Programs: A Compendium of Data Through 1981*, 11th Edition. New York: The Population Council, 1982.

Office of the United Nations High Commissioner for Refugees. "International Migration: Refugees". Paper presented to the Expert Group Meeting on Population Distribution, Migration and Development, Hammamet, Tunisia, 21-25 March 1983.

United Nations, Department of International Economic and Social Affairs. "Demographic Indicators by Countries as Assessed in 1982" (computer printout), 1 November 1983.

———. "International Migration: Levels and Trends". Paper presented to the Expert Group Meeting on Population Distribution, Migration and Development, Hammamet, Tunisia, 21-25 March 1983.

———. *International Migration Policies and Programmes: A World Survey* (United Nations publication, Sales No.E.82.XIII.4), New York, 1982.

———. Population Commission. "Concise Report on the Fifth Inquiry Among Governments: Monitoring of Government Perceptions and Policies on Demographic Trends and Levels in Relation to Development as of 1982" (E/CN.9/1984/3), 5 December 1983.

———. "Population, Resources, Environment and Development: Highlights of the Issues in the Context of the World Population Plan of Action". Paper presented to the Expert Group Meeting on Population, Resources, Environment and Development, Geneva, Switzerland, 25-29 April 1983.

———. Preparatory Committee for the International Conference on Population, 1984. "Review and Appraisal of the World Population Plan of Action: Report of the Secretary-General" (E/CONF.76/PC/10), 2 December 1983.

———. Preparatory Committee for the International Conference on Population, 1984. "Proposals for Recommendations for the Further Implementation of the World Population Plan of Action: Report of the Secretary-General" (E/CONF.76/PC/11), 6 December 1983.

———. "World Population Trends and Policies: 1983 Monitoring Report, Part One" (Population Division Working Paper, IESA/P/WP.82), 9 December 1983.

United Nations. Preparatory Committee for the International Conference on Population, 1984. "Text submitted by Mr. F. Sai, Chairman of the informal open-ended working group, on the basis of consultations held on document E/CONF.76/PC/11 and Corr.1" (E/CONF.76/PC/WG/L.1/Rev.1), 1 February 1984.

World Bank. *Health Sector Policy Paper*. Washington, D.C., 1980.

World Health Organization. *The Epidemiology of Infertility*. Technical Report Series No. 582, Geneva, Switzerland, 1975.

APPENDIX A

RECOMMENDATIONS FOR THE FURTHER IMPLEMENTATION OF THE WORLD POPULATION PLAN OF ACTION *AND* THE MEXICO CITY DECLARATION ON POPULATION AND DEVELOPMENT

Adopted by the International Conference on Population, Mexico City 6-14 August 1984.

Recommendations for the Further Implementation of the World Population Plan of Action*

CONTENTS

Report of the International Conference on Population, 1984, Mexico City, 6-14 August 1984 (United Nations publication, Sales No. E.84.XIII.8 and corrigendum), chap. I, sect. B.

I. PREAMBLE

1. During the years since the United Nations World Population Conference in 1974, the World Conference Plan of Action[a] has served as a guide to action in the field of population for Governments, for international organizations and for non-governmental organizations. The consensus of Bucharest has facilitated international co-operation and helped to bring population issues to the forefront. The principles and objectives of the Plan have shown themselves to remain valid and are reaffirmed.

2. However, the demographic, social, economic and political conditions of the world have changed considerably. In many developing countries the demographic situation has improved since 1974; fertility has declined, morbidity has diminished, infant mortality has declined and life expectancy has increased. There have also been improvements in the social sphere. In many developing countries school enrolment and literacy rates have increased, and access to health services has improved. For the developing countries as a whole, there has been an increase in per capita calorie supply, though in some regions, such as Africa, per capita calorie supply has not improved. Economic trends have, however, been less encouraging. Although per capita income did not grow as rapidly since 1974 as in the previous 10 years, it is none the less true that per capita income did grow moderately in a number of developing countries during that period. During the latter part of the decade, however, many developing countries experienced little or no growth in per capita income, and many experienced actual declines in per capita income, with the result that the gap between the per capita incomes of many developed and most developing countries widened during the period. Moreover, while progress has been made in achieving some goals of the World Population Plan of Action, other goals have not been met. Some important gaps in knowledge have been filled and new issues have emerged to challenge the international community. Therefore, as foreseen at Bucharest, some of the goals and recommendations of the Plan now call for complementing and further refinement. Though the community of nations has made considerable progress in the pursuit of the goals of the World Population Plan of Action, there is still a great need for continuation and acceleration in these efforts to realize those goals, as they have been refined at Mexico City in August 1984.

3. With respect to some major issues raised in the Plan, the following facts and trends deserve special mention:

(a) Though the global rate of population growth has declined slightly since 1974, the world population has increased by 770 million during the decade, and 90 percent of that increase has occurred in the developing countries. Furthermore, the annual additions to the world's population are increasing in size. Moreover, in many countries of Africa, Latin America and Asia growth rates have increased owing to mortality declines not accompanied by equivalent declines in fertility;

(b) At the global level, and in virtually all countries, the level of mortality has fallen. However, the targets set by the World Population Plan of Action have not been met. At the same time, new approaches in the form of primary health care have been widely adopted;

(c) At the global level, fertility declined substantially but, as with population growth, the changes in some regions were far greater than in others. For national and sub-national groups in populations and sub-populations representing about one fourth of the world's population, no decline of fertility was observed. The fertility changes were associated with progress in socio-economic development, with continued changes in the status of women, with changes in family structure in some regions, and with the increased availability of family planning services;

(d) Improvements in the status of women have been promoted by the World Population Plan of Action and the plans and programmes generated under the aegis of the United Nations Decade for Women. However, persisting inequalities between women and men are evident in the higher incidence of poverty, unemployment and illiteracy among women, the limited range of employment categories and the uneven share of home and family responsibilities borne by women. At the same time, it is increasingly recognized that socio-economic development is curtailed without the active participation of women in all fields of activity;

(e) Access to and knowledge of family planning have come to be much more widely permitted and supported by Governments as a contribution to maternal and child health, to the human rights of individuals and couples, and as a demographic measure. Nevertheless, data from the World Fertility Survey for developing countries indicate that, of women who wanted no more children and were exposed to the risk of pregnancy, on average over half were not using contraception;

(f) As a result of demographic trends, population structures have changed. In particular, the aging of populations and changes in household and family structure and composition have continued;

(g) In most regions of the world, urban populations continued to increase far more rapidly than total populations. In some developed countries, however, there was a trend towards deconcentration. Rapid urban population growth has become a matter of growing policy concern to most Governments, particularly in the developing regions in which the urban unemployment level remains extremely high. In some regions, the continued high levels of rural population growth renders rural development difficult;

(h) Persistent disparities among countries, particularly in population and economic development as also the felt needs of some host countries, have increased the potential of further international migration. These migrant workers do contribute to the economic development of receiving countries.

However, the direction, magnitude and the type of international migration flows is a matter of concern to some countries;

(i) The flows of refugees are increasing in different regions of the world and are also a matter of increasing concern;

(j) Problems relating to involuntary migration have also increased;

(k) The overall social and economic development of the developing countries and the implementation of effective measures to deal with population trends in the period 1974-1984 have been greatly hampered by the serious effects of the international economic crisis on the economies of the developing countries. In the majority of developing countries, increases in population and its aspirations have contributed to increasing imports versus exports — food in particular. Furthermore, existing population programmes have been greatly affected by a shortage of adequate resources from both national and international sources;

(l) In many countries the population has continued to grow rapidly, aggravating such environmental and natural resource problems as soil erosion, desertification and deforestation, which affect food and agricultural production. The mechanisms to deal effectively with these problems are still in an incipient stage in many countries. There is, however, increasing awareness of the need to take into account natural resources and the quality of the environment along with social and economic factors;

(m) In the years since 1974 there have been a number of hopeful developments. New agricultural technologies, including the green revolution, have made it possible to better meet the needs of growing populations. Progress in molecular biology has potential for influencing both levels of fertility and mortality and the development of communication satellites may greatly advance mass education, including education directly related to population issues. The economic and social consequences of these advances raise serious ethical questions and may have a fundamental impact on the future of society.

4. The principles and objectives of the World Population Plan of Action affirm that the principal aim of social, economic and cultural development, of which population goals and policies are integral parts, is to improve the standards of living and quality of life of the people. Achieving this goal requires co-ordinated action in population with all socio-economic fields; thus, population trends must be co-ordinated with trends of economic and social development. In helping to achieve this co-ordination, the World Population Plan of Action should become an essential component of the system of international strategies for the promotion of economic development, the quality of life, human rights and fundamental freedoms.

5. The Plan affirms that the consideration of population problems cannot be limited to the analysis of population trends, since population variables influence development variables and are influenced by them. The present population situation in developing countries is related, *inter alia*, to unequal

processes of socio-economic development, which are intensified by inequities in international relations, and by related disparities in standards of living.

6. It remains true that the basis for an effective solution of population problems is, above all, socio-economic transformation and, therefore, population policies must always be considered as a constituent element of socio-economic development policies and never as substitutes for them. However, even if social and economic development is slow or lacking, family planning programmes may have an impact on the level of fertility.

7. While the importance of integrating women into the development of society has been recognized by many Governments, much remains to be done to fulfil the recommendations adopted in 1974 by the World Population Conference as elaborated in 1975 by the World Conference of the International Women's Year, and in 1980 by the World Conference of the United Nations Decade for Women. The Plan, as well as other important international instruments, stressed the urgency of achieving the full integration of women in society on an equal basis with men and of abolishing any form of discrimination against women. In order to provide women with the freedom to participate fully in the life of society, it is equally necessary for men to share fully with women responsibilities in the areas of family planning, child-rearing and all other aspects of family life. The achievement of these objectives is integral to achieving development goals, including those related to population policy.

8. To achieve the goals of development, the formulation of national population goals and policies must take into account the need to contribute to an economic development which is environmentally sustainable over the long run and which protects the ecological balance.

9. The interdependence among countries has become ever more manifest and requires that national and international strategies pursue an integrated and balanced approach to population, resources, environment and development at national and international levels, by ensuring that the developing countries achieve significant improvement in their living standards and in the quality of life through economic and social transformation.

10. As the world enters a second decade after the World Population Conference of 1974, major challenges and problems in the area of population that are of primary concern to the international community and that are particularly relevant to the economic and social progress of the developing countries are:

(a) The task of reducing poverty, expanding employment and assuring the right to work by encouraging economic growth, which includes measures for the just distribution of wealth;

(b) The continued need to further promote the status of women and the expansion and advancement of their roles;

(c) The annual increments in population, which are projected to grow larger throughout the decade;

(d) The rate of population growth, which remains high in developing countries and which, for many countries, may even rise in the coming years;

(e) Changes in population structures, particularly the aging of populations, changes in household and family structure and composition, and the growth of the working-age populations in developing countries where economies are not growing adequately;

(f) High levels of infant and maternal mortality, and the important mortality differentials between regions, countries, social groups and sexes;

(g) The persistence of fertility rates substantially higher or lower than those desired by Governments and peoples in some countries;

(h) The unmet needs for family planning in many countries, which unless they are addressed will grow even greater as the number of couples of reproductive age increases substantially during the coming decade;

(i) The disequilibrium between rates of change in population and changes in resources, environment and development;

(j) The persistence of high rates of internal migration, new forms of mobility, high rates of urbanization, and the concentration of population in large cities in developing countries where these phenomena have negative consequences for development;

(k) The importance and diversity of international migration and its consequences for countries of origin and destination and the necessity for cooperation between these countries in this field;

(l) The need to find solutions to all problems related to refugees, whose numbers are increasing;

(m) The increasing number of persons who lack sufficient food, pure water, shelter, health care, education and the other facilities required to achieve full human potential;

(n) The consequences of progress in agricultural technology and in genetic engineering, which may lead to essential changes in the character of societies;

(o) The relatively high proportion of young people in the populations of the developing countries and the problems and consequences attendant to this which, unless addressed, will assure that populations will continue to grow for many decades to come;

(p) The need to strengthen the capacities of developing countries in data collection, analysis and utilization and to develop appropriately trained personnel in the population area;

(q) The need for increased national and international support to implement the Plan, in particular, adequate multilateral resources to support the efforts of developing countries.

11.* The Plan and the following recommendations for its further implementation should be considered within the framework of other intergovernmental strategies and plans. In this respect, they reaffirm the principles and objectives of the Charter of the United Nations, the Universal Declaration of Human Rights (General Assembly resolution 217 A (III)), the International Covenants on Human Rights (General Assembly resolution 2200 A (XXI), annex), the Declaration on Social Progress and Development (General Assembly resolution 2542 (XXIV)), the Declaration and the Programme of Action on the Establishment of a New International Economic Order (General Assembly resolutions 3201 (S-VI) and 3202 (S-VI)), the Charter of Economic Rights and Duties of States (General Assembly resolution 3281 (XXIX)) and the International Development Strategy for the Third United Nations Development Decade (General Assembly resolution 35/56, annex) and General Assembly resolutions 34/75 and 35/46 on the declaration of the 1980s as the Second Disarmament Decade. In addition, the following declarations, plans of action and other relevant texts that have emanated from intergovernmental meetings must be stressed because of their relevance to the objectives of the World Population Plan of Action:

(a) United Nations Declaration on the Rights of the Child (1959);[b]

(b) Declaration of the United Nations Conference on the Human Environment and the Action Plan for the Human Environment (Stockholm, 1972)[c] and resolution 1 adopted by the Governing Council of the United Nations Environment Programme at its session of a special character (Nairobi, 1982);[d]

(c) Universal Declaration on the Eradication of Hunger and Malnutrition (Rome, 1974);[e]

(d) World Plan of Action for the Implementation of the Objectives of the International Women's Year (Mexico City, 1975)[f] and Programme of Action for the Second Half of the United Nations Decade for Women (Copenhagen, 1980);[g]

(e) Lima Declaration and Plan of Action on Industrial Development and Co-operation (Lima, 1975);[h]

(f) Declaration of Principles and Programme of Action adopted by the Tripartite World Conference on Employment, Income Distribution and Social Progress and the International Division of Labour (Geneva, 1976);[i]

(g) Vancouver Declaration on Human Settlements, 1976;[j]

(h) Plan of Action to Combat Desertification (Nairobi, 1977);[k]

(i) Mar del Plata Action Plan adopted by the United Nations Water Conference (Mar del Plata, 1977);[l]

---

*While joining the consensus the delegation of the United States of America stated that: "The United States reserved its position on all the international agreements mentioned in this document consistent with our previous acceptance or non-acceptance of them."

(j) Declaration of Alma-Ata adopted by the International Conference on Primary Health Care (Alma-Ata, 1978);[m]

(k) Programme of Action to Combat Racism and Racial Discrimination (Geneva, 1978),[n] programme of activities to be undertaken during the second half of the Decade for Action to Combat Racism and Racial Discrimination[o] and Declaration and Programme of Action adopted by the Second World Conference to Combat Racism and Racial Discrimination (Geneva, 1983);[p]

(l) Buenos Aires Plan of Action for Promoting and Implementing Technical Co-operation among Developing Countries (Buenos Aires, 1978);[q]

(m) Declaration of Principles and Programme of Action of the World Conference on Agrarian Reform and Rural Development (Rome, 1979);[r]

(n) Vienna Programme of Action on Science and Technology for Development (Vienna, 1979);[s]

(o) Global Strategy for Health for All by the Year 2000,[t] adopted by the World Health Assembly in its resolution WHA 34.36 of 22 May 1981 and endorsed by the General Assembly in its resolution 36/43 of 19 November 1981;

(p) Nairobi Programme of Action for the Development and Utilization of New and Renewable Sources of Energy (Nairobi, 1981);[u]

(q) Substantial New Programme of Action for the 1980s for the Least Developed Countries (Paris, 1981);[v]

(r) International Plan of Action on Aging (Vienna, 1982).[w]

II. PEACE, SECURITY AND POPULATION

12. Being aware of the existing close links between peace and development, it is of great importance for the world community to work ceaselessly to promote, among nations, peace, security, disarmament and co-operation, which are indispensable for the achievement of the goals of humane population policies and for economic and social development. Creating the conditions for real peace and security would permit an allocation of resources to social and economic rather than to military programmes, which would greatly help to attain the goals and objectives of the World Population Plan of Action.

III. RECOMMENDATIONS FOR ACTION

13. Many of the following recommendations are addressed to Governments. This is not meant to preclude the efforts or initiative of international organizations, non-governmental organizations, private institutions or organizations, or families and individuals where their efforts can make an ef-

fective contribution to overall population or development goals on the basis of strict respect for sovereignty and national legislation in force.

A. Socio-economic Development, the Environment and Population

14. The World Population Plan of Action recognizes explicitly the importance of the interrelationships between population and socio-economic development and affirms, *inter alia*, that "the basis for an effective solution of population problems is, above all, socio-economic transformation" (paragraph 1) and that "population policies are constituent elements of socio-economic development policies, never substitutes for them" (paragraph 14 (d)). Consequently, the Plan of Action includes a number of recommendations dealing with socio-economic policies, the contents of which fully deserve reaffirmation and further development. The following recommendations reflect the view that if national and international policies are not adopted and implemented to increase the overall resources and the share of the world's resources going to the very poor, it will be extremely difficult for many countries to achieve the levels of fertility and mortality that they desire. The recommendations reflect the importance to be attached to an integrated approach towards population and development, both in national policies and at the international level. The recommendations also reflect the view that, although the actions of the developing countries are of primary importance, the attainment of the goals and objectives stipulated in the International Development Strategy for the Third United Nations Development Decade will require appropriate policies by the developed countries and by the international community which support the efforts of the developing countries to achieve those objectives.

Recommendation 1

Considering that social and economic development is a central factor in the solution of population and interrelated problems and that population factors are very important in development plans and strategies and have a major impact on the attainment of development objectives, national development policies, plans and programmes, as well as international development strategies, should be formulated on the basis of an integrated approach that takes into account the interrelationships between population, resources, environment and development. In this context, national and international efforts should give priority to action programmes integrating population and development.

Recommendation 2

National and international efforts should give high priority to the following development goals included in the International Development Strategy for the Third United Nations Development Decade: the eradication of mass hunger and the achievement of adequate health and nutrition levels, the eradication of mass illiteracy, the improvement of the status of women, the elimination of mass unemployment and underemployment and the elimination of inequality in international economic relations. To achieve these goals, it is further recommended that Governments should take population trends fully into account when formulating their development plans and programmes.

Recommendation 3*

In order to promote the broadly based socio-economic development that is essential to achieving an adequate quality of life as well as national population objectives and to respond effectively to the requirements posed by demographic trends, all countries are urged to co-operate in efforts to achieve the above objectives and to accelerate development, particularly in developing countries, *inter alia*, through policies to lower barriers to trade, to increase multilateral and bilateral development assistance, to improve the quality and effectiveness of this assistance, to increase real income earnings from the export of commodities, to solve the problems arising from the debt burden in a significant number of developing countries, to increase the volume and improve the terms of international lending, and to encourage various sources of investment and, wherever appropriate, entrepreneurial initiatives. To respond to the needs of populations for employment, food self-sufficiency, and improvements in the quality of life and to increase self-reliance, productive investment should be increased, appropriate industries should be encouraged and substantial investments should be fostered in rural and agricultural development.

Recommendation 4

In countries in which there are imbalances between trends in population growth and resources and environmental requirements, Governments are

---

*While joining the consensus the delegations of the Union of Soviet Socialist Republics and the Ukranian Soviet Socialist Republic stated that: "They cannot accept the unbalanced wording in recommendation 3, which implies underestimation of the role that the State sector is playing in socio-economic development as reflected in relevant United Nations documents."

While joining the consensus the delegation of the United States of America stated that: "The United States wished to underline that endorsement of this document does not change known United States positions on commodity agreements or future lending resources for international financial institutions."

urged, in the context of overall development policies, to adopt and implement specific policies, including population policies, that will contribute to redressing such imbalances and promote improved methods of identifying, extracting, renewing, utilizing and conserving natural resources. Efforts should be made to accelerate the transition from traditional to new and renewable sources of energy while at the same time maintaining the integrity of the environment. Governments should also implement appropriate policy measures to avoid the further destruction of the ecological equilibria and take measures to restore them.

B. The Role and the Status of Women

15. The World Population Plan of Action (paragraphs 15 (e), 32 (b), 42 and 43) as well as other important international instruments – in particular the 1975 Mexico City Plan of Action, the 1980 Copenhagen Programme of Action for the United Nations Decade for Women and the Convention on the Elimination of All Forms of Discrimination against Women (General Assembly resolution 34/180, annex) – stress the urgency of achieving the full integration of women in society on an equal basis with men and of abolishing any form of discrimination against women. Comprehensive strategies to address these concerns will be formulated at the 1985 Nairobi Conference which is being convened to review and appraise the achievements of the United Nations Decade for Women.

16. In view of the slow progress made since 1974 in the achievement of equality for women, the broadening of the role and the improvement of the status of women remain important goals that should be pursued as ends in themselves. The achievement of genuine equality with respect to opportunities, responsibilities and rights would guarantee that women could participate fully with men in all aspects of decision-making regarding population and development issues that affect their families, communities and countries.

17. The ability of women to control their own fertility forms an important basis for the enjoyment of other rights; likewise, the assurance of socioeconomic opportunities on an equal basis with men and the provision of the necessary services and facilities enable women to take greater responsibility for their reproductive lives. The following recommendations take into account the need for actions to ensure that women can effectively exercise rights equal to those of men in all spheres of economic, social, cultural and political life, and in particular those rights which pertain most directly to population concerns.

Recommendation 5

Governments are strongly urged to integrate women fully into all phases of the development process, including planning, policy and decision-making. Governments should pursue more aggressively action programmes aimed at improving and protecting the legal rights and status of women through efforts to identify and to remove institutional and cultural barriers to women's education, training, employment and access to health care. In addition, Governments should provide remedial measures, including mass education programmes, to assist women in attaining equality with men in the social, political and economic life of their countries. The promotion of community support and the collaboration, at the request of Governments, of non-governmental organizations, particularly women's organizations, in expediting these efforts should be given paramount importance.

Recommendation 6

Governments should ensure that women are free to participate in the labour force and are neither restricted from, nor forced to participate in, the labour force for reasons of demographic policy or cultural tradition. Further, the biological role of women in the reproductive process should in no way be used as a reason for limiting women's right to work. Governments should take the initiative in removing any existing barriers to the realization of that right and should create opportunities and conditions such that activities outside the home can be combined with child-rearing and household activities.

Recommendation 7

Governments should provide women, through education, training and employment, with opportunities for personal fulfilment in familial and non-familial roles, as well as for full participation in economic, social and cultural life, while continuing to give due support to their important social role as mothers. To this end, in those countries where child-bearing occurs when the mother is too young, Government policies should encourage delay in the commencement of child-bearing.

Recommendation 8

Governments concerned should make efforts to raise the age of entry into marriage in countries in which this age at marriage is still quite low.

Recommendation 9

Governments should promote and encourage, through information, education and communication, as well as through employment legislation and institutional support, where appropriate, the active involvement of men in all areas of family responsibility, including family planning, child-rearing and housework, so that family responsibilities can be fully shared by both partners.

Recommendation 10

All Governments which have not already done so are strongly urged to sign and ratify or accede to the Convention on the Elimination of All Forms of Discrimination against Women.

C. Development of Population Policies

18. The World Population Plan of Action urges that population policies should not be considered substitutes for socio-economic development policies but rather should be integral components of those policies (paragraph 2). In formulating population policies, Governments may aim to affect one or more of the following population trends and characteristics, among others, population growth, morbidity and mortality, reproduction, population distribution, internal and international migration and population structure. The Plan also recognizes the sovereignty of nations in the formulation, adoption and implementation of their population policies (paragraph 14), consistent with basic human rights and responsibilities of individuals, couples and families (paragraph 17).

Recommendation 11

Governments are urged to adopt population policies and social and economic development policies that are mutually reinforcing. Such policies should be formulated with particular attention to the individual, the family and community levels, as well as to other factors at the micro-level and macro-level. Special emphasis needs to be given to linkages between population trends, labour supply and demand, the problems of unemployment and the creation of productive employment. Governments are urged to share their experience in integrating population policies into other social and economic development policies.

Recommendation 12

Governments are encouraged to provide adequate resources and, where appropriate, to adopt innovative measures for the implementation of population policy. To be effective and successful, population programmes and development activities should be responsive to local values and needs, and those directly affected should be involved in the decision-making process at all levels. Moreover, in these activities, the full participation of the community and concerned non-governmental organizations, in particular women's organizations, should be encouraged.

D. Population Goals and Policies

1. Population growth

19. United Nations population projections, as assessed in 1982,* indicate that, between 1984 and the end of the present century, the growth rate of the world population will decline more slowly than during the past 10 years. This is partly due to the fact that, as a consequence of high fertility levels in the past, the number of women of child-bearing age (15-49) will continue to grow rapidly. Although, according to the medium variant projections, the total fertility rate during this period is expected to decline from 3.6 to 3.0 children per woman, the annual rate of growth is projected to reach only 1.5 per cent. For the world as a whole, the present annual increment of 78 million is projected to increase to 89 million by 1995-2000. Thus, in the 16 years from 1984 to 2000, the world population is expected to increase by 1.3 billion, from 4.8 billion in 1984 to 6.1 billion in 2000.

20. These global perspectives conceal significant demographic differences existing at the regional as well as the country levels. According to the United Nations estimates, the current total fertility rates range from 6.4 children per woman for Africa, 4.7 for South Asia, 4.1 for Latin America, 2.3 for East Asia, to 1.9 for Europe and North America. During the remainder of the present century these differences are not expected to narrow significantly. Moreover these projections assume a continuation of present efforts and policies without which uninterrupted declines in both fertility and population growth cannot be achieved. The World Population Plan of Action invites countries to consider adopting population policies, within the framework of socio-economic development, which are consistent with basic human rights and national goals and values (paragraph 17). It is in the light of that provision and the above-mentioned trends that the following recommendation is made.

Recommendation 13

Countries which consider that their population growth rates hinder the attainment of national goals are invited to consider pursuing relevant demographic policies, within the framework of socio-economic development. Such policies should respect human rights, the religious beliefs, philosophical convictions, cultural values and fundamental rights of each individual and couple, to determine the size of its own family.

---

*The United Nations demographic estimates or projections are revised every two years.

2. Morbidity and mortality

(a) Goals and general guidance for health policies

21. The World Population Plan of Action set targets for those countries with the highest mortality levels for 1985 and noted the progress necessary for each region to attain an average life expectancy of 62 years by 1985 and 74 years by 2000 (paragraphs 22 and 23). Recommendation 14 below updates the targets for countries with higher mortality levels and challenges countries with intermediate or lower mortality levels to continue and strengthen their efforts for the improvement of health and the reduction of mortality in the context of overall population and development planning. The targets are feasible, provided a commitment is made and resources are well allocated. Their achievement requires that communities become increasingly involved in efforts to promote their health and welfare, that all agencies and institutions of government be involved in this endeavour, and that each programme be evaluated. The achievement of these targets will also require that countries will not be subject to aggression (paragraph 24 (f)). The attainment of reduced levels of morbidity and mortality is in accordance with the Declaration of Alma Ata, endorsed by the General Assembly in its resolution 34/58 of 29 November 1979.

Recommendation 14

All Governments, regardless of the mortality levels of their population, are strongly urged to strive to reduce morbidity and mortality levels and socioeconomic and geographical differentials in their countries and to improve health among all population groups, especially among those groups where the morbidity and mortality levels are the highest. Countries with higher mortality levels should aim for a life expectancy at birth of at least 60 years and an infant mortality rate of less than 50 per 1,000 live births by the year 2000. Countries with intermediate mortality levels should aim to achieve a life expectancy at birth of at least 70 years and an infant mortality rate of less than 35 per 1,000 live births by the year 2000. The countries with lower mortality should continue their efforts to improve the health of all population groups and to reduce mortality even further, in keeping with their social and economic capacities. Levels, trends and differentials in mortality should be monitored in order to evaluate the success of programmes in achieving these goals.

Recommendation 15

Governmental, intergovernmental, parliamentary and non-governmental organizations should involve the community in all possible ways in the planning, implementation and evaluation of health improvement programmes.

Recommendation 16

The promotion and preservation of health should be the explicit concern of all levels and branches of government. It is strongly urged, therefore, that governmental action in the area of mortality and health should go beyond the health sector and involve all relevant sectors of national and community development. All development programmes should be monitored and analysed by the Government concerned in order to assess and to improve their impact on health.

(b) Infant, child and maternal morbidity and mortality

22. The World Population Plan of Action (paragraphs 24 and 32 (a)) gives special attention to measures aimed at reducing foetal, infant and early childhood mortality, and related maternal morbidity and mortality. The following recommendations give more precise guidelines for the implementation of the Plan, in accordance with the objective of the Global Strategy for Health for All by the Year 2000, which was adopted by the World Health Assembly and endorsed by the General Assembly in its resolution 36/43 of 19 November 1981.

Recommendation 17

Governments are urged to take immediate steps to identify the underlying causes of morbidity and mortality among infants and young children and develop special programmes to attack these conditions. Strategies to be considered include emphasis on mother and child health services within primary health care, the introduction and support of a package of specific intervention measures, and massive community-wide education and mobilization to support them. Special efforts should be made to reach under-served and deprived populations in rural areas and urban slums. The international community should take concerted action to support national efforts to this end.

Recommendation 18

All efforts should be made to reduce maternal morbidity and mortality. Governments are urged:

(a) To reduce maternal mortality by at least 50 per cent by the year 2000, where such mortality is very high (higher than 100 maternal deaths per 100,000 births);

(b) To provide prenuptial medical examinations;

(c) To provide prenatal and perinatal care, with special attention to high-risk pregnancies, and ensure safe delivery by trained attendants, including traditional birth attendants, as culturally acceptable;

(d) To give special emphasis in nutritional programmes to the needs of pregnant women and nursing mothers;

(e) To take appropriate steps to help women avoid abortion, which in no case should be promoted as a method of family planning, and whenever possible, provide for the humane treatment and counselling of women who have had recourse to abortion;*

(f) To support family planning as a health measure in maternal and child health programmes as a way of reducing births that occur too early or too late in the mother's life, of increasing the interval between births and of diminishing higher birth orders, and by giving special consideration to the needs of those in the post-partum and/or breast-feeding period;

(g) To encourage community education to change prevailing attitudes which countenance pregnancy and child-bearing at young ages, recognizing that pregnancy occurring in adolescent girls, whether married or unmarried, has adverse effects on the morbidity and mortality of both mother and child.

Recommendation 19

Governments are urged, as a special measure, to take immediate and effective action, within the context of primary health care, to expand the use of techniques such as child growth monitoring, oral rehydration therapy, immunization and appropriate birth spacing, which have the potential to achieve a virtual revolution in child survival. All available communication channels should be used to promote these techniques. The important role of the family, especially of mothers, in the area of primary health care should be recognized.

Recommendation 20

Governments are urged to promote and support breast-feeding. Information should be widely disseminated on the nutritional, immunological and psychological benefits of breast-feeding, as well as its influence on child spacing. Nursing mothers, especially those in the labour force, should be provided with appropriate maternal benefits, including day-care facilities, access

---

*While joining the consensus the Swedish representative made the following statement: "In the opinion of the Swedish delegation, effective contraception liberates women from unwanted pregnancies and induced abortions and improves considerably the health of both mothers and children. Prevention of unwanted pregnancies must always be the principal aim. However, illegal abortions performed under unsafe medical conditions represent a very serious health hazard in many countries.

"The Swedish delegation regrets very much that an amendment was adopted to delete the word "illegal" from recommendation 13 (e) as proposed by the Preparatory Committee, which suggests that this Conference failed to recognize the importance of this very serious problem. The Swedish delegation would like to reiterate that a major step towards the elimination of illegal abortions is to provide all women in the world with access to legal and safe abortions."

to proper food supplements for themselves, and complementary weaning and foods for their infants, in order to ensure adequate nutrition throughout infancy and early childhood. Governments which have accepted it should be urged to take the necessary steps to implement the International Code of Marketing of Breast-Milk Substitutes, as adopted by the 34th World Health Assembly (resolution WHA 34.22).

Recommendation 21

Governments are strongly urged to take all necessary measures, including, whenever they consider it useful, utilizing the services of non-governmental organizations, to raise the level of education attained by women as an end in itself and because of its close link to child survival and spacing. In countries where there are still many illiterate women, a supplementary effort should be made to extend mass education programmes.

(c) Adult morbidity and mortality

23. The levels of adult morbidity and mortality and their major causes are still of concern for many Governments in both developing and developed countries. The World Population Plan of Action recognizes the importance of improving health conditions for the working-age population and stresses the need for the eradication of infectious and parasitic diseases (paragraphs 24 (d) and (e)). In countries where infectious and parasitic diseases have reached low levels of incidence, chronic and non-infectious conditions still require urgent attention. As personal health practices and behaviour affect health, dissemination of the relevant information is important so that people can act on the basis of full information.

Recommendation 22

Governments of countries where mortality is still high are urged, with adequate international support, to implement intensive programmes to control infectious and parasitic diseases, provide as far as possible sufficient potable water and adequate sanitation facilities, and implement other elements of primary health care for both adults and children.

Recommendation 23

Governments, assisted by intergovernmental and non-governmental organizations, are urged to provide individuals and families with all relevant information on the ways in which personal behaviour or practices affect health, and to ensure that the necessary resources are available for them to act on the basis of this information. In this context, Governments are urged to initiate or strengthen preventive action programmes to reduce the consumption of tobacco, alcohol, drugs and other products potentially dangerous to health.

Recommendation 24

Governments are urged to take necessary preventive or corrective measures to eliminate the negative consequences for health that characterize many occupations.

3. Reproduction and the family

24. The World Population Plan of Action recognizes the family, in its many forms, as the basic unit of society and recommends that it should be given legal protection and that measures should be taken to protect both the rights of spouses and the rights of children in the case of the termination or dissolution of marriage and the right of individuals to enter marriage only with their free and full consent (paragraph 39). It also recommends that all children, regardless of the circumstances of their parentage, should enjoy equal legal and social status and the full support of both parents (paragraph 40). The family is the main institution through which social, economic and cultural change affects fertility. While the family has undergone and continues to undergo fundamental changes in its structure and function, the family continues to be recognized as the proper setting for mutual love, support and companionship of spouses, as the primary determinant of the survival of children born into it, as the first agent of the socialization of future generations, and in many societies as the only supporting institution for the aged. The family is also an important agent of social, political and cultural change. Therefore, in the design and implementation of fertility policies, Governments must respect individual rights while at the same time giving full recognition to the important role of the family.

25. The World Population Plan of Action recognizes, as one of its principles, the basic human right of all couples and individuals to decide freely and responsibly the number and spacing of their children (paragraph 14 (f)). For this right to be realized, couples and individuals must have access to the necessary education, information and means to regulate their fertility, regardless of the overall demographic goals of the Government (paragraphs 28 and 29 (a)). While this right is widely accepted, many couples and individuals are unable to exercise it effectively, either because they lack access to information, education and/or services or because, although some services are available, yet an appropriate range of methods and follow-up services are not. Indeed, data from the World Fertility Survey for developing countries indicate that, on average, over one fourth of births in the year prior to the Survey had not been desired. In addition, the decline in the prevalence of certain traditional practices, such as prolonged breast-feeding and post-partum abstinence, has increased the relative importance of non-traditional family planning as a tool for the proper spacing of births.

26. While the Plan also stresses the responsibility of individuals and couples in exercising their right to choose, the experience of the past 10 years

suggests that Governments can do more to assist people in making their reproductive decisions in a responsible way (paragraph 14 (f)). Any recognition of rights also implies responsibilities; in this case, it implies that couples and individuals should exercise this right, taking into consideration their own situation, as well as the implications of their decisions for the balanced development of their children and of the community and society in which they live. The following recommendations reaffirm the provisions of the World Population Plan of Action and suggest specific measures for the attainment of the objectives of the Plan in these areas.

Recommendation 25

Governments should, as a matter of urgency, make universally available information, education and the means to assist couples and individuals to achieve their desired number of children. Family planning information, education and means should include all medically approved and appropriate methods of family planning, including natural family planning, to ensure a voluntary and free choice in accordance with changing individual and cultural values. Particular attention should be given to those segments of the population which are most vulnerable and difficult to reach.

Recommendation 26

Governments are urged to promote the best conditions for family formation and family life, ensuring, *inter alia*, that children enjoy the most favourable environment for their physical, psychological and social development.

Recommendation 27

Governments and intergovernmental and non-governmental organizations are urged to allocate, in accordance with national policies and priorities, the necessary resources to family planning services, where these services are inadequate and are not meeting the needs of a rapidly growing population of reproductive age.

Recommendation 28

Governments are urged to improve the quality and enhance the effectiveness of family planning services and of the monitoring of those services, including appropriate follow-up. Coverage should be extended as rapidly as possible to all couples and individuals of both sexes, particularly in rural areas. Family planning services should be made available through appropriate and practicable channels, including integrated health-care programmes (especially maternal and child health and primary health care), community-based distribution, subsidized commercial retail sales, and, in particular, local distribution through retail outlets where health infrastructure and health referral services exist. Also, Governments should bear in mind the innovative role which non-governmental organizations, in particular women's organizations, can play in improving the availability and effectiveness of family planning services. All countries should ensure that fertility control methods conform to adequate standards of quality, efficacy and safety.

Recommendation 29

Governments are urged to ensure that adolescents, both boys and girls, receive adequate education, including family-life and sex education, with due consideration given to the role, rights and obligations of parents and changing individual and cultural values. Suitable family planning information and services should be made available to adolescents within the changing socio-cultural framework of each country.

Recommendation 30

Governments are urged to ensure that all couples and individuals have the basic right to decide freely and responsibly the number and spacing of their children and to have the information, education and means to do so; couples and individuals in the exercise of this right should take into account the needs of their living and future children and their responsibilities towards the community.

Recommendation 31

Legislation and policies concerning the family and programmes of incentives and disincentives should be neither coercive nor discriminatory and should be consistent with internationally recognized human rights as well as with changing individual and cultural values.

Recommendation 32

Governments which have adopted or intend to adopt national fertility goals should translate these goals into specific policies and operational steps that are clearly understood by the citizens.

Recommendation 33

Governments that have adopted or intend to adopt fertility policies are urged to set their own quantitative targets in this area. Countries implementing family planning programmes should establish programme targets at the operational level, respecting the basic right of couples and individuals to decide freely and responsibly the number and spacing of their children, taking into account the needs of their living and future children and their responsibilities, assumed freely and without coercion, towards the community.

Recommendation 34

Family policies adopted or encouraged by Governments should be sensitive to the need for:

(a) Financial and/or other support to parents, including single parents, in the period preceding or following the birth of a child, as well as the period during which parents assume the major responsibility for the care and education of children;

(b) A strengthening of child welfare services and child-care provisions;

(c) Maternity and paternity leave for a sufficient length of time to enable either parent to care for the child, with adequate remunerative compensation and without detriment to subsequent career prospects and basic communal facilities that will enable working parents to provide care for children and aged members of their families; and

(d) Assistance to young couples and parents, including single parents, in acquiring suitable housing.

Recommendation 35

Governments wishing to decrease fertility levels should adopt development policies that are known to reduce the level of fertility, such as improved health, education, integration of women and social equity. Governments that view the level of fertility in their countries as too low may consider financial and other support to families to assist them with their parental responsibilities and to facilitate their access to the necessary services. Such policies should not restrict access to education, information and services for family planning.

4. Population distribution and internal migration

27. The World Population Plan of Action makes a number of recommendations in regard to population distribution and internal migration that are of continuing relevance (paragraphs 44-50). The Plan recommends that population distribution policies should be integrated with economic and social policies. In formulating and implementing migration policies, Governments are urged to avoid infringing the right of freedom of movement and residence within States, to promote more equitable regional development, to locate services and industry so as to promote interpersonal equity as well as efficiency, to promote networks of small and medium-sized cities, and to improve economic and social conditions in rural areas through balanced agricultural development. In addition, the Plan recommends that migrants should be provided with information on economic and social conditions in urban areas, that employment creation, systems of land tenure and the provision of basic services should be improved in rural areas and that Governments should share experiences relevant to their policies. The area of

population distribution and internal migration is still one of great concern
to many Governments. The following recommendations indicate the means
for the further implementation of the Plan of Action.

Recommendation 36*

Population distribution policies must be consistent with such international
instruments as the Geneva Convention relative to the Protection of Civilian
Persons in Time of War (1949), wherein article 49 prohibits individual or mass
forcible transfers from an occupied territory and forbids the occupier from
transferring parts of its own civilian population into the territory it occupies.
Furthermore, the establishment of settlements in territories occupied by force
is illegal and condemned by the international community.

Recommendation 37

Governments are urged to base policies aimed at influencing population
distribution on a comprehensive evaluation of costs and benefits to individuals, families, different socio-economic groups, communities, regions and the
country as a whole. Population distribution goals (e.g., target growth rates
for primate cities or rural population retention goals) should be pursued to
the extent that they help to achieve broader societal goals, such as raising
per capita incomes, increasing efficiency, making the distribution of income
more equitable, protecting the environment and improving the quality of life.
In so doing, Governments should ensure that the rights of indigenous and
other groups are recognized.

Recommendation 38

Governments are urged, in formulating population distribution policies,
to take into account the policy implications of various forms of population
mobility (e.g., circular, seasonal, rural-rural, and urban-urban, as well as
rural-urban), to consider the direction, duration and characteristics of these
movements and the interrelationships between territorial mobility and levels
and characteristics of fertility and mortality.

---

*While joining the consensus the delegation of the United States of America stat-
ed that: "The United States delegation strongly protested the inclusion of this issue,
believing it politically divisive and extraneous to the work of the Conference. The
United States also challenged the competence of the Conference to interpret one of
the most critical international instruments governing the rules of war, the Geneva
Convention."

Recommendation 39

Governments are urged to review their socio-economic policies in order to minimize any adverse spatial consequences, as well as to improve the integration of population factors in territorial and sectoral planning, particularly in the sectors concerned with human settlements.

Recommendation 40

Governments wishing to minimize undesired migration should implement population distribution policies through incentives, rather than migration controls, which are difficult to enforce and may infringe human rights.

Recommendation 41

Governments which have adopted, or intend to adopt, a comprehensive urbanization policy, should seek to integrate such policies into the overall development planning process, with the aim of achieving, *inter alia*, a reduction in current high migration to capital cities and other large urban centres, the development of medium-sized towns and a reduction of rural-urban and regional inequalities. Developed countries and the international community should extend the necessary assistance to the efforts of developing countries in this direction.

Recommendation 42

Governments should support programmes of assistance, information and community action in support of internal migrants and should consider establishing networks of labour exchanges that could allow potential migrants to have adequate information about social conditions and about the availability of employment in receiving areas.

Recommendation 43

Rural development programmes should be primarily directed towards increasing rural production and efficiency, raising rural incomes and improving social conditions and rural welfare, particularly for small peasant producers and rural women. Governments should therefore improve the accessibility of basic social services and amenities to scattered populations, regularize land ownership, facilitate access to credit, new technology and other needed inputs, and adopt pricing policies geared to the needs of smallholders. Appropriate measures must be taken to carry out agrarian reform as one of the important factors which increase agricultural production and promote the development of rural areas.

Recommendation 44

Governments should adopt effective policies to assist women migrants, especially those who are agricultural workers, as well as women, children and the elderly left behind unsupported in rural areas. Governments are also urged to pay special attention to the difficulties of adaptation encountered in urban areas by migrant women of rural origin and to take appropriate measures to overcome these difficulties.

5. International migration

(a) General guidelines for formulating international migration policies

28. The general validity of the recommendations made in the World Population Plan of Action with respect to international movements is reaffirmed (paragraphs 51-62). However, recent developments regarding the trends of international migration flows demand greater attention from the international community, especially with regard to certain types of migrants, such as documented migrant workers, undocumented migrant workers and refugees. The guidelines set out below give due consideration to the basic fact that international migration is of concern to both the receiving countries and the countries of origin, particularly when the migration of skilled persons is involved. They reflect the bearing that international migration may have on the process of establishing a New International Economic Order and recognize that the effective safeguarding of the basic human rights and fundamental freedoms of all migrants, without discrimination on the basis of race, culture, religion or sex, is an essential prerequisite for the realization of their positive contributions to the host society.

Recommendation 45

International migration policies should respect the basic human rights and fundamental freedoms of individuals as set out in the Universal Declaration of Human Rights,[x] the International Covenant on Economic, Social and Cultural Rights, the International Covenant on Civil and Political Rights[y] and other pertinent international instruments. In keeping with these documents, receiving countries should adopt measures to safeguard the basic human rights of all migrants in their territory and to ensure the respect of their cultural identity. Measures should also be taken to promote the mutual adaptation of both immigrant groups and the population of the receiving country.

Recommendation 46

In formulating policies on international migration, Governments of receiving countries should take into account not only their own country's economic and social needs but also the well-being of the migrants concerned and their families and the demographic implications of migration. Governments of countries of origin concerned with the continuing outflow of skilled workers and professionals should seek to retain those workers as well as encourage their return through, *inter alia*, the promotion of an economic environment favourable to the expansion of employment opportunities. To redress the existing imbalance of skills, Governments should try to identify alternative skill resources. Governments should formulate national and international measures to avoid the brain-drain from developing countries and to obviate its adverse effects. While pursuing these purposes in a manner consistent with respect for human rights, Governments are invited to conduct, *inter alia*, consultations or negotiations, on either a bilateral or a multilateral basis, with the support, upon request, of competent international organizations.

Recommendation 47

High priority should be placed on the rehabilitation of expelled and homeless people who have been displaced by natural and man-made catastrophes. In all cases, Governments are urged to co-operate fully in order to guarantee that the parties involved allow the return of displaced persons to their homes and ensure their right to possess and enjoy their properties and belongings without interference.

(b) Documented migrant workers

29. The World Population Plan of Action calls for the proper treatment of migrant workers and their families (paragraphs 55 and 56) whose migration has been promoted by countries facing labour shortages and who are referred to hereafter as "documented migrant workers". The Plan also addresses the concerns of countries of origin (paragraph 54) and suggests concerted action at the bilateral and multilateral levels (paragraphs 54 and 62). In 1979, recognizing that, despite the efforts made by the States involved, documented migrant workers were still not able to exercise their rights as defined by the relevant international instruments, the General Assembly called for the elaboration of an international convention on the protection of the rights of all migrant workers and their families (resolution 34/172 of 17 December 1979). Many of the following recommendations reflect the contents of the draft of this convention.[z] It is hoped that upon adoption of the convention, it may serve as a guideline for the treatment of migrant workers and their families.

Recommendation 48

Governments of receiving countries should work towards extending to documented migrant workers and accompanying members of their families whose situation as regards stay and employment in the receiving country is regular, treatment equal to that accorded their own nationals with regard to the enjoyment of basic rights, including the equality of opportunity and treatment in respect of working conditions, social security, participation in trade unions and access to health, education and other social services. In achieving this aim, Governments are invited to use as guidelines all relevant international instruments, in particular, the ILO Convention concerning Migration for Employment (Revised) 1949 (No. 97) and the ILO Convention concerning Migrations in Abusive Conditions and the Promotion of Equality of Opportunity and Treatment of Migrant Workers, 1975 (No. 143), part II.aa

Recommendation 49

Governments of receiving countries that have not already done so are urged to consider adopting appropriate measures to promote the normalization of the family life of documented migrant workers in the receiving country concerned through family reunion. Demographic and other considerations should not prevent Governments from taking such measures.

Recommendation 50

Countries of origin and receiving countries should undertake information and education activities to increase the awareness of migrants regarding their legal position and rights and to provide realistic assessments of the situation of migrants, including the availability of job opportunities. Receiving countries should recognise the right of migrants to form associations so that they may participate more effectively in the receiving society while maintaining their cultural identity.

Recommendation 51

Governments of countries of origin and of receiving countries should encourage and promote the widest dissemination, *inter alia*, through the mass media, of information aimed at promoting public understanding of and preventing any activity prejudicial to the contribution of documented migrant workers to economic development and cultural interchange.

(c) Undocumented migrants

30. The World Population Plan of Action recommends that Governments bear in mind humanitarian considerations in the treatment of undocumented migrants* (paragraph 56). Owing to the irregularity of their situation, undocumented migrants are particularly vulnerable to exploitation and

---

*For the purpose of the following recommendations, undocumented migrants are persons who have not fulfilled all the legal requirements of the State in which they find themselves for admission, stay or exercise of economic activity.

mistreatment. It is therefore urgent that their basic human rights and fundamental freedoms be universally recognized and that they enjoy international protection as well as the protection of receiving countries within the framework of bilateral conventions. The widest recognition of the rights of all migrant workers and the effective safeguarding of these rights will tend to discourage exploitation of undocumented migrants, particularly exploitation in the sphere of employment, by employers who wish to reap the benefits of unfair competition.[bb]

Recommendation 52

All measures adopted or implemented by countries of departure and of arrival to reduce the illegal entry, stay or employment of undocumented migrants (including amnesties, other regularization schemes, border controls and deportations) should respect their basic human rights.

Recommendation 53

In formulating laws and regulations to limit undocumented migration, Governments of receiving countries are invited to consider the guidelines set forth in the ILO Convention concerning Migrations in Abusive Conditions and the Promotion of Equality of Opportunity and Treatment of Migrant Workers, 1975 (No. 143), part I.[cc] To be effective, such laws and regulations should address the treatment not only of the undocumented migrants themselves but also of those persons inducing or facilitating undocumented migration.

(d) Refugees

31. The World Population Plan of Action addresses the problems of refugees (paragraph 53). Since its adoption in 1974, refugees have been a source of growing concern to the international community because of their increasing numbers, the fact that a large proportion of them are from the vulnerable groups — women, children and the aged — and particularly because most refugees originate and relocate in developing countries, which have had to cope with the added economic and social burdens imposed on them. This concern has resulted in programmes by developing countries, as well as by third countries of resettlement, generally developed countries, to alleviate the dislocations associated with the influx of refugees. There seems to be broad agreement that through international co-operation within the framework of the United Nations an attempt should be made to remove the causes of new flows of refugees, having due regard to the principle of non-intervention in the internal affairs of sovereign States. In view of the existing situation, the recommendations set out below emphasize the need for

continued international co-operation in finding durable solutions to the problem of refugees and for the provision of support and assistance to countries of first asylum.

Recommendation 54

States that have not already done so are invited to consider acceding to the international instruments concerning refugees, in particular to the 1951 Convention[dd] and the 1967 Protocol[ee] relating to the Status of Refugees.

Recommendation 55

Governments and international agencies are urged to find durable solutions to problems related to refugees and refugee movements and to work towards the elimination of the causes of these problems. Governments, international organizations and non-governmental organizations are urged to continue to promote the protection of refugees and to provide support and assistance to first asylum countries in satisfying the basic needs of refugees. Efforts towards the creation of conditions in which voluntary repatriation may take place should be pursued and assistance should be provided in rehabilitating returnees. The basic freedoms and human rights of returnees and their families should be guaranteed and assistance should be provided in developing opportunities for a return to a normal and productive way of living. In situations where neither voluntary repatriation nor resettlement in third countries appears to be feasible, Governments, international organizations and non-governmental organizations are urged to provide support and assistance to the countries of first asylum in developing the capacity of the national economic and social infrastructure to sustain and, subject to the full approval of the host countries, to integrate refugees.

6. Population structure

32. The World Population Plan of Action (paragraphs 63-67) takes particular note of changing population age structures resulting from sustained demographic change, and of the effect of such changes on socio-economic development and on family and household structures. Closely linked issues such as employment for rapidly expanding working age groups, shifts from agricultural to non-agricultural occupations and health needs of particular age and sex groups are dealt with elsewhere in these recommendations. In countries where fertility levels are high, the large absolute and relative number of children and youth is a continuing burden for social and economic development, including educational development. On the other hand, the aging of the population has become an important issue in developed countries, and an emerging one in those developing countries which experienced

declines in fertility in the recent past. The rising proportion of the aged in these populations is imposing an economic burden with respect to national expenditures for social security and social services. It is noted, however, that the aged can make significant contributions to society. The following recommendations note the above and contain proposals to foster the growth and value of all age and sex groups in the community.

Recommendation 56

Governments and the international community should continue to bear in mind the considerations that led to the designation of the International Year of the Child, as well as the recommendations of the World Population Plan of Action with respect to age distribution, giving due attention to the full range of the needs of children.

Recommendation 57

Governments, specialized agencies of the United Nations system and other concerned intergovernmental and non-governmental organizations are invited to intensify their efforts in the execution of specific programmes related to youth, duly taking into account the situation, the needs, the specific aspirations of youth and the Specific Programme of Measures and Activities to be undertaken before and during the International Youth Year endorsed by the General Assembly.[ff]

Recommendation 58

Governments are urged to reaffirm their commitment to the implementation of the International Plan of Action on Aging.[w] In this context, further efforts should be made to analyse the issue of aging, particularly its implications for overall development, social services, medical care and other related fields, and on the basis of such data Governments are urged to take appropriate measures to secure the welfare and safety of older people, paying particular attention to the situation and the needs of older women. Governments and international agencies should increase their efforts and activities with a view to improving care for the aged within the family unit. Moreover, Governments should view the aging sector of the population not merely as a dependent group, but in terms of the active contribution that older persons have already made and can still make to the economic, social and cultural life of their families and community.

Recommendation 59

In planning for economic and social development, Governments should give appropriate consideration to shifts in family and household structures and their implications for requirements in different policy fields.

E. Promotion of Knowledge and Policy

1. Data collection and analysis

33. The recommendations of the World Population Plan of Action regarding data collection and analysis (paragraphs 72-77) continue to be both valid and urgent and thus every effort should be made for their full implementation. The collection and analysis of population and related statistics is an indispensable basis for a full and accurate understanding of population trends and prospects for formulating population and development plans and programmes and for monitoring effectively the implementation of these plans and programmes. During the past decade considerable progress has been achieved in the field of data collection and analysis. For example, nearly all countries have carried out a population census; well-designed fertility and other surveys were carried out in many developed and developing countries; efforts aimed at improving continuing national survey-taking capabilities were initiated in a number of developing countries; and major advances were made in the development of methods for use in the analysis of incomplete data. However, a number of critical gaps in official statistics remain, including those related to the classification of data for urban agglomerations. In view of these developments and future requirements, priority attention should be given to the following recommendations.

Recommendation 60

Governments are urged to develop durable capabilities for data collection, processing and analysis, including needed computer facilities, to provide reliable and timely information in support of population and other development programmes. They are also urged to accord priority to the development of national and regional population information systems. Required assistance should be provided to developing countries by the international community to develop these activities.

Recommendation 61

Governments are urged to monitor population trends and to assess future demographic prospects and their implications on a regular basis. Inasmuch as population projections provide basic tools for economic and social development planning, efforts should be made to prepare statistics relevant for this purpose. Co-ordination and co-operation in this work within and between countries should be promoted.

Recommendation 62

Governments are urged to ensure that population and related data are tabulated and published separately by sex, as well as data concerning other demographic, social and economic variables, so that the situation of women is rendered clearly and in order to measure the impact on women of changes that will ensue from the implementation of the World Population Plan of Action.

Recommendation 63

Governments are encouraged to tabulate and publish data about minority groups to assist in assessing the impact of the World Population Plan of Action on such groups.

Recommendation 64

Because migration is the least developed area of current demographic statistics, Governments may consider undertaking a comprehensive programme of migration statistics, in line with national priorities, focusing on such areas of concern as (1) internal migration, (2) urbanization and (3) international migration. It is also recommended that migration should be studied in the context of the family. To this end, Governments should consider ways of strengthening their national population censuses, sample surveys or administrative record systems in order to obtain needed migration data and estimates. Countries of origin and of destination are urged to exchange such pertinent statistical data, through the relevant United Nations authorities and other competent international organizations, where appropriate.

Recommendation 65

All countries are requested to participate in the 1990 World Population and Housing Census Programme and endeavour to improve further their censuses, giving particular attention to the timely publication of census results in order to assist, *inter alia*, in the evaluation of population and development trends at all levels. Required assistance in support of these activities should be provided to developing countries by the international community.

Recommendation 66

Governments, in collaboration with appropriate international organizations, are urged to establish or strengthen national sample survey programmes that can provide, in conjunction with data from other sources, a continuous flow of integrated statistics in support of population and other development programmes, and to build enduring capabilities for conducting surveys. It is recommended, in particular, that surveys should be carried out periodically on fertility, family planning, health of mothers and children, mortality and migration and that technical assistance for this purpose should be made available from international sources.

Recommendation 67

Governments are urged, in the collection, analysis and dissemination of statistical data, and in the context of national laws and practices, to ensure that confidentiality and the privacy of the individual are safeguarded.

Recommendation 68

Governments are urged to collect, compile and publish on a timely basis the full range of vital statistics, as well as other demographic and related social and economic statistics needed to plan and evaluate population and health programmes, including family planning programmes. To this end, Governments should establish or strengthen civil registration systems and make use of well-designed sample surveys, special studies and available administrative reporting systems, such as population registers.

2. Research

34. The World Population Plan of Action (paragraphs 78-80) gives great emphasis to research activities relating to population and identifies a list of research priorities related to the theoretical, operational and policy-oriented aspects of population analyses. Throughout the course of the review and appraisal of the World Population Plan of Action, in each of the expert group meetings convened as part of the preparations for the International Conference on Population, 1984, as well as in all other review activities, the continuing need for research both to fill gaps in knowledge and to support programmatic activity was made evident. Increased research efforts together with the necessary institutional and financial support are made necessary by changes in the social and economic contexts within which population policies are formulated and implemented. Similarly, changes in population policies and in demographic conditions themselves and new research findings, including those concerning contraceptive technology, call for an expansion of research activities.

Recommendation 69

Governments and funding agencies are urged to allocate increased resources for research in human reproduction and fertility regulation, including biomedical research, in order to improve the safety and efficacy of existing family planning methods, to develop new methods (including those for males), to develop better methods of recognizing the female fertile period and to address problems of infertility and subfecundity, including those caused by environmental pollution. Such research should be sensitive to the varying acceptability of specific methods in different cultures. Other important aspects requiring increased research efforts and support include epidemiological research on the short- and long-term adverse and beneficial medical effects of fertility-regulating agents. Modernization and updating of the official requirements for the preclinical and clinical assessment of new fertility regulating agents and a strengthening of the research capabilities of developing countries in these areas are also urgently needed.

Recommendation 70

Governments and intergovernmental and non-governmental organizations should give priority to service and operational research, including (a) acceptability of programmes and methods; (b) programme design and implementation; (c) management of programmes, including training of personnel, monitoring, logistics and impact evaluation; and (d) effectiveness of programmes, including information on planning the number of children. To increase the acceptance and to improve the design of family planning service programmes, priority should be given to social research into the determinants and consequences of fertility. However, substantive priorities should continue to reflect the needs of countries. The allocation of research tasks should be pragmatically divided among institutions that operate at the national, regional or global levels, in order to make the best possible use of available resources.

Recommendation 71

Governments and intergovernmental and non-governmental organizations should provide required assistance for the development and continued effectiveness of research capabilities, especially at the country level, as well as at the regional and global levels. Arrangements to facilitate the exchange of research findings within and between regions should also be further strengthened. Results of such research should be used in the implementation of action programmes, which in turn should have adequate built-in evaluation procedures.

Recommendation 72

In setting population research goals, Governments and intergovernmental and non-governmental organizations should endeavour to make them relevant to policies and programmes, with the objective of making innovations in policy formulation, implementation and evaluation. Special emphasis should be given to research on the integration of population processes with socio-economic development, considering not only applied but also theoretical and methodological topics.

3. Management, training, information, education and communication

35. The World Population Plan of Action contains a series of recommendations on management, training, information, education and communication in the field of population (paragraphs 81-93). Since its adoption, the need for the further development of management in all fields related to population has been acknowledged, both nationally and regionally, in order to enhance the effectiveness of population programmes. In view of the importance of considering the changing demographic situations as well as the interrelationships between population and development in the formulation of population policies and measures, training programmes in population and population-related studies need to be further strengthened. There is also a growing awareness of the supportive roles in population policies and programmes of dissemination of population information and of population education at national, regional and global levels. The following recommendations relate to these activities.

Recommendation 73

Governments and intergovernmental and non-governmental organizations should increase their support to the management of population programmes. They should also expand training programmes in population fields, particularly in the areas of demography, population studies, survey research, management, family life, sex education, maternal and child health, family planning and reproductive physiology. Such efforts should focus on action-oriented training, reflecting the milieu of the area, country or region concerned. Local-level training should be supplemented by programmes of technical co-operation among the developing countries and between the developed and the developing countries, so that they can learn from each other's experience. Development and expansion of national and regional population training institutes and facilities should be encouraged and strengthened. Special attention should also be given to the need to train those who will be involved in training activities. In order to ensure increased participation of women in the design, management, implementation and evaluation of population programmes, special attention should be given to the need to include women in all training activities.

Recommendation 74

Governments, with the assistance, as appropriate, of intergovernmental and non-governmental organizations, should continue to explore innovative methods for spreading awareness of demographic factors and for fostering the active involvement and participation of the public in population policies and programmes and to intensify training of national personnel who are engaged in information, education and communication activities (including the management and planning of those activities), in developing integrated communication activities and education strategies, utilizing mass media and community-level and interpersonal communication techniques.

Recommendation 75

Governments are invited to develop an adequate corps of trained persons for the effective formulation and implementation of integrated population and development policies, plans and programmes at all levels. In this regard, increased efforts should be made by Governments and training institutions, both at national and international levels, to further facilitate the integration of population studies into training curricula for policy-makers and executives who plan and implement development programmes.

Recommendation 76

Governments and intergovernmental organizations are urged to make more effective use of available population data and, for this purpose, to promote forums for assessing the priorities in the population fields, based on the results of population data and studies, and for considering their reorientation, as necessary; moreover, national and international support should be increased with a view to improving the dissemination and exchange of information at the national levels.

IV. RECOMMENDATIONS FOR IMPLEMENTATION

A. Role of National Governments

36. The World Population Plan of Action underscores the primary role of national Governments in the formulation, implementation and achievement of the principles and objectives of the Plan (paragraphs 96-99). The experience of the last decade has demonstrated the variety of policy approaches that can be effective when designed and implemented by Governments with due regard for the particular political, social, cultural, religious and economic conditions of their countries. However, many factors, including the lack of definite commitment, inadequate resources, ineffective coordination and implementation and insufficient data, have limited the effectiveness of Governments in the implementation of their national population policies. The following recommendations emphasize specific means whereby Governments can enhance the effectiveness of population policies within the context of the guidelines articulated in the Plan of Action.

Recommendation 77

Governments are urged to attach high priority to the attainment of self-reliance in the management of their population programmes. To this end, Governments are invited:

(a) To establish monitoring and evaluation systems and procedures as an important managerial tool for policy-making and programming;

(b) To strengthen the administrative and managerial capability needed for the effective implementation of population programmes;

(c) To ensure that international assistance is provided under arrangements and on conditions that are adapted to the administrative resources of the recipient country, and that such assistance is co-ordinated at the national level in a manner that will facilitate effective and efficient programmes;

(d) To involve communities more actively in the planning and implementation of population programmes.

Recommendation 78

Governments are encouraged to continue to utilize technical co-operation among developing countries; subregional, regional and interregional co-operation should be encouraged.

B. Role of International Co-operation

37. The World Population Plan of Action outlines the supportive role of the international community in providing technical and financial assistance to achieve the goals of the Plan (paragraphs 100-106). Since the Bucharest Conference, international co-operation activities of multilateral and bilateral agencies and intergovernmental and non-governmental organizations have achieved a number of notable successes in attaining these goals. Technical assistance among developing countries has also become increasingly effective. As noted in the Review and Appraisal of the World Population Plan of Action (E/CONF.76/4) the needs of developing countries for assistance in population have increased dramatically. Although the resources available have more than doubled in nominal terms, this increase has not been sufficient either to keep pace with the demand or to compensate for erosion due to inflation. The developing countries themselves are allocating increasing shares of development expenditure for population programmes. The need for assistance for population programmes as for all development programmes continues to grow. The recommendations in this section encourage further assistance for development and population, both to enlarge programmes where effective use of resources has been demonstrated and to initiate new activities.

Recommendation 79

The international community should play an important role in the further implementation of the World Population Plan of Action. For this purpose, among other things, adequate and substantial international measures of support and assistance should be provided by developed countries, other donor countries and intergovernmental and non-governmental organizations.

Recommendation 80

Organs, organizations and bodies of the United Nations system and donor countries which play an important role in supporting population programmes, as well as other international, regional and subregional organizations, are urged to assist Governments at their request in implementing these recommendations. Of no less importance will be the review of existing criteria for setting co-operation priorities, bearing in mind considerations of regional equity and the proper balance between the various phenomena in the field of international co-operation.

Recommendation 81

The international community should give particular emphasis to:
(a) Initiation and expansion of research and action programmes;
(b) Institutionalization of the integration of population planning in the development process;
(c) Improving the status and strengthening the role of women and providing appropriate financial and technical support for this purpose in population programmes;
(d) Biomedical and social science research;
(e) Collection and analysis of needed data;
(f) Identification of successful programmes, ascertaining those factors accounting for their success and disseminating such information to those developing countries which initiate programmes;
(g) Implementation of monitoring and evaluation systems in order to ascertain the effectiveness and impact of programmes and their continued responsiveness to community needs;
(h) Promotion of exchanges between countries with common experiences;
(i) Education and training in population matters.

Recommendation 82

Governments are urged to increase the level of their assistance for population activities in the light of continuing needs in the field and the increasing commitment of developing countries, with a view to reaching the goals set for this purpose in the International Development Strategy for the Third United Nations Development Decade. In this context Governments of developed countries and other donor countries are urged to allocate increased contributions for population and population-related programmes in accordance with national goals and priorities of recipient countries. This increase should not be detrimental to the levels of economic development assistance in other areas.

Recommendation 83

In view of the leading role of the United Nations Fund for Population Activities in population matters, the Conference urges that the Fund should be strengthened further, so as to ensure the more effective delivery of population assistance, taking into account the growing needs in this field. The Secretary-General of the United Nations is invited to examine this recommendation, and submit a report to the General Assembly on its implementation as soon as possible but not later than 1986.

Recommendation 84

National non-governmental organizations are invited to continue, in accordance with national policies and laws, their pioneering work in opening up new paths and to respond quickly and flexibly to requests from Governments, intergovernmental and international non-governmental organizations, as appropriate, for the further implementation of the World Population Plan of Action. Governments are urged, as appropriate, within the framework of national objectives, to encourage the innovative activities of non-governmental organizations and to draw upon their expertise, experience and resources in implementing national programmes. Donors are invited to increase their financial support to non-governmental organizations.

Recommendation 85

Members of parliament, the scientific community, the mass media, and others in influential positions are invited, in their respective areas of competence, to create an awareness of population and development issues and to support appropriate ways of dealing with these issues.

Recommendation 86

Policy makers, parliamentarians, and other persons in public life are encouraged to continue to promote and support actions to achieve an effective and integrated approach to the solution of population and development problems by arousing public awareness and working towards the implementation of national population policies and programmes. The United Nations Fund for Population Activities and the other international organizations concerned are invited to continue providing support for such actions.

Recommendation 87

The General Assembly, the Economic and Social Council, the Governing Council of the United Nations Development Programme and legislative and policy-making bodies of the specialized agencies and other intergovernmental organizations are urged to examine and support the recommendations for the further implementation of the World Population Plan of Action and to include population questions among their major priorities.

C. Monitoring, Review and Appraisal

Recommendation 88*

The monitoring of population trends and policies and review and appraisal of the World Population Plan of Action should continue to be undertaken by the Secretary-General of the United Nations, as specified in the Plan. The monitoring of multilateral population programmes of the United Nations system aimed at the further implementation of the World Population Plan of Action should be undertaken by the Secretary-General of the United Nations, through appropriate arrangements. The next comprehensive and thorough review and appraisal of progress made towards achieving the goals and recommendations of the World Population Plan of Action will be undertaken in 1989.

---

*While joining the consensus the Mexican representative made the following statement: "The Mexican delegation expressed its reservation concerning the text of recommendation 88, noting that it is not for the Secretary-General to keep the implementation of population programmes funded by multilateral assistance under review, as this is exclusively the prerogative of Governments. In this sense, the Secretary-General may only keep under review the use of the assistance provided by United Nations agencies to governmental programmes in regard to population."

The representative of India associated himself with the statement by the representative of Mexico.

NOTES

a. See *Report of the United Nations World Population Conference, 1974, Bucharest, 19-30 August 1974* (United Nations publication, Sales No. E.75.XIII.3), chap. 1.

b. General Assembly resolution 1386 (XIV).

c. *Report of the United Nations Conference on the Human Environment, Stockholm, 5-16 June 1972* (United Nations publication, Sales No. E.73.II.A.14 and corrigendum), chaps. I and II.

d. See *Official Records of the General Assembly, Thirty-seventh Session, Supplement No. 25* (A/37/25), part one, annex 1.

e. *Report of the World Food Conference, Rome, 5-16 November 1974* (United Nations publication, Sales No. E.75.II.A.3), chap. I.

f. *Report of the World Conference of the International Women's Year, Mexico City, 19 June-2 July 1975* (United Nations publication, Sales No. E.76.IV.1), chap. II, sect. A.

g. *Report of the World Conference of the United Nations Decade for Women: Equality, Development and Peace, Copenhagen, 14-30 July 1980* (United Nations publication, Sales No. E.80.IV.3 and corrigendum), chap. I, sect. A.

h. See A/10112, chap. IV.

i. See *Meeting Basic Needs: Strategies for Eradicating Mass Poverty and Unemployment* (Geneva, International Labour Office, 1977).

j. *Report of Habitat: United Nations Conference on Human Settlements, Vancouver, 31 May-11 June 1976* (United Nations publication, Sales No. E.76.IV.7 and corrigendum), chap. I.

k. *Report of the United Nations Conference on Desertification, Nairobi, 29 August-9 September 1977* (A/CONF.74/36), chap. I.

l. *Report of the United Nations Water Conference, Mar del Plata, 14-25 March 1977* (United Nations publication, Sales No. E.77.II.A.12), chap. I.

m. See *Primary Health Care: Report of the International Conference on Primary Health Care, Alma-Ata, USSR, 6-12 September 1978* (Geneva, World Health Organization, 1978).

n. *Report of the World Conference to Combat Racism and Racial Discrimination, Geneva, 14-25 August 1978* (United Nations publication, Sales No. E.79.XIV.2), chap. II.

o. General Assembly resolution 34/24, annex.

p. *Report of the Second World Conference to Combat Racism and Racial Discrimination, Geneva, 1-12 August 1983* (United Nations publication, Sales No. E.83.XIV.4 and corrigendum), chap. II.

q. *Report of the United Nations Conference on Technical Co-operation among Developing Countries, Buenos Aires, 30 August-12 September 1978* (United Nations publication, Sales No. E.78.II.A.11 and corrigendum), chap. I.

r. *Report of the World Conference on Agrarian Reform and Rural Development, Rome, 12-20 July 1979* (WCARRD/REP) (Rome, Food and Agriculture Organization of the United Nations, 1979), part one.

s. *Report of the United Nations Conference on Science and Technology for Development, Vienna, 20-31 August 1979* (United Nations publication, Sales No. E.79.I.21 and corrigenda), chap. VII.

t. *Global Strategy for Health for All by the Year 2000*, "Health for All" Series, No. 3 and corrigenda (Geneva, World Health Organization, 1981).

u. *Report of the United Nations Conference on New and Renewable Sources of Energy, Nairobi, 10-21 August 1981* (United Nations publication, Sales No. E.81.I.24), chap. I, sect. A.

v. *Report of the United Nations Conference on the Least Developed Countries, Paris, 1-14 September 1981* (United Nations publication, Sales No. E.82.I.8), part one, sect. A.

w. *Report of the World Assembly on Aging, Vienna, 26 July-6 August 1982* (United Nations publication, Sales No. E.82.I.16), chap. VI, sect. A.

x. General Assembly resolution 217 A (III).

y. General Assembly resolution 2200 A (XXI), annex.

z. See A/C.3/38/WG.1/CRP.2/Rev.1; for the deliberations of the Working Group on the drafting of an international Convention on the Protection of the Rights of All Migrant Workers and Their Families, see A/C.3/35/13, A/36/378, A/36/383, A/C.3/36/10, A/C.3/37/1, A/C.3/37/7 and Corr.1 and 2, A/C.3/38/1 and A/C.3/38/5.

aa. See *International Labour Conventions and Recommendations, 1919-1981* (Geneva, International Labour Office, 1982).

bb. See, in this connection, the draft Convention on the Protection of the Rights of All Migrant Workers and Their Families (A/C.3/38/WG.1/CRP.2/Rev.1), preambular paragraph 18 and proposed preambular paragraph 19, and the report of the Working Group on its meetings during the thirty-sixth session of the General Assembly (A/C.3/36/10), para. 25.

cc. See *International Labour Conventions and Recommendations, 1919-1981* (Geneva, International Labour Office, 1982).

dd. United Nations, *Treaty Series*, vol. 189, No. 2545, p. 137.

ee. *Ibid.*, vol. 606, No. 8791, p. 267.

ff. General Assembly resolution 36/28.

Mexico City Declaration on Population and Development*

1. The International Conference on Population met in Mexico City from 6 to 14 August 1984, to appraise the implementation of the World Population Plan of Action, adopted by consensus at Bucharest, 10 years ago. The Conference reaffirmed the full validity of the principles and objectives of the World Population Plan of Action and adopted a set of recommendations for the further implementation of the Plan in the years ahead.

2. The world has undergone far-reaching changes in the past decade. Significant progress in many fields important for human welfare has been made through national and international efforts. However, for a large number of countries it has been a period of instability, increased unemployment, mounting external indebtedness, stagnation and even decline in economic growth. The number of people living in absolute poverty has increased.

3. Economic difficulties and problems of resource mobilization have been particularly serious in the developing countries. Growing international disparities have further exacerbated already serious problems in social and economic terms. Firm and widespread hope was expressed that increasing international co-operation will lead to a growth in welfare and wealth, their just and equitable distribution and minimal waste in use of resources, thereby promoting development and peace for the benefit of the world's population.

---

*Report of the International Conference on Population, 1984, Mexico City, 6-14 August 1984 (United Nations publication, Sales No. E.84.XIII.8 and corrigendum), chap. I, sect. A.

4. Population growth, high mortality and morbidity, and migration problems continue to be causes of great concern requiring immediate action.

5. The Conference confirms that the principal aim of social, economic and human development, of which population goals and policies are integral parts, is to improve the standards of living and quality of life of the people. This Declaration constitutes a solemn undertaking by the nations and international organizations gathered in Mexico City to respect national sovereignty, to combat all forms of racial discrimination, including *apartheid*, and to promote social and economic development, human rights and individual freedom.

* * *

6. Since Bucharest the global population growth rate has declined from 2.03 to 1.67 per cent per year. In the next decade the growth rate will decline more slowly. Moreover, the annual increase in numbers is expected to continue and may reach 90 million by the year 2000. Ninety per cent of that increase will occur in developing countries and at that time 6.1 billion people are expected to inhabit the Earth.

7. Demographic differences between developed and developing countries remain striking. The average life expectancy at birth, which has increased almost everywhere, is 73 years in developed countries, while in developing countries it is only 57 years and families in developing countries tend to be much larger than elsewhere. This gives cause for concern since social and population pressures may contribute to the continuation of the wide disparity in welfare and the quality of life between developing and developed countries.

8. In the past decade, population issues have been increasingly recognized as a fundamental element in development planning. To be realistic, development policies, plans and programmes must reflect the inextricable links between population, resources, environment and development. Priority should be given to action programmes integrating all essential population and development factors, taking fully into account the need for rational utilization of natural resources and protection of the physical environment and preventing its further deterioration.

9. The experience with population policies in recent years is encouraging. Mortality and morbidity rates have been lowered, although not to the desired extent. Family planning programmes have been successful in reducing fertility at relatively low cost. Countries which consider that their population growth rate hinders their national development plans should adopt appropriate population policies and programmes. Timely action could avoid the accentuation of problems such as overpopulation, unemployment, food shortages, and environmental degradation.

10. Population and development policies reinforce each other when they are responsive to individual, family and community needs. Experience from the past decade demonstrates the necessity of the full participation by the entire community and grass-roots organizations in the design and implementation of policies and programmes. This will ensure that programmes are relevant to local needs and in keeping with personal and social values. It will also promote social awareness of demographic problems.

11. Improving the status of women and enhancing their role is an important goal in itself and will also influence family life and size in a positive way. Community support is essential to bring about the full integration and participation of women into all phases and functions of the development process. Institutional, economic and cultural barriers must be removed and broad and swift action taken to assist women in attaining full equality with men in the social, political and economic life of their communities. To achieve this goal, it is necessary for men and women to share jointly responsibilities in areas such as family life, child-caring and family planning. Governments should formulate and implement concrete policies which would enhance the status and role of women.

12. Unwanted high fertility adversely affects the health and welfare of individuals and families, especially among the poor, and seriously impedes social and economic progress in many countries. Women and children are the main victims of unregulated fertility. Too many, too close, too early and too late pregnancies are a major cause of maternal, infant and childhood mortality and morbidity.

13. Although considerable progress has been made since Bucharest, millions of people still lack access to safe and effective family planning methods. By the year 2000 some 1.6 billion women will be of child-bearing age, 1.3 billion of them in developing countries. Major efforts must be made now to ensure that all couples and individuals can exercise their basic human right to decide freely, responsibly and without coercion, the number and spacing of their children and to have the information, education and means to do so. In exercising this right, the best interests of their living and future children as well as the responsibility towards the community should be taken into account.

14. Although modern contraceptive technology has brought considerable progress into family planning programmes, increased funding is required in order to develop new methods and to improve the safety, efficacy and acceptability of existing methods. Expanded research should also be undertaken in human reproduction to solve problems of infertility and subfecundity.

15. As part of the overall goal to improve the health standards for all people, special attention should be given to maternal and child health services within a primary health care system. Through breast-feeding, adequate nutrition, clean water, immunization programmes, oral rehydration therapy and

birth spacing, a virtual revolution in child survival could be achieved. The impact would be dramatic in humanitarian and fertility terms.

16. The coming decades will see rapid changes in population structures with marked regional variations. The absolute numbers of children and youth in developing countries will continue to rise so rapidly that special programmes will be necessary to respond to their needs and aspirations, including productive employment. Aging of populations is a phenomenon which many countries will experience. This issue requires attention particularly in developed countries in view of its social implications and the active contribution the aged can make to the social, cultural and economic life in their countries.

17. Rapid urbanization will continue to be a salient feature. By the end of the century, 3 billion people, 48 per cent of the world's population, might live in cities, frequently very large cities. Integrated urban and rural development strategies should therefore be an essential part of population policies. They should be based on a full evaluation of the costs and benefits to individuals, groups and regions involved, should respect basic human rights and use incentives rather than restrictive measures.

18. The volume and nature of international migratory movements continue to undergo rapid changes. Illegal or undocumented migration and refugee movements have gained particular importance; labour migration of considerable magnitude occurs in all regions. The outflow of skills remains a serious human resource problem in many developing countries. It is indispensable to safeguard the individual and social rights of the persons involved and to protect them from exploitation and treatment not in conformity with basic human rights; it is also necessary to guide these different migration streams. To achieve this, the co-operation of countries of origin and destination and the assistance of international organizations are required.

19. As the years since 1974 have shown, the political commitment of Heads of State and other leaders and the willingness of Governments to take the lead in formulating population programmes and allocating the necessary resources are crucial for the further implementation of the World Population Plan of Action. Governments should attach high priority to the attainment of self-reliance in the management of such programmes, strengthen their administrative and managerial capabilities, and ensure co-ordination of international assistance at the national level.

20. The years since Bucharest have also shown that international co-operation in the field of population is essential for the implementation of recommendations agreed upon by the international community and can be notably successful. The need for increased resources for population activities is emphasized. Adequate and substantial international support and assistance will greatly facilitate the efforts of Governments. It should be provided wholeheartedly and in a spirit of universal solidarity and enlightened self-interest. The United Nations family should continue to perform its vital responsibilities.

21. Non-governmental organizations have a continuing important role in the implementation of the World Population Plan of Action and deserve encouragement and support from Governments and international organizations. Members of Parliament, community leaders, scientists, the media and others in influential positions are called upon to assist in all aspects of population and development work.

* * *

22. At Bucharest, the world was made aware of the gravity and magnitude of the population problems and their close interrelationship with economic and social development. The message of Mexico City is to forge ahead with effective implementation of the World Population Plan of Action aimed at improving standards of living and quality of life for all peoples of this planet in promotion of their common destiny in peace and security.

23. IN ISSUING THIS DECLARATION, ALL PARTICIPANTS AT THE INTERNATIONAL CONFERENCE ON POPULATION REITERATE THEIR COMMITMENT AND REDEDICATE THEMSELVES TO THE FURTHER IMPLEMENTATION OF THE PLAN.

APPENDIX B

WORLD POPULATION PLAN OF ACTION

Adopted by the World Population Conference Bucharest, 19-30 August 1974.

Text of World Population Plan of Action*

CONTENTS

The World Population Conference,

Having due regard for human aspirations for a better quality of life and for rapid socio-economic development,

Taking into consideration the interrelationship between population situations and socio-economic development,

Decides on the following World Population Plan of Action as a policy instrument within the broader context of the internationally adopted strategies for national and international progress:

Report of the United Nations World Population Conference, Bucharest, 19-30 August 1974 (United Nations publication, Sales No. E.75.XIII.3), chap. I.

A. Background to the Plan

1. The promotion of development and improvement of quality of life require co-ordination of action in all major socio-economic fields including that of population, which is the inexhaustible source of creativity and a determining factor of progress. At the international level a number of strategies and programmes whose explicit aim is to affect variables in fields other than population have already been formulated. These include the Provisional Indicative World Plan for Agricultural Development of the Food and Agriculture Organization of the United Nations, the United Nations/FAO World Food Programme, the International Labour Organisation's World Employment Programme, the Action Plan for the Human Environment, the United Nations World Plan of Action for the Application of Science and Technology to Development, the Programme of Concerted Action for the Advancement of Women, and, more comprehensively, the International Development Strategy for the Second United Nations Development Decade. The Declaration on the Establishment of a New International Economic Order and the Programme of Action to achieve it, adopted by the United Nations General Assembly at its sixth special session (resolutions 3201 (S-VI) and 3202 (S-VI) of 1 May 1974), provide the most recent overall framework for international co-operation. The explicit aim of the World Population Plan of Action is to help co-ordinate population trends and the trends of economic and social development. The basis for an effective solution of population problems is, above all, socio-economic transformation. A population policy may have a certain success if it constitutes an integral part of socio-economic development; its contribution to the solution of world development problems is hence only partial, as is the case with the other sectoral strategies. Consequently, the Plan of Action must be considered as an important component of the system of international strategies and as an instrument of the international community for the promotion of economic development, quality of life, human rights and fundamental freedoms.

2. The formulation of international strategies is a response to universal recognition of the existence of important problems in the world and the need for concerted national and international action to achieve their solution. Where trends of population growth, distribution and structure are out of balance with social, economic and environmental factors, they can, at certain stages of development, create additional difficulties for the achievement of sustained development. Policies whose aim is to affect population trends must not be considered substitutes for socio-economic development policies but as being integrated with those policies in order to facilitate the solution of certain problems facing both developing and developed countries and to promote a more balanced and rational development.

3. Throughout history the rate of growth of world population averaged only slightly above replacement levels. The recent increase in the growth rate

began mainly as a result of the decline in mortality during the past few centuries, a decline that has accelerated significantly during recent decades. The inertia of social structures and the insufficiency of economic progress, especially when these exist in the absence of profound socio-cultural changes, partly explain why in the majority of developing countries the decline in mortality has not been accompanied by a parallel decline in fertility. Since about 1950, the world population growth rate has risen to 2 per cent a year. If sustained, this will result in a doubling of the world's population every 35 years. However, national rates of natural growth range widely, from a negative rate to well over 3 per cent a year.

4. The consideration of population problems cannot be reduced to the analysis of population trends only. It must also be borne in mind that the present situation of the developing countries originates in the unequal processes of socio-economic development which have divided peoples since the beginning of the modern era. This inequity still exists and is intensified by lack of equity in international economic relations with consequent disparity in levels of living.

5. Although acceleration in the rate of growth of the world's population is mainly the result of very large declines in the mortality of developing countries, those declines have been unevenly distributed. Thus, at present, average expectation of life at birth is 63 years in Latin America, 57 years in Asia and only a little over 46 years in Africa, compared with more than 71 years in the developed regions. Furthermore, although on average less than one in 40 children dies before reaching the age of 1 year in the developed regions, 1 in 15 dies before reaching that age in Latin America, 1 in 10 in Asia and 1 in 7 in Africa. In fact, in some developing regions, and particularly in African countries, average expectation of life at birth is estimated to be less than 40 years and 1 in 4 children dies before the age of 1 year. Consequently, many developing countries consider reduction of mortality, and particularly reduction of infant mortality, to be one of the most important and urgent goals.

6. While the right of couples to have the number of children they desire is accepted in a number of international instruments, many couples in the world are unable to exercise that right effectively. In many parts of the world, poor economic conditions, social norms, inadequate knowledge of effective methods of family regulation and the unavailability of contraceptive services result in a situation in which couples have more children than they desire or feel they can properly care for. In certain countries, on the other hand, because of economic or biological factors, problems of involuntary sterility and of subfecundity exist, with the result that many couples have fewer children than they desire. Of course, the degree of urgency attached to dealing with each of these two situations depends upon the prevailing conditions within the country in question.

7. Individual reproductive behaviour and the needs and aspirations of society should be reconciled. In many developing countries, and particularly in the large countries of Asia, the desire of couples to achieve large families is believed to result in excessive national population growth rates and Governments are explicitly attempting to reduce those rates by implementing specific policy measures. On the other hand, some countries are attempting to increase desired family size, if only slightly.

8. Throughout the world, urban populations are growing in size at a considerably faster rate than rural populations. As a result, by the end of this century, and for the first time in history, the majority of the world's population will be living in urban areas. Urbanization is an element of the process of modernization. Moreover, while in certain countries this process is efficiently managed and maximum use is made of the advantages this management presents, in others urbanization takes place in an uncontrolled manner and is accompanied by overcrowding in certain districts, an increase in slums, deterioration of the environment, urban unemployment and many other social and economic problems.

9. In most of the developing countries, although the rate of urban population growth is higher than the growth rate in rural areas, the latter is still significant. The rural population of developing countries is growing at an average rate of 1.7 per cent a year, and in some instances at a faster rate than that of the urban population in developed countries. Furthermore, many rural areas of heavy emigration, in both developed and developing countries, are being depleted of their younger populations and are being left with populations whose age distribution is unfavourable to economic development. Thus, in many countries, the revitalization of the countryside is a priority goal.

10. For some countries international migration may be, in certain circumstances, an instrument of population policy. At least two types of international migration are of considerable concern to many countries in the world: the movement of migrant workers with limited skills, and the movement of skilled workers and professionals. Movements of the former often involve large numbers and raise such questions as the fair and proper treatment in countries of immigration, the breaking up of families and other social and economic questions in countries both of emigration and immigration. The migration of skilled workers and professionals results in a "brain drain", often from less-developed to more-developed countries, which is at present of considerable concern to many countries and to the international community as a whole. The number of instruments on these subjects and the increased involvement of international organizations reflect international awareness of these problems.

11. A population's age structure is greatly affected by its birth rates. For example, declining fertility is the main factor underlying the declining proportion of children in a population. Thus, according to the medium projections

of the United Nations, the population of less than 15 years of age in the developing countries is expected to decline from an average of more than 41 per cent of total population in 1970 to an average of about 35 per cent in 2000. However, such a decline in the proportion of children will be accompanied by an increase in their numbers at an average of 1.7 per cent a year. The demand for educational services is expected to increase considerably, in view of both the existing backlog and the continuously increasing population of children which ought to enter and remain in schools; therefore the supply of educational services must be increased. With regard to the population 15 to 29 years of age, an increase in both their proportion and number is expected in the developing countries. Consequently, unless very high rates of economic development are attained, in many of these countries, and particularly where levels of unemployment and underemployment are already high, the additional difficulties will not be overcome at least until the end of this century. Furthermore, in both developed and developing countries, the greatly changing social and economic conditions faced by youth require a better understanding of the problems involved and the formulation and implementation of policies to resolve them.

12. Declining birth rates also result in a gradual aging of the population. Because birth rates have already declined in developed countries, the average proportion of the population aged 65 years and over in these countries makes up 10 per cent of the total population, whereas it makes up only 3 per cent in developing countries. However, aging of the population in developing countries has recently begun, and is expected to accelerate. Thus, although the total population of these countries is projected to increase by an average of 2.3 per cent a year between 1970 and 2000, the population 65 years and over is expected to increase by 3.5 per cent a year. Not only are the numbers and proportions of the aged increasing rapidly but the social and economic conditions which face them are also rapidly changing. There is an urgent need, in those countries where such programmes are lacking, for the development of social security and health programmes for the elderly.

13. Because of the relatively high proportions of children and youth in the populations of developing countries, declines in fertility levels in those countries will not be fully reflected in declines in population growth rates until some decades later. To illustrate this demographic inertia, it may be noted that, for developing countries, even if replacement levels of fertility — approximately two children per completed family — had been achieved in 1970 and maintained thereafter, their total population would still grow from a 1970 total of 2.5 billion to about 4.4 billion before it would stabilize during the second half of the twenty-first century. In these circumstances, the population of the world as a whole would grow from 3.6 billion to 5.8 billion. This example of demographic inertia, which will lead to a growing population for many decades to come, demonstrates that whatever population poli-

cies may be formulated, socio-economic development must accelerate in order to provide for a significant increase in levels of living. Efforts made by developing countries to speed up economic growth must be viewed by the entire international community as a global endeavour to improve the quality of life for all people of the world, supported by a just utilization of the world's wealth, resources and technology in the spirit of the new international economic order. It also demonstrates that countries wishing to affect their population growth must anticipate future demographic trends and take appropriate decisions and actions in their plans for economic and social development well in advance.

B. Principles and Objectives of the Plan

14. This Plan of Action is based on a number of principles which underlie its objectives and are observed in its formulation. The formulation and implementation of population policies is the sovereign right of each nation. This right is to be exercised in accordance with national objectives and needs and without external interference, taking into account universal solidarity in order to improve the quality of life of the peoples of the world. The main responsibility for national population policies and programmes lies with national authorities. However, international co-operation should play an important role in accordance with the principles of the United Nations Charter. The Plan of Action is based on the following principles:

(a) The principal aim of social, economic and cultural development, of which population goals and policies are integral parts, is to improve levels of living and the quality of life of the people. Of all things in the world, people are the most precious. Man's knowledge and ability to master himself and his environment will continue to grow. Mankind's future can be made infinitely bright;

(b) True development cannot take place in the absence of national independence and liberation. Alien and colonial domination, foreign occupation, wars of aggression, racial discrimination, *apartheid* and neo-colonialism in all its forms continue to be among the greatest obstacles to the full emancipation and progress of the developing countries and all the people involved. Co-operation among nations on the basis of national sovereignty is essential for development. Development also requires recognition of the dignity of the individual, appreciation for the human person and his self-determination, as well as the elimination of discrimination in all its forms;

(c) Population and development are interrelated: population variables influence development variables and are also influenced by them; thus the formulation of a World Population Plan of Action reflects the international community's awareness of the importance of population trends for socio-economic development, and the socio-economic nature of the recommendations contained in this Plan of Action reflects its awareness of the crucial role that development plays in affecting population trends;

(d) Population policies are constituent elements of socio-economic development policies, never substitutes for them: while serving socio-economic objectives, they should be consistent with internationally and nationally recognized human rights of individual freedom, justice and the survival of national, regional and minority groups;

(e) Independently of the realization of economic and social objectives, respect for human life is basic to all human societies;

(f) All couples and individuals have the basic right to decide freely and responsibly the number and spacing of their children and to have the information, education and means to do so; the responsibility of couples and individuals in the exercise of this right takes into account the needs of their living and future children, and their responsibilities towards the community;

(g) The family is the basic unit of society and should be protected by appropriate legislation and policy;

(h) Women have the right to complete integration in the development process particularly by means of an equal access to education and equal participation in social, economic, cultural and political life. In addition, the necessary measures should be taken to facilitate this integration with family responsibilities which should be fully shared by both partners;

(i) Recommendations in this Plan of Action regarding policies to deal with population problems must recognize the diversity of conditions within and among different countries;

(j) In the democratic formulation of national population goals and policies, consideration must be given, together with other economic and social factors, to the supplies and characteristics of natural resources and to the quality of the environment and particularly to all aspects of food supply including productivity of rural areas. The demand for vital resources increases not only with growing population but also with growing *per capita* consumption; attention must be directed to the just distribution of resources and to the minimization of wasteful aspects of their use throughout the world;

(k) The growing interdependence among nations makes international action increasingly important to the solution of development and population problems. International strategies will achieve their objective only if they ensure that the underprivileged of the world achieve, urgently, through structural, social and economic reforms, a significant improvement in their living conditions;

(l) This Plan of Action must be sufficiently flexible to take into account the consequences of rapid demographic changes, societal changes and changes in human behaviour, attitudes and values;

(m) The objectives of this Plan of Action should be consistent with the purposes and principles of the Charter of the United Nations, the Universal

Declaration of Human Rights and with the objectives of the Second United Nations Development Decade; however, changes in demographic variables during the Decade are largely the result of past demographic events and changes in demographic trends sought during the Decade have social and economic repercussions up to and beyond the end of this century.

15. Guided by these principles, the primary aim of this Plan of Action is to expand and deepen the capacities of countries to deal effectively with their national and subnational population problems and to promote an appropriate international response to their needs by increasing international activity in research, the exchange of information, and the provision of assistance on request. In pursuit of this primary aim, the following general objectives are set for this Plan of Action:

(a) To advance understanding of population at global, regional, national and subnational levels, recognizing the diversity of the problems involved;

(b) To advance national and international understanding of the interrelationship of demographic and socio-economic factors in development: on the one hand, of the nature and scope of the effect of demographic factors on the attainment of goals of advancing human welfare, and, on the other hand, the impact of broader social, economic and cultural factors on demographic behaviour;

(c) To promote socio-economic measures and programmes whose aim is to affect, *inter alia*, population growth, morbidity and mortality, reproduction and family formation, population distribution and internal migration, international migration and, consequently, demographic structures;

(d) To advance national and international understanding of the complex relations among the problems of population, resources, environment and development, and to promote a unified analytical approach to the study of these interrelationships and to relevant policies;

(e) To promote the status of women and the expansion of their roles, their full participation in the formulation and implementation of socio-economic policy including population policies, and the creation of awareness among all women of their current and potential roles in national life;

(f) To recommend guidelines for population policies consistent with national values and goals and with internationally recognized principles;

(g) To promote the development and implementation of population policies where necessary, including improvement in the communication of the purposes and goals of those policies to the public and the promotion of popular participation in their formulation and implementation;

(h) To encourage the development and good management of appropriate education, training, statistical research, information and family health services as well as statistical services in support of the above principles and objectives.

C. Recommendations for Action

1. Population goals and policies

(a) Population growth

16. According to the United Nations medium population projections, little change is expected to occur in average rates of population growth either in the developed or in the developing regions by 1985. According to the United Nations low variant projections, it is estimated that, as a result of social and economic development and population policies as reported by countries in the Second United Nations Inquiry on Population and Development, population growth rates in the developing countries as a whole may decline from the present level of 2.4 per cent per annum to about 2 per cent by 1985 and may remain below 0.7 per cent per annum in the developed countries. In this case the worldwide rate of population growth would decline from 2 per cent to about 1.7 per cent.

17. Countries which consider that their present or expected rates of population growth hamper their goals of promoting human welfare are invited, if they have not yet done so, to consider adopting population policies, within the framework of socio-economic development, which are consistent with basic human rights and national goals and values.

18. Countries which aim at achieving moderate or low population growth should try to achieve it through a low level of birth and death rates. Countries wishing to increase their rate of population growth should, when mortality is high, concentrate efforts on the reduction of mortality, and where appropriate, encourage an increase in fertility and encourage immigration.

19. Recognizing that *per capita* use of world resources is much higher in the developed than in the developing countries, the developed countries are urged to adopt appropriate policies in population, consumption and investment, bearing in mind the need for fundamental improvement in international equity.

(b) Morbidity and mortality

20. The reduction of morbidity and mortality to the maximum feasible extent is a major goal of every human society. It should be achieved in conjunction with massive social and economic development. Where mortality and morbidity rates are very high, concentrated national and international efforts should be applied to reduce them as a matter of highest priority in the context of societal change.

21. The short-term effect of mortality reduction on population growth rates is symptomatic of the early development process and must be viewed as beneficial. Sustained reductions in fertility have generally been preceded

by reductions in mortality. Although this relationship is complex, mortality reduction may be a prerequisite to a decline in fertility.

22. It is a goal of this Plan of Action to reduce mortality levels, particularly infant and maternal mortality levels, to the maximum extent possible in all regions of the world and to reduce national and subnational differentials therein. The attainment of an average expectation of life of 62 years by 1985 and 74 years by the year 2000 for the world as a whole would require by the end of the century an increase of 11 years for Latin America, 17 years for Asia and 28 years for Africa.

23. Countries with the highest mortality levels should aim by 1985 to have an expectation of life at birth of at least 50 years and an infant mortality rate of less than 120 per thousand live births.

24. It is recommended that national and international efforts to reduce general morbidity and mortality levels be accompanied by particularly vigorous efforts to achieve the following goals:

(a) Reduction of foetal, infant and early childhood mortality and related maternal morbidity and mortality;

(b) Reduction of involuntary sterility, subfecundity, defective births and illegal abortions;

(c) Reduction or, if possible, elimination of differential morbidity and mortality within countries, particularly with regard to differentials between regions, urban and rural areas, social and ethnic groups, and the sexes;

(d) Eradication, wherever possible, or control of infections and parasitic diseases, undernutrition and malnutrition; and the provision of a sufficient supply of potable water and adequate sanitation;

(e) Improvement of poor health and nutritional conditions which adversely affect working-age populations and their productivity and thus undermine development efforts;

(f) Adoption of special measures for reducing mortality from social and environmental factors and elimination of aggression as a cause of death and poor health.

25. It is recommended that health and nutrition programmes designed to reduce morbidity and mortality be integrated within a comprehensive development strategy and supplemented by a wide range of mutually supporting social policy measures; special attention should be given to improving the management of existing health, nutrition and related social services and to the formulation of policies to widen their coverage so as to reach, in particular, rural, remote and underprivileged groups.

26. Each country has its own experience in preventing and treating diseases. Promotion of interchange of such experience will help to reduce morbidity and mortality.

(c) Reproduction, family formation and the status of women

27. This Plan of Action recognizes the variety of national goals with regard to fertility and does not recommend any world family-size norm.

28. This Plan of Action recognizes the necessity of ensuring that all couples are able to achieve their desired number and spacing of children and the necessity of preparing the social and economic conditions to achieve that desire.

29. Consistent with the Proclamation of the International Conference on Human Rights, the Declaration on Social Progress and Development, the relevant targets of the Second United Nations Development Decade and the other international instruments on the subject, it is recommended that all countries:

(a) Respect and ensure, regardless of their overall demographic goals, the right of persons to determine, in a free, informed and responsible manner, the number and spacing of their children;

(b) Encourage appropriate education concerning responsible parenthood and make available to persons who so desire advice and the means of achieving it;

(c) Ensure that family planning, medical and related social services aim not only at the prevention of unwanted pregnancies but also at the elimination of involuntary sterility and subfecundity in order that all couples may be permitted to achieve their desired number of children, and that child adoption may be facilitated;

(d) Seek to ensure the continued possibility of variations in family size when a low fertility level has been established or is a policy objective;

(e) Make use, wherever needed and appropriate, of adequately trained professional and auxiliary health personnel, rural extension, home economics and social workers, and non-governmental channels, to help provide family planning services and to advise users of contraceptives;

(f) Increase their health manpower and health facilities to an effective level, redistribute functions among the different levels of professionals and auxiliaries in order to overcome the shortage of qualified personnel and establish an effective system of supervision in their health and family planning services;

(g) Ensure that information about, and education in, family planning and other matters which affect fertility are based on valid and proven scientific knowledge, and include a full account of any risk that may be involved in the use or non-use of contraceptives.

30. Governments which have family planning programmes are invited to consider integrating and co-ordinating those services with health and other services designed to raise the quality of family life, including family allowances and maternity benefits, and to consider including family planning services in their official health and social insurance systems. As concerns couples themselves, family planning policy should also be directed towards the promo-

tion of the psycho-social harmony and mental and physical well-being of couples.

31. It is recommended that countries wishing to affect fertility levels give priority to implementing development programmes and educational and health strategies which, while contributing to economic growth and higher standards of living, have a decisive impact upon demographic trends, including fertility. International co-operation is called for to give priority to assisting such national efforts in order that these programmes and strategies be carried into effect.

32. While recognizing the diversity of social, cultural, political and economic conditions among countries and regions, it is nevertheless agreed that the following development goals generally have an affect on the socioeconomic context of reproductive decisions that tends to moderate fertility levels:

(a) The reduction of infant and child mortality, particularly by means of improved nutrition, sanitation, maternal and child health care, and maternal education;

(b) The full integration of women into the development process, particularly by means of their greater participation in educational, social, economic and political opportunities, and especially by means of the removal of obstacles to their employment in the non-agricultural sector wherever possible. In this context, national laws and policies, as well as relevant international recommendations, should be reviewed in order to eliminate discrimination in, and remove obstacles to, the education, training, employment and career advancement opportunities for women;

(c) The promotion of social justice, social mobility and social development, particularly by means of a wide participation of the population in development and a more equitable distribution of income, land, social services and amenities;

(d) The promotion of wide educational opportunities for the young of both sexes, and the extension of public forms of pre-school education for the rising generation;

(e) The elimination of child labour and child abuse and the establishment of social security and old-age benefits;

(f) The establishment of an appropriate lower limit for age at marriage.

33. It is recommended that Governments consider making provision, in both their formal and non-formal educational programmes for informing their people of the consequences of existing or alternative fertility behaviour for the well-being of the family, for educational and psychological development of children and for the general welfare of society, so that an informed and responsible attitude to marriage and reproduction will be promoted.

34. Family size may also be affected by incentive and disincentive schemes. However, if such schemes are adopted or modified it is essential that they should not violate human rights.

35. Some social welfare programmes, such as family allowances and maternity benefits, may have a positive effect on fertility and may hence be strengthened when such an effect is desired. However, such programmes should not, in principle, be curtailed if the opposite effect on fertility is desired.

36. The projections in paragraph 16 of future declines in rates of population growth, and those in paragraph 22 concerning increased expectation of life, are consistent with declines in the birth-rate of the developing countries as a whole from the present level of 38 per thousand to 30 per thousand by 1985; in these projections, birth-rates in the developed countries remain in the region of 15 per thousand. To achieve by 1985 these levels of fertility would require substantial national efforts, by those countries concerned, in the field of socio-economic development and population policies, supported, upon request, by adequate international assistance. Such efforts would also be required to achieve the increase in expectation of life.

37. In the light of the principles of this Plan of Action, countries which consider their birth-rates detrimental to their national purposes are invited to consider setting quantitative goals and implementing policies that may lead to the attainment of such goals by 1985. Nothing herein should interfere with the sovereignty of any Government to adopt or not to adopt such quantitative goals.

38. Countries which desire to reduce their birth-rates are invited to give particular consideration to the reduction of fertility at the extremes of female reproductive ages because of the salutary effects this may have on infant and maternal welfare.

39. The family is recognized as the basic unit of society. Governments should assist families as far as possible to enable them to fulfil their role in society. It is therefore recommended that:

(a) The family be protected by appropriate legislation and policy without discrimination as to other members of society;

(b) Family ties be strengthened by giving recognition to the importance of love and mutual respect within the family unit;

(c) National legislation having direct bearing on the welfare of the family and its members, including laws concerning age at marriage, inheritance, property rights, divorce, education, employment and the rights of the child, be periodically reviewed, as feasible, and adapted to the changing social and economic conditions and with regard to the cultural setting;

(d) Marriages be entered into only with the free and full consent of the intending spouses;

(e) Measures be taken to protect the social and legal rights of spouses and children in the case of dissolution or termination of marriage by death or other reason.

40. It is also recommended that:

(a) Governments should equalize the legal and social status of children born in and out of wedlock as well as children adopted;

(b) The legal responsibilities of each parent towards the care and support of all their children should be established.

41. Governments should ensure full participation of women in the educational, social, economic and political life of their countries on an equal basis with men. It is recommended that:

(a) Education for girls as well as boys should be extended and diversified to enable them to contribute more effectively in rural and urban sectors, as well as in the management of food and other household functions;

(b) Women should be actively involved both as individuals and through political and non-governmental organizations, at every stage and every level in the planning and implementation of development programmes, including population policies;

(c) The economic contribution of women in households and farming should be recognized in national economies;

(d) Governments should make a sustained effort to ensure that legislation regarding the status of women complies with the principles spelled out in the Declaration on the Elimination of Discrimination against Women and other United Nations declarations, conventions and international instruments, to reduce the gap between law and practice through effective implementation, and to inform women at all socio-economic levels of their legal rights and responsibilities.

42. Equal status of men and women in the family and in society improves the overall quality of life. This principle of equality should be fully realized in family planning where each spouse should consider the welfare of the other members of the family.

43. Improvement of the status of women in the family and in society can contribute, where desired, to smaller family size, and the opportunity for women to plan births also improves their individual status.

(d) Population distribution and internal migration

44. Urbanization in most countries is characterized by a number of adverse factors: drain from rural areas through migration of individuals who cannot be absorbed by productive employment in urban areas, serious disequilibrium in the growth of urban centres, contamination of the environment, inadequate housing and services and social and psychological stress. In many developing countries, adverse consequences are due in large part to the economic structures resulting from the dependent situation of those countries in the international economic system; the correction of these shortcomings requires as a matter of priority the establishment of equitable economic relations among peoples.

45. Policies aimed at influencing population flows into urban areas should be co-ordinated with policies relating to the absorptive capacity of urban centres as well as policies aimed at eliminating the undesirable consequences of excessive migration. In so far as possible, those policies should be integrated

into plans and programmes dealing with overall social and economic development.

46. In formulating and implementing internal migration policies, Governments are urged to consider the following guidelines, without prejudice to their own socio-economic policies:

(a) Measures should be avoided which infringe the right of freedom of movement and residence within the borders of each State as enunciated in the Universal Declaration of Human Rights and other international instruments;

(b) A major approach to a more rational distribution of the population is that of planned and more equitable regional development, particularly in the advancement of regions which are less favoured or developed by comparison with the rest of the country;

(c) In planning development, and particularly in planning the location of industry and business and the distribution of social services and amenities, Governments should take into account not only short-term economic returns or alternative patterns but also the social and environmental costs and benefits involved as well as equity and social justice in the distribution of the benefits of development among all groups and regions;

(d) Population distribution patterns should not be restricted to a choice between metropolitan and rural life: efforts should be made to establish and strengthen networks of small and medium-size cities to relieve the pressure on the large towns, while still offering an alternative to rural living;

(e) Intensive programmes of economic and social improvement should be carried out in the rural areas through balanced agricultural development which will provide increased income to the agricultural population, permit an effective expansion of social services and include measures to protect the environment and conserve and increase agricultural resources;

(f) Programmes should be promoted to make accessible to scattered populations the basic social services and the support necessary for increased productivity, for example, by consolidating them in rural centres.

47. Internal migration policies should include the provision of information to the rural population concerning economic and social conditions in the urban areas, including information on the availability of employment opportunities.

48. In rural areas and areas accessible to rural populations, new employment opportunities, including industries and public works programmes, should be created, systems of land tenure should be improved and social services and amenities provided. It is not sufficient to consider how to bring the people to existing economic and social activities; it is also important to bring those activities to the people.

49. Considerable experience is now being gained by some countries which have implemented programmes for relieving urban pressures, revitalizing the countryside, inhabiting sparsely populated areas and settling newly reclaimed agricultural land. Countries having such experience are invited to share it

with other countries. It is recommended that international organizations make available upon request co-ordinated technical and financial assistance to facilitate the settlement of people.

50. The problems of urban environment are a consequence not only of the concentration of inhabitants but also of their way of life which can produce harmful effects, such as wasteful and excessive consumption and activities which produce pollution. In order to avoid such effects in those countries experiencing this problem, a development pattern favouring balanced and rational consumption is recommended.

(e) International migration

51. It is recommended that Governments and international organizations generally facilitate voluntary international movement. However, such movements should not be based on racial considerations which are to the detriment of indigenous populations. The significance of international migration varies widely among countries, depending upon their area, population size and growth rate, social and economic structure and environmental conditions.

52. Governments which consider international migration to be important to their countries, either in the short or the long run, are urged to conduct, when appropriate, bilateral or multilateral consultations, taking into account the principles of the Charter of the United Nations, the Universal Declaration of Human Rights, the relevant resolutions of the United Nations system and other international instruments, with a view to harmonizing those of their policies which affect these movements. It is recommended that international organizations make available upon request co-ordinated technical and financial assistance to facilitate the settlement of people in countries of immigration.

53. Problems of refugees and displaced persons arising from forced migration, including their right of return to homes and properties, should also be settled in accordance with the relevant principles of the Charter of the United Nations, the Universal Declaration of Human Rights and other international instruments.

54. Countries that are concerned with the outflow of migrant workers and wish to encourage and assist those remaining workers or returning workers should make particular efforts to create favourable employment opportunities at the national level. More developed countries should co-operate, bilaterally or through regional organizations and the international community, with less developed countries, to achieve these goals through the increased availability of capital, technical assistance, export markets and more favourable terms of trade and choice of production technology.

55. Countries receiving migrant workers should provide proper treatment and adequate social welfare services for them and their families, and should ensure their physical safety and security, in conformity with the provisions

of the relevant conventions and recommendations of the International Labour Organisation and other international instruments.

56. Specifically, in the treatment of migrant workers, Governments should work to prevent discrimination in the labour market and in society through lower salaries or other unequal conditions, to preserve their human rights, to combat prejudice against them and to eliminate obstacles to the reunion of their families. Governments should enable permanent immigrants to preserve their cultural heritage *inter alia* through the use of their mother tongue. Laws to limit illegal immigration should relate not only to the illegal migrants themselves but also to those inducing or facilitating their illegal action and should be promulgated in conformity with international law and basic human rights. Governments should bear in mind humanitarian considerations in the treatment of aliens who remain in a country illegally.

57. Since the outflow of qualified personnel from developing to developed countries seriously hampers the development of the former, there is an urgent need to formulate national and international policies to avoid the "brain drain" and to obviate its adverse effects, including the possibility of devising programmes for large-scale communication of appropriate technological knowledge mainly from developed countries to the extent that it can be properly adjusted and appropriately absorbed.

58. Developing countries suffering from heavy emigration of skilled workers and professionals should undertake extensive educational programmes, manpower planning, and investment in scientific and technical programmes. They should also undertake other programmes and measures to better match skills with employment opportunities and to increase the motivation of such personnel to contribute to the progress of their own country. Measures should be taken to encourage the return of scientists and skilled personnel to specific job vacancies.

59. Foreign investors should employ and train local personnel and use local research facilities to the greatest possible extent in conformity with the policies of the host country. Subject to their consent, the location of research facilities in host countries may aid them to a certain extent in retaining the services of highly skilled and professional research workers. Such investment should, of course, in no circumstances inhibit national economic development. International co-operation is needed to improve programmes to induce skilled personnel to return to, or remain in, their own countries.

60. Where immigration has proved to be of a long-term nature, countries are invited to explore the possibilities of extending national civil rights to immigrants.

61. The flow of skilled workers, technicians and professionals from more developed to less developed countries may be considered a form of international co-operation. Countries in a position to do so should continue and increase this flow with full respect for the sovereignty and equality of recipient countries.

62. Countries affected by significant numbers of migrant workers are urged, if they have not yet done so, to conclude bilateral or multilateral agreements which would regulate migration, protect and assist migrant workers, and protect the interests of the countries concerned. The International Labour Organisation should promote concerted action in the field of protection of migrant workers, and the United Nations Commission on Human Rights should help, as appropriate, to ensure that the fundamental rights of migrants are safeguarded.

(f) Population structure

63. All Governments are urged, when formulating their development policies and programmes, to take fully into account the implications of changing numbers and proportions of youth, working-age groups and the aged, particularly where such changes are rapid. Countries should study their population structures to determine the most desirable balance among age groups.

64. Specifically, developing countries are urged to consider the implications which the combination of the characteristically young age structure and moderate to high fertility has on their development. The increasing number and proportion of young persons in the populations of developing countries requires appropriate development strategies, priority being accorded to their subsistence, health, education, training and incorporation in the labour force through full employment as well as their active participation in political, cultural, social and economic life.

65. Developing countries are invited to consider the possible economic, social and demographic effects of population shifts from agriculture to non-agricultural industries. In addition to fuller utilization of labour and improvements in productivity and the levels of living, promotion of non-agricultural employment should aim at such changes in the socio-economic structure of manpower and population as would affect demographically relevant behaviour of individuals. All countries are invited to consider fully giving appropriate support and assistance to the World Employment Programme and related national employment promotion schemes.

66. Similarly, the other countries are urged to consider the contrary implications of the combination of their aging structure with moderate to low or very low fertility. All countries should carry out, as part of their development programmes, comprehensive, humanitarian and just programmes of social security for the elderly.

67. In undertaking settlement and resettlement schemes and urban planning, Governments are urged to give adequate attention to questions of age and sex balance and, particularly, to the welfare of the family.

2. Socio-economic policies

68. This Plan of Action recognizes that economic and social development is a central factor in the solution of population problems. National efforts of developing countries to accelerate economic growth should be assisted by the entire international community. The implementation of the International Development Strategy for the Second United Nations Development Decade, and the Declaration and the Programme of Action on the New International Economic Order as adopted at the sixth special session of the General Assembly should lead to a reduction in the widening gap in levels of living between developed and developing countries and would be conducive to a reduction in population growth rates particularly in countries where such rates are high.

69. In planning measures to harmonize population trends and socio-economic change, human beings must be regarded not only as consumers but also as producers. The investment by nations in the health and education of their citizens contributes substantially to productivity. Consequently, plans for economic and social development and for international assistance for this purpose should emphasize the health and education sectors. Likewise, patterns of production and technology should be adapted to each country's endowment in human resources. Decisions on the introduction of technologies affording significant savings in employment of manpower should take into account the relative abundance of human resources. To this end it is recommended that efforts should be intensified to determine for each country the technologies and production methods best suited to its working population situation and to study the relationship between population factors and employment.

70. It is imperative that all countries, and within them all social sectors, should adapt themselves to more rational utilization of natural resources, without excess, so that some are not deprived of what others waste. In order to increase the production and distribution of food for the growing world population it is recommended that Governments give high priority to improving methods of food production, the investigation and development of new sources of food and more effective utilization of existing sources. International co-operation is recommended with the aim of ensuring the provision of fertilizers and energy and a timely supply of food-stuffs to all countries.

3. Promotion of knowledge and policies

71. In order to achieve the population objectives of this Plan of Action and to put its policy recommendations adequately into effect, measures need to be undertaken to promote knowledge of the relationships and problems

involved, to assist in the development of population policies and to elicit the co-operation and participation of all concerned in the formulation and implementation of these policies.

(a) Data collection and analysis

72. Statistical data on the population collected by means of censuses, surveys or vital statistics registers, are essential for the planning of investigations and the provision of a basis for the formulation, evaluation and application of population and development policies. Countries that have not yet done so are urged to tabulate and analyse their census and other data and make them available to national policy-making bodies in order to fulfil these objectives.

73. It is up to each country to take a population census in accordance with its own needs and capabilities. However, it is recommended that a population census be taken by each country between 1975 and 1985. It is also recommended that those censuses give particular attention to data relevant to development planning and the formulation of population policies. In order to be of greatest value, it is recommended that the data be tabulated and made available as quickly as possible, together with an evaluation of the quality of the information and degree of coverage of the census.

74. All countries that have not yet done so are encouraged to establish a continuing capability for taking household sample surveys and to establish a long-term plan for regular collection of statistics on various demographic and interrelated socio-economic variables, particularly those relating to the improvement of levels of living, well-being and level of education of individuals, factors which relate closely to problems affecting population. All countries are invited to co-operate with the World Fertility Survey.

75. In line with the objectives of the World Programme for the Improvement of Vital Statistics, countries are encouraged to establish or improve their vital registration system, as a long-term objective, and to enact laws relevant to the improvement of vital registration. Until this improvement is completed, the use of alternative methods is recommended, such as sample surveys, to provide up-to-date information on vital events.

76. Developing countries should be provided with technical co-operation, equipment and financial support to develop or improve the population and related statistical programmes mentioned above. Provision for data-gathering assistance should cover fully the need for evaluating, analysing and presenting the data in a form most appropriate to the needs of users.

77. Governments that have not yet done so are urged to establish appropriate services for the collection, analysis and dissemination of demographic and related statistical information.

(b) Research

78. This Plan of Action gives high priority to research activities in population problems (including unemployment, starvation and poverty) and to related fields, particularly to research activities that are important for the formulation, evaluation and implementation of the population policies consistent with full respect for human rights and fundamental freedoms as recognized in international instruments of the United Nations. Although research designed to fill gaps in knowledge is very urgent and important, high priority should be given to research oriented to the specific problems of countries and regions, including methodological studies. Such research is best carried out in the countries and regions themselves and by competent persons especially acquainted with national and regional conditions. The following areas are considered to require research in order to fill existing gaps in knowledge:

(a) The social, cultural and economic determinants of population variables in different developmental and political situations, particularly at the family and micro levels;

(b) The demographic and social processes occurring within the family cycle through time and, particularly, in relation to alternative modes of development;

(c) The development of effective means for the improvement of health, and especially for the reduction of maternal, foetal, infant and early childhood mortality;

(d) The study of experiences of countries which have major programmes of internal migration with a view to developing guidelines that are helpful to policy makers of those countries and of countries that are interested in undertaking similar programmes;

(e) Projections of demographic and related variables including the development of empirical and hypothetical models for simulating possible future trends;

(f) The formulation, implementation and evaluation of population policies including: methods for integrating population inputs and goals in development plans and programmes; means for understanding and improving the motivations of people to participate in the formulation and implementation of population programmes; study of education and communication aspects of population policy; analysis of population policies in their relationship to other socio-economic development policies, laws and institutions, including the possible influences of the economic system on the social, cultural and economic aspects of population policies; translation into action programmes of policies dealing with the socio-economic determinants of fertility, mortality, internal migration and distribution, and international migration;

(g) The collection, analysis and dissemination of information concerning human rights in relation to population matters and the preparation of studies designed to clarify, systematize and more effectively implement those human rights;

(h) The review and analysis of national and international laws which bear directly or indirectly on population factors;

(i) The assessment and improvement of existing and new methods of fertility regulation by means of research, including basic biological and applied research; the evaluation of the impact, both in short-term and long-term effects, of different methods of fertility regulation on ethical and cultural values and on mental and physical health; and the assessment and study of policies for creating social and economic conditions so that couples can freely decide on the size of their families;

(j) The evaluation of the impact of different methods of family planning on the health conditions of women and members of their families;

(k) The interrelationships among patterns of family formation, nutrition and health, reproductive biology, and the incidence, causes and treatment of sterility;

(l) Methods of improving the management, delivery and utilization of all social services associated with population, including family welfare and, when appropriate, family planning;

(m) Methods for the development of systems of social, demographic and related economic statistics in which various sets of data are interlinked, with a view to improving insight into the interrelationships of variables in these fields;

(n) The interrelations of population trends and conditions and other social and economic variables, in particular the availability of human resources, food and natural resources, the quality of the environment, the need for health, education, employment, welfare, housing and other social services and amenities, promotion of human rights, the enhancement of the status of women, the need for social security, political stability, discrimination and political freedom;

(o) The impact of a shift from one family size pattern to another on biological and demographic characteristics of the population;

(p) The changing structure, functions and dynamics of the family as an institution, including the changing roles of men and women, attitudes towards and opportunities for women's education and employment; the implications of current and future population trends for the status of women; biomedical research on male and female fertility, and the economic, social and demographic benefits to be derived from the integration of women in the development process;

(q) Development of social indicators, reflecting the quality of life as well as the interrelations between socio-economic and demographic phenomena, should be encouraged. Emphasis should also be given to the development of socio-economic and demographic models.

79. National research requirements and needs must be determined by Governments and national institutions. However, high priority should be given, wherever possible, to research that has wide relevance and international applicability.

80. National and regional research institutions dealing with population and related questions should be assisted and expanded as appropriate. Special efforts should be made to co-ordinate the research of those institutions by facilitating the exchange of their research findings and the exchange of information on their planned and ongoing research projects.

(c) Management, training, education and information

81. There is a particular need for the development of management in all fields related to population, with national and international attention and appropriate support given to programmes dealing with its promotion.

82. A dual approach to training is recommended: an international programme for training in population matters concomitant with national and regional training programmes adapted and made particularly relevant to conditions in the countries and regions of the trainees. While recognizing the complementarity of these two approaches, national and regional training should be given the higher priority.

83. Training in population dynamics and policies, whether national, regional or international, should, in so far as possible, be interdisciplinary in nature. The training of population specialists should always be accompanied by relevant career development for the trainees in their fields of specialization. Training should deal not only with population variables but also with interrelationships of these variables with economic, social and political variables.

84. Training in the various aspects of population activities, including the management of population programmes should not be restricted to the higher levels of specialization but should also be extended to personnel at other levels, and, where needed, to medical, paramedical and traditional health personnel, and population programme administrators. Such training should impart an adequate knowledge of human rights in accordance with international standards and an awareness of the human rights aspect of population problems.

85. Training in population matters should be extended to labour, community and other social leaders, and to senior government officials, with a view to enabling them better to identify the population problems of their countries and communities and to help in the formulation of policies relating to them.

86. Owing to the role of education in the progress of individuals and society and the impact of education on demographic behaviour, all countries are urged to further develop their formal and informal educational

programmes; efforts should be made to eradicate illiteracy, to promote education among the youth and abolish factors discriminating against women.

87. Educational institutions in all countries should be encouraged to expand their curricula to include a study of population dynamics and policies, including, where appropriate, family life, responsible parenthood and the relation of population dynamics to socio-economic development and to international relations. Governments are urged to co-operate in developing a worldwide system of international, regional and national institutions to meet the need for trained manpower. Assistance to the less developed countries should include, as appropriate, the improvement of the educational infrastructure such as library facilities and computer services.

88. Governments are invited to use all available means for disseminating population information.

89. Governments are invited to consider the distribution of population information to enlighten both rural and urban populations, through the assistance of governmental agencies.

90. Voluntary organizations should be encouraged, within the framework of national laws, policies and regulations, to play an important role in disseminating population information and ensuring wider participation in population programmes, and to share experiences regarding the implementation of population measures and programmes.

91. International organizations, both governmental and non-governmental, should strengthen their efforts to distribute information on population and related matters, particularly through periodic publications on the world population situation, prospects and policies, the utilization of audio-visual and other aids to communication, the publication of non-technical digests and reports, and the production and wide distribution of newsletters on population activities. Consideration should also be given to strengthening the publication of international professional journals and reviews in the field of population.

92. In order to achieve the widest possible dissemination of research results, translation activities should be encouraged at both the national and international levels. In this respect, the revision of the *Multilingual Demographic Dictionary* and its publication in additional languages are strongly recommended.

93. The information and experience resulting from the World Population Conference and the World Population Year relating to the scientific study of population and the elaboration of population policies should be synthesized and disseminated by the United Nations.

(d) Development and evaluation of population policies

94. Where population policies or programmes have been adopted, systematic and periodic evaluations of their effectiveness should be made with a view to their improvement.

95. Population measures and programmes should be integrated into comprehensive social and economic plans and programmes and this integration should be reflected in the goals, instrumentalities and organizations for planning within the countries. In general, it is suggested that a unit dealing with population aspects be created and placed at a high level of the national administrative structure and that such a unit be staffed with qualified persons from the relevant disciplines.

D. Recommendations for Implementation

1. Role of national Governments

96. The success of this Plan of Action will largely depend on the actions undertaken by national Governments. To take action, Governments are urged to utilize fully the support of intergovernmental and non-governmental organizations.

97. This Plan of Action recognizes the responsibility of each Government to decide on its own policies and devise its own programmes of action for dealing with the problems of population and economic and social progress. Recommendations, in so far as they relate to national Governments, are made with due regard to the need for variety and flexibility in the hope that they may be responsive to major needs in the population field as perceived and interpreted by national Governments. However, national policies should be formulated and implemented without violating, and with due promotion of, universally accepted standards of human rights.

98. An important role of Governments with regard to this Plan of Action is to determine and assess the population problems and needs of their countries in the light of their political, social, cultural, religious and economic conditions; such an undertaking should be carried out systematically and periodically so as to promote informed, rational and dynamic decision-making in matters of population and development.

99. The effect of national action or inaction in the fields of population may, in certain circumstances, extend beyond national boundaries; such international implications are particularly evident with regard to aspects of morbidity, population concentration and international migration, but may also apply to other aspects of population concern.

2. *Role of international co-operation*

100. International co-operation, based on the peaceful coexistence of States having different social systems, should play a supportive role in achieving the goals of the Plan of Action. This supportive role could take the form of direct assistance, technical or financial, in response to national and regional requests and be additional to economic development assistance, or the form of other activities, such as monitoring progress, undertaking comparative research in the area of population, resources and consumption, and furthering the exchange among countries of information and policy experiences in the field of population and consumption. Assistance should be provided on the basis of respect for sovereignty of the recipient country and its national policy.

101. The General Assembly of the United Nations, the Economic and Social Council, the Governing Council of the United Nations Development Programme/United Nations Fund for Population Activities and other competent legislative and policy-making bodies of the specialized agencies and the various intergovernmental organizations are urged to give careful consideration to this Plan of Action and to ensure an appropriate response to it.

102. Countries sharing similar population conditions and problems are invited to consider jointly this Plan of Action, exchange experience in relevant fields and elaborate those aspects of the Plan that are of particular relevance to them. The United Nations regional economic commissions and other regional bodies of the United Nations system should play an important role towards this end.

103. There is a special need for training in the field of population. The United Nations system, Governments and, as appropriate, non-governmental organizations are urged to give recognition to that need and priority to the measures necessary to meet it, including information, education and services for family planning.

104. Developed countries, and other countries able to assist, are urged to increase their assistance to developing countries in accordance with the goals of the Second United Nations Development Decade and, together with international organizations, make that assistance available in accordance with the national priorities of receiving countries. In this respect, it is recognized, in view of the magnitude of the problems and the consequent national requirements for funds, that considerable expansion of international assistance in the population field is required for the proper implementation of this Plan of Action.

105. It is suggested that the expanding, but still insufficient, international assistance in population and development matters requires increased co-operation; the United Nations Fund for Population Activities is urged, in

co-operation with all organizations responsible for international population assistance, to produce a guide for international assistance in population matters which would be made available to recipient countries and institutions and be revised periodically.

106. International non-governmental organizations are urged to respond to the goals and policies of this Plan of Action by co-ordinating their activities with those of other non-governmental organizations, and with those of relevant bilateral and multilateral organizations, by expanding their support for national institutions and organizations dealing with population questions, and by co-operating in the promotion of widespread knowledge of the goals and policies of the Plan of Action, and, when requested, by supporting national and private institutions and organizations dealing with population questions.

3. Monitoring, review and appraisal

107. It is recommended that monitoring of population trends and policies discussed in this Plan of Action should be undertaken continuously as a specialized activity of the United Nations and reviewed biennially by the appropriate bodies of the United Nations system, beginning in 1977. Because of the shortness of the intervals, such monitoring would necessarily have to be selective with regard to its informational content and should focus mainly on new and emerging population trends and policies.

108. A comprehensive and thorough review and appraisal of progress made towards achieving the goals and recommendations of this Plan of Action should be undertaken every five years by the United Nations system. For this purpose the Secretary-General is invited to make appropriate arrangements taking account of the existing structure and resources of the United Nations system, and in co-operation with Governments. It is suggested that the first such review be made in 1979 and be repeated each five years thereafter. The findings of such systematic evaluations should be considered by the Economic and Social Council with the object of making, whenever necessary, appropriate modifications of the goals and recommendations of this Plan.

109. It is urged that both the monitoring and the review and appraisal activities of this Plan of Action be closely co-ordinated with those of the International Development Strategy for the Second United Nations Development Decade and any new international development strategy that might be formulated.

REPORTS ON THE
STATE OF WORLD POPULATION
1980-1984

Rafael M. Salas, Executive Director
United Nations Fund for Population Activities

Editors' note: The Executive Director of UNFPA issued his first *State of World Population Report* in June 1978. The *Reports* for 1978 and 1979 have been reprinted in his volume *International Population Assistance: The First Decade* (1979). The *Reports* for 1980, 1981, 1982, 1983 and 1984 are reprinted here in their entirety.

The State of
World Population 1980

INTRODUCTION

In the decade of the 1980s, the decline in world fertility will continue notice-
ably. The United Nations has estimated that the annual average rate of growth
of world population would decline from about 2 per cent in the mid-1960s
to about 1.8 per cent in the early 1980s and to about 1.6 per cent at the end
of the century.[1] However, this does not in any way reduce the magnitude
of the "population problem" since the annual growth rate would continue
to exceed 2 per cent for the less developed countries till the end of this decade.[2] In fact, during the remaining two decades of this century, close to
2 billion would be added to the world population and this would be almost
equal to what was added between 1950 and 1980. Over 90 per cent of this
increase will occur in the less developed countries and their population alone
by the year 2000 would be nearly twice the total population the world had
in 1950. By the year 2000, nearly 80 per cent of the world population would
be living in the less developed countries. Given these facts, there is no cause
for complacency even though we have entered a phase of declining world
fertility.

The full implications of population growth can be understood only if we
take into account the regional dimensions of the distribution of world population. First, most of the increase in world population between now and the
year 2000 would take place again in the areas which have already experienced
the largest increases in population between 1950 and 1980. Second, the countries and regions where such growth would take place are the poorest areas
of the world.

Between now and the year 2000, it is likely that there will be a further
increase in the numbers of the poor and a worsening of the depth of depriva-

tion unless urgent measures are taken to alter the living conditions in these areas. Third, for the very same reason, the international disparity in incomes would widen farther.

These configurations of population growth have already generated a number of differing population trends of far-reaching consequences which will be accentuated further during the next two decades. The growth of population in the poorest areas of the world is acting as a powerful "push" factor forcing an increase in the rates of migration of population. Since, in most of these less developed areas, poverty and lack of employment opportunities are most persistent in the rural areas, migrants tend to move towards urban areas. In many developing countries the pattern of urbanization is highly skewed, thus giving rise to high growth rates in certain urban centres. This will result in the emergence of large metropolitan centres which will be hard pressed to deal with this growth and will increasingly become centres of concentrated urban poverty. Finally, world resources, including technology and human resources, are not distributed in the same manner as population, and this lack of matching of resources with population will continue to affect the capability of less developed countries to progress economically. This report is confined largely to a discussion of these issues.

Regional distribution of population

The most striking feature of population growth in the next two decades is that the largest increases in population will occur in the poorest countries and regions of the world. Countries which feel the greatest need to balance resources and population growth are the least able to achieve this end.

An examination of the shares of world population in different regions among the less developed countries shows that these have been rising for quite some time and will continue to do so during the next two decades. The only exception is the East Asian region, where, due to the projected decline in the birth rate for China, the share would decline from about 28 per cent in 1980 to about 23 per cent by the year 2000.[3] The share of the rest of Asia is projected to rise from 32 per cent to 36 per cent, Africa from 11 per cent to 13 per cent, and Latin America from 8 per cent to 10 per cent during the same period.[4]

These changes in the shares of total world population among the less developed countries still do not fully indicate the nature of regionalization of population problems. Since resources and efforts have to be matched with the increase in numbers of population, it is necessary to study these numbers and how they will be distributed. It is estimated that between 1950 and 2000, while 600 million would be added to the combined total population of Africa and Latin America, the addition to the population of Asia will exceed 100 million. However, most of this increase in Asia would be confined to South Asia, amounting there to over 780 million.

Mortality

The growth in numbers not only indicates the disparate movements of fertility and mortality rates but also mirrors the degree of success of programmes aimed at modifying the effects of these trends in fertility and mortality rates. In most cases greater declines are indicated for mortality rates than for fertility rates. This is a result of it being easier to bring about a reduction in the mortality rate than to bring about a similar reduction in the birth rate since the former appears to respond more quickly to public policy implementation. At the same time, a number of studies on population change have indicated that a decline in mortality rates is a necessary pre-condition for bringing about rapid declines in population growth rate. However, its proximate effect is a rise in population growth rate. Herein lies a paradox of population trends. The lower the death rate, the greater the likelihood of the population growth rate falling. It appears inevitable that before world population could settle down to an era of stable population, the population of less developed countries would have to pass through various phases of this process.

Africa

An examination of the rates of population growth, fertility and mortality shows that various countries and regions are indeed at different stages of this process of demographic transition. By far the highest rates seem to persist in the different sub-regions of the African continent. It is estimated that the average annual growth rate of population would vary between 3.2 per cent for Western Africa and 2.6 per cent for Middle Africa during the period 1980-1985.[5] Most of the countries in the African continent appear to be in the very early phase of demographic transition in which, due to a fall in death rates, their population growth rates are still rising from the previous levels. While fertility rates continue to be high in most of these countries, this decline in mortality rates is attributed to medical intervention and the spread of health care facilities. This is clearly illustrated in the case of Kenya. Kenya has a birth rate close to 50 per 1000 and a death rate of 12 per 1000, resulting in a growth rate of 3.8 per cent per annum.[6] The birth rates of most of the African countries, excluding Egypt, Tunisia and a few islands, are in the mid-40's or higher, and, depending on the rates of mortality decline, most of the countries are experiencing a phase of increasing population growth rates during this decade.

Latin America

Latin America depicts great variations in fertility. While some countries are in the early phase of demographic transition, there are others, especially in the Caribbean and Temperate South America, whose growth rates are tending towards the replacement level of fertility. However, there is a uniform factor which clearly distinguishes the Latin American situation from that of Africa. Mortality rates are uniformly low in all countries of Latin America, except Bolivia, Haiti, Honduras, Nicaragua and Peru. There is hardly any country with a fertility level comparable to rates prevailing in African countries. But due to the time-lag in fertility decline, the very low rate of mortality in some of the Latin American countries has resulted in an initial increase in population growth rate. However, only the Middle American region seems to have a rate of population growth comparable to regions in Africa and this is largely due to the high growth rate of Mexico. The population of Mexico may nearly double between now and the year 2000 if United Nations projections hold true.

Asia

Nearly 60 per cent of the increase in total world population between now and the year 2000 would be in Asia, and therefore what happens in Asia will largely determine the over-all trends in world population. The aggregate projections for Asia conceal wide sub-regional variations and include figures for East Asia where fertility levels have declined significantly (the only exception being Mongolia). Much of this decline can be attributed to the projected fall in the birth rate of China. It is also a fact that mortality rates are uniformly low in all countries of this sub-region. The rest of Asia can be divided broadly into three groups. There is the group consisting of Singapore, Sri Lanka, and possibly Malaysia where a distinct demographic transition is already under way. India, due to her size, should be treated separately. Fertility and mortality rates in India lie somewhere between those of East Asia and the rest of Asia. In the remaining Asian countries birth rates range from the mid-30s to the upper-40s and death rates lie between 15 and 20 per 1000 population. Almost all Muslim nations in this region have fertility rates around 45 per 1000: Countries such as Afghanistan, Bangladesh and Pakistan belong to the poorest among Asian nations and also have very high mortality rates.

POPULATION MIGRATION

An important aspect of population growth in the less developed countries has been the inability of employment to keep pace with population growth. This has turned out to be one of the most intractable problems of development in these countries in the past, leading to considerable internal migration of populations, or between countries or regions. Within the developing countries themselves, labour migration and the movement of population have been from rural areas to mainly urban areas. This has led to unprecedented growth in urbanization in many less developed countries.

Apart from internal migration, there has been an increase in international migration of skilled and unskilled labour from the less developed countries. Such migration has become, for some countries, a major element in their population trends. The nature and extent of migration between countries is generally determined by income differentials, but the number of immigrants is often restricted by the recipient countries. In spite of such restrictions, it seems clear from an examination of available data on international migration that it does reflect a salient population trend in various regions of the world.

International migration

The recent migrations are of a modest scale compared to the mass migrations of population that took place from Europe to the New World in the latter part of the 19th century and the early part of the 20th century. However, they represent a resumption of earlier patterns of international migration. It is estimated that at least 52 million people migrated from Europe to the United States, Canada, Latin America and Oceania between 1840 and 1930, and this amounted to 20 per cent of the population of Europe at the beginning of this period.[7] There has also been a significant change in this pattern of migration from Europe and since 1960 there is a positive net migration to Western Europe.

The largest inflows of migrants within Western Europe have been to the Federal Republic of Germany and to France. The average annual net migration per 1000 population in the Federal Republic of Germany was +3.5 in the period 1960-1970 and +5.9 during 1970-1974.[8] The natural rate of increase of population in Western Europe has become close to zero and in a few countries it is negative. If these trends continue, in a number of countries of Western Europe, migration from the less developed countries may be the only source of population growth.

A United Nations estimate for mid-1974 gives 9.5 million immigrants from the less developed countries as residing in the industrialized countries of Northern and Western Europe, North America and Oceania, compared to 3.2 million in 1960.[9] These estimates are considered to be on the low side since they exclude illegal immigrants who escape inclusion in official statistics. Nearly 60 per cent of the total immigrants from the less developed countries in 1974 are in North America and Oceania. It is also estimated that for the period 1970-1974, 70 per cent of the total immigrants to the United States came from less developed countries.[10] Of these, 40 per cent were from Latin America and 40 per cent from Asia (1974 figure).

The migration from Asia reflects both the pressure of population and the lack of economic opportunities. Latin America, however, had been a region of net immigration from Europe for a considerable length of time. A reversal of this trend has taken place since 1960 and despite lower population densities in the region, Latin American migration is spurred by the uneven distribution of both resources and economic benefits as well as by the extent of differential advantage one gains by migrating to the United States (almost the whole of Latin American out-migration is to North America).

Though there has been an increase in the number of Asian immigrants to industrialized countries, in most countries of Asia emigration has not reached any significant level as a proportion of their populations. Since 1974, there has been considerable flow of labour to the oil exporting countries of the Gulf region and the Middle East. While this emigration has benefited a number of countries, especially in South Asia, through the repatriation of valuable foreign exchange, the numbers are small compared to their populations and it is also of a temporary nature. Migrants of this kind raise a number of issues which need international agreements and solutions. It is essential to protect the human rights of such immigrants, and mechanisms and safeguards need to be devised for this purpose. When such immigrants return home problems of resettlement arise. Some plans already exist to deal with such problems, for example, the schemes for resettlement of labourers who have returned as a consequence of the Sri Lanka-India agreement on the repatriation of plantation labour. With the increase in temporary migration of labour, such problems may assume greater importance in the future.

Refugees

A second type of migration which is of great international concern is the problem of refugees and their rights and rehabilitation. Large-scale forced migration of population for political reasons not only affects the development and economic structure of the country where it happens, but also leads to considerable strain on the resources of neighbouring countries to which such movements take place. Unlike labour migration, such refugee movements include women and children. In recent years the number of refugees in Asia has grown enormously and now many Asian countries are finding themselves unable to cope with such a volume of refugees. The same is true of the refugee problem in other parts of the world, particularly in Africa, and refugees are rapidly becoming an important international population issue.

Internal migration

Cities have always attracted people. They have been seats of government, the headquarters of trading and financial houses, the centres of culture and the sites of town houses for the aristocracy and landed gentry from the countryside. Then, with the beginning of the industrial revolution cities became the hub of economic activity and of transportation networks, and also the location of the means of livelihood for a growing industrial proletariat. In those days, cities were designed to solve problems, to provide various types of external services to the growing industrial sector and to promote the growth of consumption of the products of industry. Now many of these have become problems due to rapid and unplanned growth.

Urbanization in the second half of the 20th century represents an antithesis of the earlier phase of the growth of cities. Latest United Nations estimates suggest that world urban population has doubled since 1950 and will double again before the end of the century. By then about three-fourths of the population in the more developed countries will be living in urban areas. While only about one-third of the population of less developed countries lives today in urban areas, the proportion is likely to increase to nearly one-half by the year 2000. These changes would be brought about by a higher rate of urbanization in the less developed countries than in the more developed countries.

The expected growth in urbanization in the less developed countries largely reflects population growth between now and the year 2000. It is the result not only of the natural increase in urban population but also of massive migrations of population to these areas in search of employment. It is estimated that the largest cities will grow more rapidly than the smaller cities and some of these are likely to reach proportions which are totally unfamiliar to town planners. In 1950, only four of the fifteen largest cities were in the less developed countries, but this number rose to seven by 1975. It is projected that twelve of the fifteen largest cities would be in the less developed countries by the year 2000.[11]

There were only six cities with populations of five million and over in 1950 and their combined population was only 47 million. This has already risen to 26 cities in 1980 with a combined population of 252 million. Projections indicate that this number will rise to approximately 60 with an estimated population of nearly 650 million by the year 2000.[12]

The seriousness of these trends in metropolitan growth can be understood only if again, we analyze these regionally. In 1980, of the 26 cities of five million or more, 16 were in the less developed countries with a total population of 141 million, compared to only one city in 1950. By the year 2000, of the 60 cities, 45 will be in the less developed countries. In 1980, there is only one city in Africa with a population exceeding five million, but this number is expected to rise to five by 2000. The largest number of cities in this category are in Asia, and their numbers will rise from ten in 1980 to 29 in the year 2000, and their combined population will increase from 80 million to nearly 300 million. These figures clearly indicate how closely the trends in urbanization and metropolitization follow the general trends in population growth and the regional distribution of world population. Due to migration from rural areas to urban centres, the rates of urbanization are much higher than the rates of natural increase in population.

Though the entire world is moving towards bigger and more numerous urban agglomerations, the urbanization trends vary between more and less developed countries. The urban future has become a subject of great concern in both groups of countries, though for different reasons. While the less developed countries are facing an explosive growth in the cities a reverse trend has begun in the last two decades in some of the metropolitan areas of the more developed countries, where due to their inability to cope with the problems of urban growth, there has been an escalation of economic costs. These factors have resulted in either a stagnation in their population or a reduction due to movement of population from city to suburbs and further afield. The reverse flow of population from New York City to the Sun Belt is an example of this trend.

The growth of urbanization in the less developed countries reflects as much the lack of rural development as the growth of industry and employment opportunities in the urban agglomerations. Thus, the problems of the urban future and the growth of the metropolitan areas in the less developed countries are equally a problem of "total" development of the country just like any other population or socio-economic problem. The solution to the urban problem lies as much in the rural areas as in the cities themselves. Only a contented countryside can provide a lasting solution to the ills afflicting the urban world.

Considering the manifold dimensions involved in the urban problem and with a view to exploring the possibilities of integrating these issues within a framework of population and development, the UNFPA is sponsoring an International Conference on the Urban Future in Rome in September this year, where mayors from 60 cities and national planners from the same countries will participate.

POPULATION-RESOURCE BALANCE

The next two decades of this century will be a hard testing-time for the world community's ability to cope with the demands for food, education, health care and employment caused by this rapid increase in numbers. While the so-called "population bomb" may have been defused, the aspiration bomb has not. Every one of the 125 million babies born each year is a bundle of aspirations and the drive to fulfill these will become the most dynamic and unpredictable force in world affairs in the years ahead. And the explosion of aspirations in the last two decades and the next two is likely to become a tremendous problem in its impact on limited resources, fragile ecosystems, on the struggle against mass poverty and on the world's political, economic and social fabric.

In the developing world, today's young people know more about the world and expect more from it than their parents did. They are increasingly educated, increasingly unemployed, and increasingly concentrated in cities.

In the developed world, where each person born will consume 20 to 40 times more in his or her lifetime than a person born in a developing country, the drive to fulfill continuously rising material aspirations will have a major impact on the environment, on the possibilities for meeting the most basic needs for the poor majority in the developing world and on the struggle for more just economic relationships within and between nations. In this context it is worth remembering that population growth is a problem only when resources cannot meet the needs of people, and that by definition, it is as much a problem of regulating the use of resources as it is of regulating birth.

Just as the decade of the 1970s saw the emergence of a deeper understanding of the interrelationship between population and development issues, we are also now witnessing the delineation of a similar relationship between population and the world's resources. For instance, the Report of the Independent Commission on International Development Issues under the Chairmanship of Willy Brandt states:[13]

"A question we cannot overlook is whether the resources and the ecological system of the earth will suffice to meet the needs of a greatly increased world population at the economic standard that is hoped for. So far the bulk of the depletion of nonrenewable resources and the pressure on the oceans and the atmosphere have been caused by the spectacular industrial growth of the developed countries where only one-fifth of the world's population live. But population growth in some parts of the Third World is already a source of alarming ecological changes, and its industrialization is bound to lead to greater pressure on resources and environment."

Food needs

The United Nations Food and Agriculture Organization (FAO)[14] has estimated that the number of malnourished people in the less developed countries (excluding China and other centrally planned economies of Asia) rose from about 400 million in 1969-1971 to 450 million in 1972-1974. They constituted about a quarter of the population of these countries. The prospects for dramatic increases in food output appear dim unless significant technological breakthroughs in high yielding varieties of seeds for a number of crops materialize or a considerable increase in inputs enables a rise in agricultural productivity. The estimated annual rate of increase in food production in the 1970s in less developed countries has been less than three per cent. Unless a substantial increase in the rate takes place, the number of un-dernourished is unlikely to diminish. Even under the optimistic assumption that the proportion of undernourished is halved by the year 2000, it is ap-parent that their absolute number may still remain around 450 million in the less developed countries.

Estimates indicate that in the decade of the 1970s the rate of growth of agricultural production in Africa has been less than half that achieved in other developing regions. In fact, per capita food output in Africa declined at an annual rate of 1.3 per cent during the period 1970-1977. The situation is no less true in the case of the most seriously affected countries in the Asian region. In their case also, per capita food production has declined. Latin America is the only region where food output has risen slightly above the rate of growth of population, but it is feared that this has been achieved at considerable cost. The FAO Report on the State of Food and Agriculture for 1978 points out with reference to Latin America that "the expansion of the modern sector appears to have been accomplished by a breakdown of the traditional sector, so that rural socio-economic disequilibria have been accentuated".[15]

The implications of these trends are clear. In Africa, the self-sufficiency ratio for food declined from 98 per cent in 1962-1964 to 90 per cent in 1972-1974.[16] During the same period, the total food imports into the region trebled. In South and South East Asia, where rice is the staple food, the aver-age increase in rice production was only 2.2 per cent per annum, which was well below the population growth rate of 2.5 per cent per annum.[17]

The growth of population and its regional distribution between 1950 and 1975 is already bringing about a major transformation in the world food economy. While world grain output nearly doubled between 1950 and 1975, per capita grain production increased only one-third in the same period. Taken along with the fact that in the most densely populated countries belonging to the less developed group, there has hardly been any increase in per capita output, one can infer where such increases have taken place. Some develop-ing countries which were net exporters of grain in the past have now become net importers of grain. The imbalances in the distribution of food and popu-lation are likely to be with us for some time and it is imperative that mechan-isms are developed for the transfer of grain from surplus to deficit regions of the world. While there is a global responsibility to eliminate starvation irrespective of whether it leads to socio-economic development or changes in population parameters, there is considerable scope to increase food out-put in the less developed countries if appropriate policy measures are im-plemented. Such measures should include redistribution of land, provision of credit, expansion of irrigation and support of agricultural prices.

Human resources

The problem of resources for the less developed countries is not only a problem of availability of natural resources but also a problem of inadequate development of human resources. The less developed countries often lack technical, administrative and managerial resources. The bulk of their labour force constitutes unskilled labour and their productivity is also affected by factors such as malnutrition, poor health, inadequate health care and lack of educational facilities. Some of these factors have affected most the conditions of children and women.

The significance of health care for the welfare of the population and for the success of population programmes is obvious. Life expectancy figures provide a good summary measure of the status of the health of a population. Life expectancy in 1975-1980 was only 54 years for the less developed countries compared to 68 years for the more developed countries.[18] Life expectancy figures reflect mortality rates and an increase in life expectancy is, therefore, closely linked to the expansion of health care facilities and to improvement in nutritional levels. Among the less developed countries themselves there are pockets of high mortality and these areas will need special programmes. The highest mortality rates among the less developed countries are to be found in Africa. The whole region of Africa, with the exception of some countries in the extreme North and South of the continent, suffers from high mortality rates. Bangladesh, Bhutan, Nepal and Pakistan are a group of high mortality countries in the Asian region. On the whole, countries in Latin America have been able to bring down mortality rates and do not appear to require as much assistance in this area.

The picture that emerges is not very different when we examine the prospects for the development of education and the projected figures of literacy rates. Estimates of literacy provided by UNESCO[19] show that in most of Africa over 50 per cent of population over age 15 would be illiterate in 1980. The same is true for South Asia and the Middle East. There are also a few countries in Africa, South Asia and the Middle East where the proportion of illiterates in the total population is over 90 per cent. Unless a significant effort is made in these countries to improve literacy levels, the regional disparities in levels of education will continue to persist.

All the above factors affect most severely the conditions and opportunities available to children and to women. High infant mortality rates and lack of educational opportunities not only affect the present living conditions but also affect the future development of human resources. We have just completed the International Year of the Child and a lasting service to children would be to make an all-out effort to reduce infant mortality and to provide universal literacy. This year marks the half-way point of the International Decade for Women. The brunt of poverty in the home is invariably borne by women and they are also the ones who suffer the consequences of high fertility rates. If women are excluded from taking part in the development process, this detracts from the human resources required for development and is itself a denial of basic human rights. Improvement in the status of women is closely related to over-all development in these countries.

When all these regional variations are taken into account, it is quite apparent that the employment problem is not only one of creating additional jobs for over 600 million people but also of creating jobs that will take into account the nature and characteristics of the labour force. Since there are regional concentrations of population, employment generation would also have to be concentrated. At the same time, a substantial increase in the unskilled labour force in countries with very low incomes would only complicate this process because the potential for employment generation could be the lowest in these countries. Low incomes, high unemployment and poverty are also bound to affect not only the implementation of population programmes but even their effectiveness during their implementation.

LOOKING AHEAD

There is a great deal of misunderstanding of the nature and consequences of the current demographic transition in the less developed countries. A demographic transition took place in Western European countries in the 19th century, when their base populations were much smaller so that even when their growth rates rose the absolute numbers added to their populations were not large. This period also coincided with colonial expansionism on the one hand and industrialization of their domestic economies on the other. Colonies assured them that the resouces — food supply and other natural resources — necessary for sustaining high levels of population growth and industrialization were available at comparably low economic costs. At the same time, the increases in the supply of labour resulting from the higher growth rate of population could be absorbed by the expanding industrial sector. Besides, opportunities for migration to the United States, South America and Australia were also open to the populations of Europe.

These favourable conditions which were then available to Europe were not then and are not now available to the less developed countries. To begin with, some of the large countries, such as India and China, belonging to the less developed countries always contained within themselves a major share of the world population. With an increase in the growth of population, their share of world population has risen further. The process of mortality decline which began in the 19th century in Western Europe did not spread to the currently less developed countries at that time. On the other hand, advances made in medical technology in the 20th century have made effective control of communicable diseases possible. This has led to larger declines in mortality rates within a shorter time-span in the less developed countries than it took in Western Europe in the 19th century. While paucity of resources is limiting the capacity of these countries to develop, restrictions on immigration are also limiting the scope for migration of population. All these factors need to be borne in mind when analyzing the current trends and devising population programmes and policies.

In my last report I indicated the need for an ever-widening array of "New Integrations" in the 1980s between demographic policies and development policy. The Colombo Conference of Parliamentarians on Population and Development held in September 1979 called for such an integration and for the strengthening of population programmes. The Brandt Commission Report, too, has emphasized the need for such integration. We are about to enter the Third Development Decade—an opportunity to begin such an integration by incorporating population programmes into development strategies.

But, such "integrations" require a pledge by all concerned that the programmes, which have had considerable success and need to be enlarged and extended, will not suffer from lack of resources. Such resources are needed on a wide front and population programmes form only one element of such a scheme. The Colombo Conference has called for a total volume of international population assistance of $1 billion by 1984.

UNFPA is aware of the wide disparities that exist among the less developed countries and has considered a number of countries for assistance on a priority basis. It is clear from the studies on various interrelationships between population and socio-economic variables that the success of population programmes is closely linked to the implementation of various other socio-economic programmes such as health care, education, adult literacy and maternal care. What we do now about population and development will determine the living conditions and opportunities for unborn generations of the next century.

REFERENCES

1. United Nations, *World Population Trends and Prospects by Country, 1950-2000: Summary Report of the 1978 Assessment*, (ST/ESA/Series R/33), New York, 1979.
2. *Ibid.*
3. *Ibid.*
4. *Ibid.*
5. *Ibid.*
6. *Ibid.*
7. *Trends and Characteristics of International Migration Since 1950* (United Nations publication, Sales No. 78.XIII.5), New York, 1979.

8. *Ibid.*

9. *Ibid.*

10. *Ibid.*

11. United Nations, "Trends and Prospects in the Populations of Urban Agglomerations, 1950-2000, As Assessed in 1973-1975" (Population Division Working Paper, ESA/P/WP.58), New York, November 1975.

13. Independent Commission on International Development Issues, *North-South, A Program for Survival* (Cambridge, Massachusetts: The MIT Press, 1980).

14. Food and Agriculture Organization of the United Nations, *The State of Food and Agriculture*, Rome, 1978.

15. *Ibid.*

16. *Ibid.*

17. *Ibid.*

18. United Nations, *World Population Trends and Prospects.* . . .

19. United Nations Educational, Scientific and Social Organization, *Estimates and Projections of Illiteracy*, Paris, 1978.

The State of
World Population 1981

BEYOND 2000

The United Nations estimates that the global population could stabilize at 10.5 billion in the year 2110.[1] The rate of decline in fertility in the future will be crucial in determining when and at what level population stabilization can be achieved. The United Nations projects three scenarios for stabilization, high, medium and low, based on modest, moderate and significant rates of decline in fertility. The high variant results in a projected population of 14.2 billion, and the low variant in 8.0 billion.[2] The fact that the low level could be reached in 60 years, by the year 2040, whereas the high level would be reached in 150 years, by the year 2130, shows that the ultimate level of stable population is sensitive to the speed and extent of decline in fertility. If we are able to sustain the present tempo of population programmes and policies then stabilization appears feasible at the medium variant of 10.5 billion in the year 2110.

Though the 10.5 billion stable population projected by the United Nations medium variant is less alarmist than the figures projected by other studies, it still means that the global population would have grown to be nearly two and a half times larger than the present 4.4 billion. A number of studies have indicated the nature of the impact of population growth on global resources, the global environment and global development. Therefore, we cannot afford to be complacent about the nature of these interrelationships, minimize the pressures they generate, or underestimate the instability they perpetuate.

Even during the present century we might not be able to claim to have provided for the basic needs of nearly half of the world's population, spread not only across the developing countries but also living in some pockets of highly advanced societies. While imbalances created by poverty, malnutrition or ill-health persist, the social tensions arising out of population pressures will permeate every aspect of the quality of life on earth, even impinging on populations outside and setting up a chain reaction. Social consequences of overcrowding, for example, have already led to increase in crime and violence in the over-populated metropolitan centres of the world. The rural areas of many countries have so far been relatively free of similar tensions, but given the patterns of future population growth and its distribution, such problems are likely to spread over much larger areas of the developing world. The 9.1 billion people who will be living in the developing countries will most acutely feel the impact of population growth on their resources and living conditions.

HISTORICAL PATTERNS

Fertility began to decline in the high fertility societies of Europe and North America with industrialization in the 19th century. It took 150 years for them to reach low fertility levels without any conscious public policy interventions. During the first half of the 20th century it took the Soviet Union about 40 years to achieve this transition. And, during the latter half of the 20th century, Japan has taken only 25 years to undergo this transformation.

The demographic changes established by individual response to industrialization can be read as: first, an articulation of an abundant future — leading to more children; secondly, improved living conditions leading to longer life expectancy for future generations; and thirdly, regulation of family size, by lowering birth rates to enjoy the fruits of science and new technology. Conscious public policies in planning for even more rapid industrial development over shorter spans of time therefore cannot ignore the knowledge we now have of how crucially family size is determined by socio-economic factors. A couple's conscious decision on family size, in turn, establishes fertility behaviour. Reduction of infant mortality has an impact on fertility decline, and this can be achieved by assured maternal or child health care, supplementary nutritional programmes, upgrading of the quality of environmental health and extension of medical care facilities. The industrial development of Japan, the Soviet Union, Europe and North America has been accompanied by such programmes, thus creating the conditions for fertility decline.

With this historical hindsight, it is possible for the less developed regions of the world to gain valuable lessons in planning their own population growth. Scattered evidence from a few countries or regions in the less developed parts of the world where fertility rates have begun to fall show that the rates are declining faster. Moreover, it is happening within a shorter span of time than it took for Europe to achieve similar rates of decline in birth rates. It is from such an historical path analysis over different periods of time and under different historical conditions that one feels confident in suggesting that it is within our capability now to bring about the demographic transition in the less developed countries in the remaining two decades of this century. Integration of population with development planning which is supported by UNFPA will certainly strengthen this capability.

QUICKENING DECLINE

The latest United Nations[3] assessment of population trends supported by independent evidence such as the findings of the World Fertility Survey undoubtedly signals a quickening of the rate of decline in world fertility. When the United Nations assessed world population trends in 1973, an annual average growth rate of 1.95 per cent was projected for 1975-1980.[4] The 1978 assessment lowered the rate to 1.81 per cent.[5] The latest assessment, undertaken last year, has further lowered the estimated growth rate to 1.73 per cent per annum for the period 1975-1980.[6] It was based on more reliable population data for a much larger number of countries than was possible during the assessment in 1973. By now, population censuses have been completed also in a number of countries where none had ever been conducted. Such a small revision of the growth rate might appear inconsequential but its significance lies in confirming the probably irreversible downward trend in global population growth, the anticipated acceleration of this trend and its immense implications for development. United Nations estimates of population growth rates for the developing countries show an annual average growth rate of 2.10 per cent in 1980, declining to 2.00 by 1985. By the year 2000 the growth rate in developing countries is projected to decline to 1.80 per cent compared with a total world rate of 1.50 per cent per annum. The earlier projections were for rates of 1.90 per cent and 1.60 per cent per annum, respectively. These downward revisions in no way lessen the global and regional implications of development and population growth.

The decline in global population growth which began in 1965 was brought about initially by dramatic declines in growth rates in the developed countries — from a 1.2 per cent annual population growth rate in 1965 to 0.8 per cent in 1975.[7] During the same period the population growth rate of the developing countries rose from 2.25 per cent to 2.35 per cent,[8] an increase which occurred in spite of a declining birth rate because of a proportionately greater decline in mortality rates. Recent data show that the rate of mortality decline had probably levelled off in the 1970s.[9]

Comparisons of data obtained by the World Fertility Survey and various other studies, and deeper analysis and evaluation of the data, show the range and validity of the factors affecting fertility in the developing countries. We know that during the early phases of the demographic transition, it is comparatively easier to bring about a quick and significant decline through comprehensive public measures in mortality rates than a similar decline in birth rates.

The decline in the birth rate is dependent on a host of social, economic and cultural factors which influence a couple's decision about family formation and ideal family size. Reduction of disparities in income and wealth, the opportunities offered for women to move from traditional occupations to newer occupations, number of years of schooling, population education aimed at helping people to make their socio-economic decisions and information about the best means to act on those decisions — all these contribute to a decline in fertility rate.

Two caveats have to be made in regard to declining global fertility, and lower growth rate. First, the current population growth rate in the developing countries is still higher than the growth rate that prevailed during the period 1950-1955. All our efforts have only helped to arrest the rising trend in the population growth rate in the developing countries and to set it in reverse. Secondly, annual increments in total population will continue to be higher during the rest of this century in spite of the fact that the annual global growth rate is declining. It is estimated that in 1980 the net addition to global population was of the order of 80 million, and the net increments will be close to 90 million by the year 2000 because of annual increments continuing to rise. Even a declining birth rate when applied to an ever-expanding population base yields larger and larger annual increments in total population. Hence the warning in last year's *State of World Population Report* that the decline should not be taken to mean that "the population problem" had been solved. On the contrary, in the coming years the pressures generated by increases in the annual numbers will intensify problems associated with population growth. (See Chart 1.)

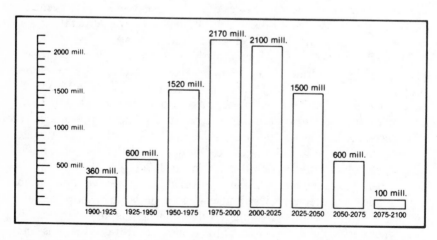

Chart 1. Net Additions to World Population at 25-Year Intervals, 1900-2100

The relationship between increases in absolute numbers and the global growth rate is illustrated by examining population growth in this century. During the first quarter of this century the global growth rate was 0.8 per cent, and the net increase amounted to 360 million. During the second quarter of the century the growth rate rose to 1.1 per cent and the net increase which resulted was 600 million. During the next quarter, 1950-1975, the growth rate peaked at 1.9 per cent and the net addition to global population jumped to 1.5 billion. Since then the growth rate has declined, and yet the net addition to the total world population will be 2.2 billion in the last quarter of this century.[10]

REGIONAL DEMOGRAPHIC DIVERSITY

The differences in fertility levels and in rates of decline in different regions of the world will result in different regions attaining stabilization at different times in the future.[11]

While the largest number will be added to the population of South Asia, that region is expected to reach the stable level in the year 2100, with an increase in population from the present 1.4 billion to 4.1 billion. East Asia, including China and Japan, will reach a stable population of 1.7 billion in the year 2090, because of the already low population growth rate attained by China, adding only 0.5 billion to its current population of 1.2 billion. Africa, the region where stable population could be attained only by the year 2110, is expected to add 1.6 billion to its current population and reach 2.1 billion. Latin America, achieving stabilization by the year 2100, will add 0.8 billion to level at 1.2 billion. Europe, reaching stabilization earliest, in the year 2030, will have a population of 0.5 billion, adding only 50 million to its current population, whereas the Soviet Union will have 0.38 billion people when it achieves stabilization in the year 2100. North America, stabilizing its population in the year 2060, will account for 0.32 billion.

South Asia and Africa will thus between themselves account for over 60 per cent of the world's total population at the time of stabilization. These two regions not only contain the greatest proportions of poor people, whatever the criteria we use to define poverty, but also include some of the poorest sub-regions and countries of the world. Malnutrition, ill-health, illiteracy and the lowest life expectations are predominant in South Asia and Africa, accompanied by inadequate technology and economic organization. It is not very difficult to imagine the crippling burden their resources will have to bear even at stabilization from a combined population of 6.2 billion. In this context, one cannot help wondering whether such regional pressures of population on resources might not still pose some threat to global peace and stability even in the 21st century.

During the 20th century the decade of the 1970s has been marked by the dividends in hope issued by a global fertility decline, the only such dividends issued during a decade which began to generate disequilibrating forces in the international economic system. Have these last 10 years not reassured us that it is worth continuing to strive towards eliminating disparities caused by lack of population planning? (See Chart 2.)

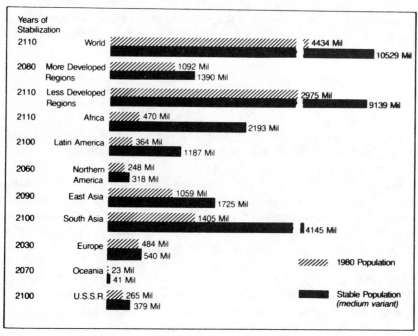

Chart 2. Ultimate Stable Population Compared with 1980 Population for Various Geographical Regions

Africa

Fertility behaviour in African countries clearly represents an exception to the prevailing global pattern. The crude birth rate for the whole continent of Africa has remained practically constant between 1950 and 1980, changing only from 48 to 46 per thousand.[12] There are a number of countries where the crude birth rates are close to 50. In fact, high fertility rates — crude birth rates over 45 per thousand — are the general rule in all countries and areas of Africa, except a few such as Egypt, Gabon, Réunion, South Africa, and Tunisia. The highest birth rate estimated for any country in the world is for Kenya, 54 per thousand in 1980.[13] These high birth rates are reflected in the estimates of African populations at the times of stabilization. Most of the African countries are undergoing tremendous changes in social structure and in economic organization. The interrelationships between these profound changes in African societies and the demographic variables need much further investigation for an understanding of the forces determining fertility in these countries.

One of the factors which possibly discourages a reduction in fertility in African countries is the prevalence of high levels of infant and general mortality rates. Since decline in mortality usually precedes decline in fertility, it appears that African fertility levels will continue to be high unless mortality rates are brought down. In many African countries crude death rates exceed 20 per 1000 population and the highest death rates anywhere in the world are found in this region.

Asia

On the basis of the levels of birth rates, the countries of Asia can be divided into three broad groups, though exceptions can be found in each group.[14] The highest fertility level, with an estimated birth rate during 1975-1980 of around 45 per 1000 population, is in the West Asian region, comprising the geographical area lying between Pakistan and Turkey. The lowest birth rate is in the East Asian region including China, which has made considerable headway in the demographic transition. China's crude birth rate is estimated at 18.3 per 1000 population in 1978 and the aim is to bring down the natural rate of increase in population to 5 per 1000 by 1985. China's one-child family policy incorporates both financial incentives and disincentives.

Intermediate levels of crude birth rates characterize the countries of the rest of Asia, in South and Southeast Asia. In this group, a few countries, such as Sri Lanka and Singapore, have succeeded in reducing their birth rates to a significant extent. Bangladesh, on the other hand, still has a crude birth rate of around 45. But there are clear indications that this region is poised for a significant reduction in birth rates.

Mortality rates have declined considerably everywhere in this region during the recent past with a few exceptions. The East Asian region has the lowest mortality rates, below 10 per 1000 population, thus accelerating the decline in fertility in this region. Mortality rates in the West Asian region are generally lower than in South Asia. However, in some countries of Asia, such as Afghanistan, Bhutan and Nepal, crude death rates continue to be high, at 20 or more per 1000. At the time of population stabilization Asia's population will still constitute nearly 60 per cent of global population.

Latin America

On the basis of crude birth rates the Latin American countries can also be classified into three broad groups.[15] Argentina, Chile and Uruguay, in the Temperate zone, have the lowest birth rates in this region, between 20 and 25 per 1000 population. All the Caribbean Islands, except Haiti and the Dominican Republic, are in the second group with a crude birth rate well below 30 per 1000 population, which is also the dividing line for birth rates between the developed and developing countries. The countries of Middle America and the Tropical South American regions form a third group, and crude birth rates for many within this group exceed 35 per 1000 population. Generally speaking, there has been hardly any significant decline in the overall birth rate in this area, although Mexico, Panama and Guyana may be poised for declines in birth rates. The Mexican crude birth rate which declined by 19 per cent during the period 1970-1978 might decline further as a result of a new population policy.

Mortality rates almost everywhere in Latin America are among the lowest in the less developed group, and, therefore, the resistance of fertility rates to decline cannot be attributed to the prevalence of high mortality rates. The population growth rates in Middle America and Tropical South America are even higher than the growth rate of South Asia due to this difference between birth and death rates. All these factors will affect both the time-frame and the numbers when stabilization of population is reached in this region.

More developed regions

When the global population is stabilized the share of the more developed regions will decline from 24 per cent in 1980 to 13 per cent. Uniformly low levels of fertility characterize this group, and in 14 out of 22 countries the fertility rate in 1977 had fallen below the replacement level of 2.1. Within this group, the countries of Northern and Western Europe have the lowest fertility rate. This group, on the other hand, has to consider initiating major cultural, social and economic policies to cope with their rising percentages of people over 65 years old. Whereas in 1980 people over 65 constituted 11 per cent of their population, by the year 2000 this will increase to 13 per cent and by 2025 to 16.7.[16] Europe and North America will reach population stabilization in the years 2030 and 2060, respectively.

FAMILY SIZE

The decline in fertility accompanied by lowering of growth rates depends on the decisions of couples and individuals regarding family size. It is indeed in recognition of this reality that the World Population Plan of Action emphasizes the right of couples and individuals to decide freely and responsibly the number and spacing of their children and to have access to the information and means to do so. This has been further endorsed in the Colombo Declaration on Population and Development and the Rome Declaration on Population and the Urban Future. The World Plan of Action also re-emphasizes the sovereign right of each nation to choose the population programme most appropriate for its needs and requirements. In pursuance of this, UNFPA maintains strict neutrality, leaving it to governments themselves to make available the information, education and means for couples and individuals to exercise this right, in the context of their own population characteristics and social and cultural traditions.

The data collected by the World Fertility Survey shed some light on the spread of family planning information, the extent and availability of choices, the practices followed, and the impediments still prevailing in knowledge and means for couples and individuals to exercise their right.[17]

In 14 out of 20 developing countries, although nearly 90 per cent of the ever-married women of reproductive age know of one or more family planning methods, practices fell far short of knowledge because access to means were often unavailable. For example, in Pakistan, whereas 75 per cent had knowledge of family planning only 32 per cent had access to the means to practice it; and whereas nearly half of the women did not want to have another child, only 6 per cent of currently-married women in Pakistan practised limitation of family size.

On the other hand, in the Republic of Korea, almost all the women of reproductive age know of a method, and 86 per cent also had access to the means to exercise their choice; and, similarly, while 74 per cent did not want any more children, 35 per cent of married women in the Republic of Korea were using a method to limit family size. Meanwhile, in a country like Nepal only one-fifth of currently married women even have information and knowledge to limit family size. The crude birth figures for these countries reflect the differences in access to knowledge and means. In Pakistan the crude birth rate declined from 46.8 per 1000 in 1960-1965 to 43.1 per 1000 in 1975-1980; in Nepal, it declined from 45.8 per 1000 to 43.7, a comparatively minor decline; in the Republic of Korea the decline was from 39.6 to 24.3.[18]

In general, impressive gains have been made during the last decade in enabling people to exercise their basic right to plan their family size. For example, in India, the proportion of married women in the reproductive age group of 15-44 who practise family planning has increased from 8 per cent in 1969 to 23 per cent in 1979; and in Malaysia, from 6 per cent to 36 per cent during the same 10 years.[19] In Mexico, between 1973 and 1978 the increase has been from 13 per cent to 40 per cent; and in Thailand, between 1971 and 1979, from 10 per cent to 39 per cent.[20] Progress has been comparatively slow in countries ranging from Bangladesh to most of the countries of the African region, and some of the countries in Middle America and Tropical South America.

It has been found that the age at marriage, which is influenced by prevailing cultural and social norms, is another of the most important determinants of family size. In the less developed countries women who marry early invariably have, on average, more pregnancies than women who choose to marry later.

The results of the World Fertility Survey data collected also show that women who reside in urban areas and whose husbands are engaged in non-agricultural occupations have lower fertility compared with women in rural areas whose menfolk are in agricultural occupations. Age at marriage, choice of occupation and location of residence, are all closely related to education, and the higher the levels of education the lower the fertility. It is thus clear that the spread of education and changes in traditional patterns of occupation have a significant impact on fertility. Public policies adopted in Sri Lanka and other areas in the less developed regions show that, even in societies with low per capita incomes, fertility can decline when rural populations have access to health and education.

ASSISTANCE FOR POPULATION PROGRAMMES

The World Population Plan of Action, while recognizing the basic right of couples and individuals to determine family size, also emphasizes that population policies should be an integral part of over-all development policies geared to optimize available resources for balanced growth. The integration of population policies in the social and economic goals and strategies of some countries has already hastened their demographic transition. Generally speaking, countries which are making significant strides towards self-reliant socio-economic advance are also the ones which are succeeding in implementing population programmes. Several of the less developed countries have committed substantial human and developmental resources to their population programmes. To supplement this, international assistance for these programmes has averaged about $250 million per annum in the 1970s. This assistance becomes either critical, crucial or catalytic in implementing population programmes.

It is critical in the case of the poorest among the less developed countries, especially in Africa, where even the data base was lacking, let alone the training and skills needed to implement these programmes. In Africa, 43 per cent of UNFPA assistance was for data collection and 24 per cent for family planning.

International assistance is of crucial importance to a number of medium-sized countries in which family planning programmes receive a small portion of limited domestic resources. For instance, Bangladesh clearly illustrates the crucial nature of international assistance for population programmes, which was $6.2 million of a total of $9.4 million in 1974; and $9.3 million of a total of $14.4 million in 1976.[21]

In Asia and Latin America, however, international assistance is catalytic, as is shown by the increasingly large amount of their domestic resources allocated to population programmes. In these areas international assistance for research, equipment, experts and local costs supplements large-scale domestic investment in these programmes. During 1979-1981, 65 per cent of the assistance of UNFPA for Asia was for family planning and 54 per cent of the allocation for Latin America was also for family planning.

In India and China, which have committed substantial domestic resources to population programmes, international assistance has been largely supplementary. India spent $600 million on family planning during the period 1974-1979, of which the foreign assistance component was $84 million.[22] China has mostly depended on its own resources for implementing its population programmes, by sustained inputs of human skills and energies and by creating the climate for the participation of its people in achieving their population goals. Of late, China has accepted some international assistance through UNFPA for its data collection and family planning programmes.

UNFPA has emerged as the principal multilateral funding organization for integrated population and development programmes. Its neutral and flexible policies have encouraged countries in the world to make efforts towards correcting the imbalances between global population growth and global resources.

TOWARDS GREATER COMMITMENT

The year 1980 is a watershed in our assessment of the global future. The Report of the International Commission on North-South Dialogue, and the conclusions of such conferences as the Toronto Conference on the Global Future, and the Rome Conference on the Urban Future, have helped to clarify many of the major issues that lie ahead. We have almost reached a consensus that integrated global development and the prospects for global stability are intertwined and depend on an enlightened understanding of the emerging demographic profile.

Population stabilization, indeed, will be a crucial determinant of the prospects for global stability beyond the year 2000 and with a time horizon of the next century. Last year's *State of World Population Report* was a reminder that although global fertility had begun to decline, a greater international commitment would still be needed to resolve the population problem at the global level. Although in the long run it might be possible to overcome the limitations of economic growth imposed by resources, through the development of new technology to find substitutes for scarce natural resources and to harness renewable energy sources, imbalances may persist in the developing countries between population and resources. In this context it may be worthwhile to undertake a long-term exercise to assess the need for population assistance with a view to achieving stable population within the time-framework laid down by the United Nations. Such an exercise could identify the quantum of total population assistance, the time-profile for such assistance, the relative significance of the various components of population changes, the regional distribution of assistance, and the options available.

The success of population programmes, as indeed of all development programmes, ultimately depends on the participation of people. A particular kind of future therefore becomes thinkable if the goals of development embody the wishes of people.

REFERENCES

1. United Nations, "Long-range Population Projections, Based on Data as Assessed in 1978" (Population Division Working Paper, ESA/P/WP.75), New York, August 1978.
2. *Ibid.*
3. *World Population Prospects as Assessed in 1980* (United Nations publication, Sales No.E.81.XIII.8), New York, 1981.
4. United Nations, *World Population Trends and Prospects by Country, 1950-2000: Summary Report of the 1978 Assessment* (ST/ESA/SER.R/33), New York, 1979.
5. *Ibid.*
6. *World Population Prospects. . . .*
7. United Nations, "Report on Monitoring of Population Trends" (Population Division Working Paper, ESA/P/WP.68), New York, December 1980.
8. *Ibid.*
9. Davidson R. Gwatkin, "Indicators of Change in Developing Country Mortality Trends: The End of an Era?" *Population and Development Review*, vol.6, No.4 (December 1980).
10. United Nations, "Long-range Global Population Projections . . .".
11. *Ibid.*
12. *World Population Prospects. . . .*
13. *Ibid.*
14. *Ibid.*
15. *Ibid.*
16. United Nations, "World Demographic Indicators: Estimates and Projections – As Assessed in 1980", January 1981.
17. United Nations, "Report on Monitoring . . .".
18. *World Population Prospects. . . .*
19. Dorothy L. Nortman and Ellen Hofstatter, *Population and Family Planning Programs*, 10th Edition (New York: The Population Council, 1980).
20. *Ibid.*
21. *Ibid.*
22. *Ibid.*

The State of World Population 1982

SIGNPOSTS TO 1984

The current United Nations medium variant projection of world population for the year 2000 is 6.1 billion.[1] If the conditions of stable fertility and declining mortality prevailing in the 1950s had continued to the end of this century, the projected world population for the year 2000 would have been 7.5 billion.[2] The difference between the two projections is 1.4 billion people. This is the real significance of the impact of national population policies and programmes, changes in social and economic conditions, and of international population assistance. The present estimate of 6.1 billion is almost 20 per cent lower than the earlier projection. During the 1970s, birth rates in developing countries declined at twice the rate of the 1960s, and the decline continues. The perspectives and experiences drawn from over a decade of global population activities augur well for the future, as we approach the Orwellian year of 1984, when the next International Conference on Population is to be held. Based on these declining trends in fertility the United Nations has also held out the prospect of world population stabilizing at 10.5 billion in the year 2110.[3]

In the light of the decision to hold the next International Conference on Population in 1984, this year's *State of World Population Report* provides a preliminary review of significant achievements in global population programmes during the first phase of 1971 to 1981 and seeks to identify the major issues that will require attention during the rest of this century. The achievements have been essentially due to national efforts, with financial and technical assistance from the global community.

A review of the responses to population growth and development during the first phase shows that these have taken shape in five ways.

First, the number of governments whose perceptions of population issues have sharpened and which have recognized the need to intervene through policies and programmes has vastly increased. Second, research and analysis undertaken mainly in the 1970s assigned a central role to population in development policies and a large number of governments formulated policies and programmes taking into account linkages between population, resources, environment and development. Third, a number of countries made considerable progress in building up the necessary infrastructure and facilities for the implementation of their programmes. Fourth, in the course of implementation of programmes there was an increase in the country's own allocations. Fifth, international assistance for population programmes has become a significant factor with the recognition that global population growth has implications for the eradication of poverty and the achievement of a more balanced growth between population and income.

Changing perceptions

The world population growth rate rose from 1.76 per cent in 1950-1955 to 1.99 per cent in 1960-1965. Thenceforth it began to decline and reached 1.72 per cent in 1975-1980. The United Nations projects that the annual rate of world population growth could come down to 1.5 per cent by the end of this century.[4]

The combined effect of the unprecedented growth in the 1950s and 1960s and deficiencies in conventional development strategies was to increase the number of poor living below minimum levels. This generated a sense of urgency for the integration of national population factors into development planning.

A significant number of governments which had earlier subscribed to the notion that larger populations would not be detrimental to future economic growth, and had viewed population policy interventions as unnecessary or even harmful to development, reversed their position in the 1970s. They recognized their existing levels of fertility as high and realized that remedial measures were necessary. The new perceptions that developed during this period not only resulted in the formulation of policies and programmes for reducing birth rates but also encompassed such other areas as mortality and morbidity, spatial distribution, and different aspects of internal and international migration. Two-thirds of the world's governments representing four-fifths of the world population had already adopted population policies by the mid-1970s. The World Population Conference held at Bucharest in 1974 provided impetus to this movement and the World Population Plan of Action consolidated in a single document the objectives, actions and policies which had crystallized by that time.

The population policy and programme of each individual government is shaped by that government's perceptions concerning the nature of its particular population problems. India was the first country to adopt policies to lower the rate of growth of population; that was in 1952. Barbados and China followed in 1956. By 1980, 59 developing nations had programmes aimed at lowering or maintaining their respective fertility levels, compared with only 26 countries in 1969. Another 21 countries now consider their fertility levels to be too high, but have not yet chosen to adopt interventionist policies. On the other hand, in 1980, 21 governments considered fertility levels too low, and 17 have policies to raise them.[5]

The significance of these changes in the perceptions of the governments can be fully grasped only if we take into account the size of the population affected by them. About 80 per cent of the total population of the developing world reside in countries which consider the levels of their fertility too high and would like them reduced. By contrast, countries with only three per cent of the population of the developing world would like their fertility rates increased. The remaining 17 per cent of the population live in countries which are satisfied with their current levels of fertility.

Many more governments concerned with the welfare of their populations consider the present levels of mortality and morbidity to be too high and the average expectation of life at birth to be unacceptable. In 1980, 107 governments out of a total of 165 considered the average life expectancy at birth in their countries as low. Of these 107 governments, 98 are in developing countries. All the governments desire a reduction of their morbidity and mortality levels and have embarked on policies in this area primarily as health and social policies rather than as demographic ones. A large number of governments also consider that the spatial distribution of their populations and the trends in internal migration and the growth of metropolitan urban centres require policies to modify the current directions. In 1980, 110 developing countries out of a total of 126 considered the distribution of their population as unacceptable to a varying degree.

Policy integrations

The recognition by many governments that population problems generate different types of social and economic impacts has culminated in the formulation of policies and programmes to counter these effects. The integration of population with development has been facilitated by research and analysis at two levels. At the macro-level, a body of research has broadly indicated the linkages between population, resources, environment and development, and the implications of alternative policy options. The deterioration of soil fertility and the consequential loss in land productivity in the long run, brought about by improper land use practices in efforts to feed a growing population or by soil erosion arising from a decline in forest area as a consequence of the felling of trees are examples of such macro-level interrelationships. At the micro-level, studies have shown that population has a circular relationship with a number of social and economic variables and that these relationships can, therefore, reinforce the demographic impact of population programmes if mutually supportive social and economic policies and programmes are simultaneously implemented. Some of the most important relationships uncovered by this research relate to fertility behaviour.

The rapid demographic transition in the 1970s in a number of developing countries, where much lower levels of economic development existed than in Western Europe in the nineteenth century (when they underwent their demographic transition), elicited a great deal of interest in the various factors involved in this transition. The World Fertility Survey[6] undertaken in the mid- and late 1970s collected data on a comparable basis for a number of countries and provided a data base for comparative studies on fertility variations under differing social and economic conditions. These studies indicate that the relationships between fertility and social and economic variables are complex, but that policies in certain sectors could help to bring about a faster decline in fertility. Intercountry comparisons generally indicate a negative relationship between fertility level and socio-economic status. Negative relationships are also seen between fertility levels and female education, and the occupational status of women. The WFS studies reveal that women who had worked at some time since marriage had fewer children compared to those who had never worked. Women in white-collar and professional occupations tended to have smaller families than blue-collar women workers, while agricultural workers generally had the highest fertility levels.

Women's education has been found to be a major influence on the level of infant and child mortality. There is extensive evidence indicating that maternal education plays a major role in influencing infant and child mortality, presumably reflecting personal health behaviour, care and access to and use of medical facilities. It was found in Latin America, for instance, that the probability of death between birth and age two years declined almost linearly with increase in the level of mothers' education. Children of illiterate women had a risk 3.5 times that of children whose mothers had 10 or more years of education.[7] Thus, from research and studies done in the 1970s it appears that the most important policy integrations for reducing both birth and mortality rates in developing countries would have to include: education of women, changes in the status of women brought about by shifts from traditional to new occupations, access to health and family planning, and changes in attitudes towards family formation.

Mexico provides an excellent example of a country which has integrated demographic policies and programmes as components of its development strategy.[8] The twin objectives of the demographic policy are a reduction in fertility to lower the growth rate of population and the rationalization of migratory movements of population in order to achieve a better regional balance within Mexico. Mexico has spelt out a new reproductive model for achieving a reduction in fertility levels, whose parameters include (a) raising the age of marriage; (b) determining in advance the number of children desired; (c) lengthening the period between the time of marriage and the first birth, and between the first birth and later births. The objective of harmonizing the spatial distribution of population with balanced regional development is to be achieved by modifying the intensity and the orientation of migratory movements and by integrating the actual growth rates in the states and counties with the national growth target.

Mexico has set up a National Population Council to implement the programme by "establishing mechanisms for inter-institutional co-ordination with the Budget and Planning Ministry, for the incorporation of elements of the demographic policy in the over-all development plan; with the Human Settlements Sector, providing an impact of socio-demographic information and analyses for the formulation and readjustment of urban development plans; with the Advisory Commission on Employment, headed by the Ministry of Labour and Welfare, in the development of the National Employment Plan, and particularly in estimating the labour supply at the national and state levels; with the health sector in the systematic administration of the national family planning programme through establishing user-coverage goals, strategies for regional medical services, and in family planning and sex education; with the Ministry of Public Education, for the formation and institutionalization of the sex education and education in population programmes; and to establish its own planning for future educational demand; and with the agriculture and animal husbandry sector, in establishing work groups formed by the Council and the Ministry of Agriculture and Water Resources, to collaborate in this sector's long- and short-term programming".[9]

Programme delivery

While research has indicated that a number of variables and relationships affect the outcome of population programmes, this is not in any case a substitute for the building of the requisite infrastructure and facilities for implementation. Reductions in mortality depend not only on the access to and use of medical care but also on the elimination of common communicable diseases through improvement of sanitation and public health measures. But an examination of the programmes in different countries shows that there are many routes for the delivery of the programmes to the people who need them most. A major factor in the decline in fertility in many developing countries is the extent of the use of contraceptives. A comparative country analysis shows a high level of awareness of contraception in most of the countries surveyed by the World Fertility Survey.[10] However, knowledge does not necessarily imply practice; since the percentage of women who knew of a family planning outlet was lower than the percentage who knew of a suitable modern method. The results also indicate that women with little education and women living in rural areas are even less likely to know of a family planning outlet. The survey shows that the proportion of currently married women in the reproductive ages who have ever used contraceptives varies widely between countries. Some of the Latin American countries have reported the highest use of contraceptives among the developing countries, followed by countries of Asia. Contraceptive use is least prevalent among Sub-Saharan African countries. Costa Rica, Colombia, Indonesia and Thailand, where contraceptive use has substantially risen in the 1970s, have also reported substantial declines in their birth rates. In all these countries, the programmes have succeeded because they have experimented with and developed novel methods of effective delivery suitable to their own population sizes, desired levels of fertility decline and local conditions.

A natural family planning movement has made some headway during the past five years. In "natural" family planning, medication, the use of appliances and the use of surgical procedures are avoided; it is based only on the physiological cycle of a woman's fertile and infertile phases. Biomedical research to develop reliable tests of these phases is being undertaken in a number of countries and by the World Health Organization (WHO). It may become an important programme method for providing solutions to problems of fertility control or problems of apparent infertility.

National allocations

Irrespective of a country's population size, allocations for population programmes have dramatically increased in the 1970s. Although data on this is still being collated, it can be said that the level of resources allocated by countries committed to population programmes has become substantial and is still rising. Data collected by the Population Council and by the United Nations Fund for Population Activities for a few developing countries indicate that the bulk of expenditure on population is met by the countries themselves. There has also been an increase in the commitment of internal resources even in countries which were initially dependent on external assistance for population programmes. This is borne out by some UNFPA data from the field summarized in Table 1.

Increased national allocations have made it possible for a country such as Indonesia to compensate for the decline in external population assistance. In Kenya, where the birth rate has actually risen, the government expenditure during the period 1976-1980 was about twelve times that of 1971-1975.

The average of national shares of family planning expenditures, in 15 developing countries for which data have been collected by the Population Council, comes to about 67 per cent of total expenditure, the ratio of inter-

Table 1. Government expenditure and international assistance for population programmes in selected countries (in million US $)

Country	Government Expenditure	Percentage Rise Over the Previous Period	International Assistance
Indonesia			
1971-1975	37.9		10.6
1976-1980	111.4	194.0	38.4
Kenya			
1971-1975	1.1		1.5
1976-1980	13.1	1090.9	37.0
Thailand			
1972-1976	3.67		13.35
1977-1981	12.88	250.9	39.23
Tunisia			
1974-1977	8.3		16.0
1978-1981	12.7	53.0	15.3

nal expenditure to external assistance being 2 to 1.[11] This ratio is even higher when applied to UNFPA assistance. During 1979-1981, for each dollar budgeted by UNFPA the countries themselves have budgeted 4.6 dollars. The higher average ratio in UNFPA's programming reflects a massive commitment of funds in 1980 by India and Mexico for their population projects.

It is essential to bear in mind, while examining these figures, how difficult it is for countries at low levels of development to allocate large amounts of internal resources for population programmes which do not yield immediately tangible results. These internal resource commitments would not have been possible but for the groundwork laid by the creation of awareness on population issues.

International assistance

Meanwhile, international population assistance has continued to be a catalytic agent to sustain and expand the population programmes of the developing countries. In 1961, when external development aid was $5.2 billion, population assistance amounted to only $6 million, or 0.1 per cent of total aid. By 1970, when population rise began to be recognized as a crucial factor in development, there was a spurt in assistance specifically earmarked for population activity. In 1970 for the first time it exceeded $100 million, or 1.8 per cent of total development aid. International population assistance has, indeed, increased in constant prices from $125 million in 1970 to $249 million in 1980, but it is still less than 2.0 per cent of development aid.[12] The Colombo Declaration adopted by the International Conference of Parliamentarians on Population and Development in 1979, has called for a target of $1 billion in population assistance by the year 1984.

Impact on fertility and mortality

The downward turn in the global population growth rate is closely related to the extent and nature of the efforts in the individual countries and regions. There are, however, wide variations in the performances of individual countries as reflected in the rates of decline in birth rates, and in reducing mortality. During the period 1965-1970 to 1975-1980, the global birth rate declined by 13.97 per cent and, in the less developed regions, the decline was 16.2 per cent.[13]

The World Population Plan of Action had expressed the hope in 1974 that "population growth rates in the developing countries as a whole may decline from the present level of 2.4 per cent per annum to about 2 per cent by 1985".[14] The United Nations projects the attainment of this level for the less developed regions by 1985. Similarly, the 1974 Plan of Action's expectations of 0.7 per cent annual rate of growth for the developed countries will also be realized by 1985. The efforts of the countries themselves are the main driving force behind this decline in birth rate. Table 2 classifies developing countries with populations of 10 million or more into six groups, based on their percentage changes in birth rates during 1965-1970 and 1975-1980. The total population of these countries constitutes 88 per cent of the total population of the developing world.

China, with an estimated population of 1.02 billion in 1982, shows a 34 per cent decline in its birth rate during this period.[15] There are seven countries in the next group, with an aggregate population of over 1.0 billion, whose percentage declines lie between 15 to 25 per cent. There are 16 countries with an aggregate population of 450 million which have registered birth rate declines below 5 per cent. The two countries in the last group (Kenya and Uganda) show an increase in the levels of birth rate.

The countries which have experienced the largest declines in birth rates contain about two-thirds of the total population of the developing countries. Most of these are in the Asian region, where the rate of decline accelerated in the 1970s. For Asia as a whole, a target of one per cent population growth rate in the year 2000 was set by the Asian Parliamentarians Conference on Population and Development in Beijing in October 1981. The least impact of population on birth rates is noticeable in the African continent. Birth rates of 45 and above are still common, particularly in Western and Eastern Africa. Out of 50 developing African nations, 32 governments have not yet decided on interventions to reduce their birth rates whereas 22 out of the 32 developing countries in Asia (including the West Asian countries) have perceived a need for government policies to maintain or to bring down their birth rates. In Latin America, 10 out of 30 governments presently consider intervention as appropriate to lower their current birth rates.

Table 2. Developing countries with populations of 10 million and over; classified according to the percentage rate of decline in birth rates between 1965-70 and 1975-80

% Change in Birth Rates	Number of Countries	% of Total Population of Developing Countries (1982)	Countries
>-25	1	29.67	China
>-15, <-25	7	29.67	Chile, Colombia, India, Indonesia, Malaysia, Republic of Korea, Thailand
>-10, <-15	4	6.22	Brazil, Peru, Philippines, Sri Lanka
>-5, <-10	5	9.30	Bangladesh, Egypt, Mexico, Pakistan, Venezuela
< 0, <-5	16	13.47	Afghanistan, Algeria, Argentina, Burma, Ethiopia, Ghana, Iran, Iraq, Morocco, Mozambique, Nepal, Nigeria, Sudan, United Republic of Tanzania, Viet Nam, Zaire
>0, <+5	2	0.09	Kenya, Uganda

Calculations based on data provided in reference 1.

It is clear that the rates of decline of the countries with the largest share of the population of the developing countries are crucial to the global decline in fertility. Although the impact of the decline in birth rates of smaller countries may not be perceptible in the global rate of decline, population programmes are still vital to them for balancing their resources with their population.

The spread of public health services has been an important factor in the mortality reductions achieved during the 1960s and 1970s. A slow-down in the rate of decline in mortality suggests that unless access to health and medical care is made available to the rural and outlying regions of many countries, further reductions in mortality may be difficult to achieve.

The prevalence of high infant and child mortality rates in many developing countries is a crucial factor inhibiting the attainment of the targets on life expectancy. The continent of Africa again appears to be the one region where mortality rates continue to be the highest. Infant mortality rates in almost all countries of Sub-Saharan Africa are in the range of 90-170 deaths per 1000 live births. In the Indian sub-continent the rates remain well above 120. How acute this problem is in these countries can be realized only when one compares their rates with those now prevailing in the developed countries where these are in the range of 7 to 15 deaths per 1000 live births. The World Population Plan of Action had suggested the attainment of an average expectation of life of 74 years for the world as a target by the year 2000. While the developed countries may exceed this level, United Nations projections indicate that by the year 2000, the developing countries may reach an expectation of life of only 63 or 64 years.[16]

Tasks ahead

The 1984 International Conference on Population offers the global community an opportunity to assess the achievements and the problems thus far encountered and to give new directions for the next phase of integration of population with development. The tasks to be undertaken fall into three categories: to strengthen and sustain the momentum already generated; to initiate programmes in those areas where no significant impact has yet been achieved; and to identify the emerging problems for concerted action.

Family planning, including natural methods, was the main focus of population activities in the 1970s. In several other areas, such as statistical data collection and analysis, research on determinants of population variables under different conditions of development, demographic projections, and studies on legislation and population, impressive strides have been made with international inputs of technical and financial assistance. However, in South Asia and Africa, as stated earlier, the impact of programmes on fertility and mortality has still to be felt. There is a continuing need to intensify programmes in these regions.

Nor can we ignore, as we prepare for the 1984 Conference, some of the emerging population problems for the next two decades and beyond. Rapid urbanization and uncontrolled urban growth will call for fresh policies. The United Nations Fund for Population Activities organized an International Conference on Population and the Urban Future, in September, 1980, in Rome. The Rome Declaration suggested a number of measures to meet challenges posed by rapid urbanization. Another problem which is now occupying the attention of the developed countries is the large increase in the numbers of aged in their populations. Some of the countries of the developing world, notably China, where fertility and mortality rates show steep declines, will, by the year 2000, begin to face the problems of an aging population. The kind of socio-economic response that may be needed to face this shift in the age structure of populations will therefore have to be considered.

The 1970s were marked by a shift in the pattern of international migration. While there was a reduction in the scale of migration from the developing countries to Northern and Western Europe, there was a substantial increase in the number of migrants to West Asia from the poorer areas of the developing nations. Further research will have to be undertaken on the nature of the impact of migration both on the host countries and the areas of out-migration.

The experience of countries where family planning is integrated with development planning shows that programmes to improve the status of women, access to health care and contraceptive methods, reduction of infant mortality, and population education converge to produce a decline in fertility. The findings of the World Fertility Survey have already highlighted the importance of improved conditions for women in reducing fertility and mortality. The role of women can be strengthened by providing further education and employment opportunities in non-traditional sectors. The WFS also noted that increased usage of contraceptive methods by women is dependent both on increased education and easier access. While government intervention has proved essential in starting or giving the necessary impetus to family planning programmes, effective delivery cannot be maintained without active community participation. Community involvement not only can ensure the regular supply of contraceptives but also can provide a forum to educate women on the benefits of family planning. The notable success in family planning in China and Indonesia is due to active community participation in the programmes. More bio-medical research on contraceptives is also needed to strengthen the available family planning methods, including natural methods.

Four workshops are planned in preparation for the International Conference on Population. These will re-examine the achievements and problems still prevalent in fertility, mortality and morbidity, migration, and the inter-relationships between population issues and development. Meanwhile, the debate on the complexities of relationships between population growth and development continues. Governments themselves clearly perceive now that population programmes are of the utmost importance to their development plans and the international community can help governments to achieve their objectives.

REFERENCES

UNFPA gratefully acknowledges the information provided by the United Nations Population Division, the Population Council and the International Planned Parenthood Federation for the preparation of this *Report*.

1. *World Population Prospects as Assessed in 1980* (United Nations publication, Sales No.E.81.XIII.8), New York, 1981.
2. *World Population Prospects as Assessed in 1963* (United Nations publication, Sales No.66.XIII.2), New York, 1966.
3. United Nations, "Long-range Global Population Projections" (Population Division Working Paper, ESA/P/WP.75), New York, August 1981.
4. *World Population Prospects as Assessed in 1980.*
5. United Nations, "Report on Monitoring of Population Policies" (Population Division Working Paper, ESA/P/WP.69), New York, January 1981.
6. United Nations, "Report on Monitoring of Population Trends" (Population Division Working Paper, ESA/P/WP.68), New York, December 1980.
7. *Ibid.*, p.13.
8. Statement of Lic. Gustavo Cabrera at the XII Ordinary Session of the National Population Council, Mexico.
9. *Ibid.*, p.4.
10. United Nations, "Report on Monitoring of Population Trends".
11. Dorothy L. Nortman and Ellen Hofstatter, *Population and Family Planning Programs, A Population Council Factbook*, 11th Edition (New York: The Population Council, 1982).
12. Compiled by UNFPA from OECD and UNFPA data.
13. *World Population Prospects as Assessed in 1980.*
14. *Report of the United Nations World Population Conference, 1974, Bucharest, 19-30 August 1974* (United Nations publication, Sales No.E.75.XIII.3), part one, chap.I, para.16.
15. Cuba, whose population will be close to 10 million in 1982, experienced the greatest decline of all countries in its birth rate, namely 47 per cent between 1965-1970 and 1975-1980.
16. *World Population Prospects as Assessed in 1980.*

The State of
World Population 1983

THE BIG QUESTION

In August 1984, with the convening of the International Conference on Population in Mexico, ten years will have passed since the World Population Conference in Bucharest. The record of the intervening decade is remarkable. Population growth in the developing countries has declined from 2.4 per cent annually during 1965-1970 to an estimated 2.0 per cent during 1980-1985.[1] Stabilization of the global population is possible by the end of the 21st century, if the downward trend can be sustained.[2] How to sustain it will be the question in 1984.

Family size

The key to stabilization is family size. According to the World Fertility Survey, the average number of children born to a woman[3] in 20 developing countries surveyed varied from 8.3 in Kenya to 3.8 in Sri Lanka. The United Nations estimates that the average for all developing countries during 1975-1980 was 4.64. By comparison, the average for the developed countries was 2.05 children per woman in the late 1970s.[4]

Stabilization of population will become a reality only when the average size of completed families in the developing countries declines to a level comparable to what it is now in the developed countries.

Birth rates

Differences in family size parallel marked differences in birth rates between developing and developed countries. The yearly average for developing countries was 33 per 1000 population during 1975-1980, compared to 16 per 1000 population in the developed.[5]

Though they are declining, high birth rates are still a primary concern of population programmes. Other concerns of population are closely related:

high infant mortality rates in the developing countries, for example, are a cause as well as an effect of high birth rates. Migration, both internal and international, may be spurred by the pressure of population in predominantly agricultural and rural economies. The question of population-resource balance and its impact on the environment arises directly from rapid population growth.

Recognizing that each of these related issues will have an effect on efforts to achieve a stable world population, the preparatory discussions for the International Population Conference in 1984 are grouped under four headings: 1) fertility and the family; 2) mortality and health policy; 3) population distribution, migration and development; and 4) population, resources, environment and development. This year's *State of World Population Report* examines each of these issues as a step towards evolving operational policies.

FERTILITY AND THE FAMILY

The question of what determines family size is at the core of the attempt to explain levels and variations of fertility rates. Modes of production, economic value of children, social customs, systems of property ownership and the extent and control of disease, to give a few examples, all influence desired family size.

Rural families are on average larger than in urban industrial communities. Industrialization and urbanization used to be considered essential to bring down fertility rates in the developing countries.

Smaller families

In the early 1960s, one of the distinctions between developed and developing countries was the level of their birth rates: there was no developed country where the birth rate was higher than 30 per 1000 population and there was no developing country where it was lower. During the 1970s, this distinction became blurred; the trend in many developing countries is now towards smaller families. The crude birth rate in developing countries is projected to decline from 37 per 1000 population during 1970-1975 to 31.4 during 1980-1985.[6]

The World Fertility Survey has completed several comparative studies of national fertility. The data were gathered during 1974-1978 and therefore provide a broad demographic picture at about the time of the Bucharest World Population Conference.

Chart 1 compares three indicators of fertility in 20 developing countries.[7] Of the 20 countries, 13 countries have populations exceeding 10 million. Nine of the 13 have estimated birth rate declines of between 10 and 25 per cent

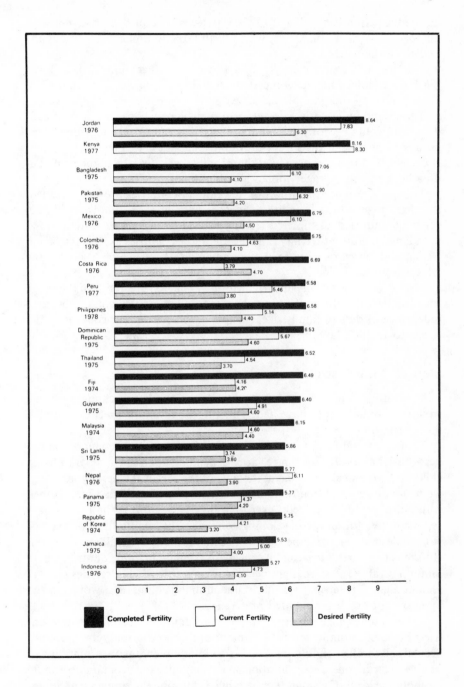

Chart 1. Completed, Current and Desired Fertility for Selected Countries

during the period 1965-1970 to 1975-1980. Kenya is representative of a large number of countries in Africa, where birth rates continue to be among the highest in the world.

The first indicator is *completed fertility*, the average number of children born to a woman who had completed her child-bearing years within the five years preceding the date of the survey.

The second indicator is *current fertility*, which gives the number of children who would be born to a woman if fertility rates for the different age-groups at the time of the survey prevail throughout her child-bearing years. If current fertility rates are lower than completed rates, the number of children born to the average woman is going down.

Though a number of important developing countries are not included, the chart gives a broad picture of what is happening to family size in developing countries. Completed fertility ranged from 8.64 in Jordan to 5.3 in Indonesia. Current fertility is lower for all the countries except Kenya and Nepal, and lowest of all in Sri Lanka and Costa Rica, which also have the largest fertility declines.[8]

The range of variations in current fertility is much greater than the range for completed fertility, reflecting changes in demographic conditions, attitudes towards desired family size, changes in socio-economic conditions and access to family planning.

Desired family size

The third indicator is *desired fertility*, or the number of children women would like to have or to have had. This was the result of direct questioning during the survey.[9]

The average number of children desired in 17 out of the 20 countries ranged between 3.7 and 4.7. This figure varies depending upon the number of living children a woman already had at the time of the survey. Generally speaking, women with few children desired more than they already had and women with more would have liked fewer than they had.[10] But if the findings are representative for all the developing countries, they imply that the average woman desired to have somewhere between three and five children. The conclusion is that birth rates can be expected to remain high in countries where infant mortality rates are high, because the number of children desired will remain high. But fertility would decline in many countries if women acted in accordance with their stated preferences.

These findings have important implications for policy in developing countries. First, programmes to reduce infant and child mortality are essential. Second, all families should have access to family planning information and services. Third, population education and communication programmes should promote the ideal of a small family, while respecting the principle of voluntary decisions and in keeping with cultural and religious values.

Issues for the Conference

The preparatory expert group on fertility and the family which met in New Delhi, January 5-11, 1983, considered a number of issues which the Conference may be expected to take up.

The World Population Plan of Action "recognizes the necessity of ensuring that all couples are able to achieve their desired number and spacing of children". Considering the family as the fundamental social unit, the first issue will be how fertility decisions are made within the family, the implications for national population policy, and what principles would ensure that the importance of the family is recognized in making policy.

Second will be age at marriage. Besides having an effect on completed family size, marriage too early damages the health of women and reduces their status in the family and community. Child marriage is recognized as a violation of human rights. The expert group recommended that the Conference consider what legislative and social measures would promote later marriage.

The third issue concerns the rights and responsibilities of individuals in relation to national population policy. The World Population Plan of Action emphasized that all couples and individuals have the basic right to decide freely and responsibly the number and spacing of their children. The exercise of this right takes into account their responsibility to the community. The Conference may be expected to consider what measures are needed to make national population policy universally known and assure voluntary individual co-operation in achieving its goals.

Finally, stabilization of population will be feasible only through comprehensive population programmes, which can only be carried out successfully through active co-operation between governments and communities. A fourth issue for the Conference will be to suggest how to secure the full involvement of the community in population policy.

MORTALITY AND HEALTH POLICY

Death is a demographic as well as a humanitarian concern; mortality rates affect the age distribution and the sex composition of a country's population, the structure and growth of its labour force, and the proportions of children and the aged in a population. Infant (0-1 year old) and child (1-5 years) mortality rates, affect fertility decisions. History shows that when mortality rates begin to go down there is a delay before birth rates decline. The very high population growth rates of the 1950s and 1960s were the result of this delay, following rapid declines in mortality.

Life expectancy

A refined measure of mortality in a country is provided by the expectation of life at birth. Enabling people to live longer is an important goal of welfare policy of all nations. The United Nations estimates that average life expectancy at birth rose from 47.0 years during 1950-1955 to 57.5 years during 1975-1980 for the world as a whole.[11] Life expectancy in developing countries rose at a higher annual rate, largely because of the development of low-cost and easily imported technologies in public health and disease control such as antibiotics, vaccines and pesticides.

However, there is still a big discrepancy between life expectancy in developed and developing countries. Life expectancy at birth in the developed countries had already reached 65.2 years during 1950-1955 and is estimated to have risen to 71.9 years during 1975-1980.[12]

Life expectancy in the developed countries is not only longer than in developing countries, but does not vary much between countries within the group. Among developing countries on the other hand, there is considerable variation, from 62.5 years in Latin America to 48.6 in Africa.[13]

Infant mortality

Lower life expectancy at birth in many developing countries is the result of high infant mortality. The United Nations estimates[14] and projections show a fall in infant mortality from 56 per thousand live births to 19 in the developed countries in the thirty years up to 1980. In the same period in the developing countries the fall was from 164 to 100. The highest infant mortality rates are found in Africa, exceeding 150 per thousand in several countries (Chart 2).

According to a recent United Nations study,[15] average infant mortality in the developing countries is about 100 per thousand live births. That is, each year in these countries about 10 million children die before reaching their first birthday. In Middle South Asia, which includes the Indian subcontinent, over 4 million of approximately 35 million children born annually die before their first birthday.[16] As the previous section shows, declines in infant mortality are considered essential for lower birth rates.

The dramatic improvement in mortality rates in the 1950s was the result of improvements in sanitation and public health. Once epidemic diseases have been controlled, however, further reduction in mortality depends on better health services, living conditions and nutrition. It is also determined by ease of access, social and personal attitudes towards different systems of medicine, levels of education, and economic and social class.

There is overwhelming evidence that easy access to health and medical care is the most important influence on levels of mortality. The main reason for the difference between urban and rural mortality rates is that health facilities in most developing countries are located in urban areas and are therefore more easily accessible to the urban population.

For the world as a whole, the speed of decline in infant mortality slowed down in the 1970s. However, in a number of developing countries with easy access to health care, low medical costs, and high literacy rates, especially among women, infant and general death rates declined substantially.

It is of the greatest importance for health policy to attempt to reduce social inequality. Variation in death rates between social classes is more pronounced in developing countries, but can be seen even in such countries as the United Kingdom and France where particular care has been taken to introduce egalitarian health and medical care.[17]

Aging

An important effect of longer life expectancy is growth in the numbers of older people. According to United Nations estimates, the number of people 60 years of age and over will rise from 200 million in 1953 to over 590 million by the year 2000. In the developing countries this will mean a change from 6 per cent to 7 per cent of the whole population. In developed countries, however, the proportion of older people will rise from 15 per cent in 1975 to 18 per cent by the end of the century. There will be an increasing need for physical, economic and social services for the elderly and important implications for the family as a social institution.

Issues for the Conference

The World Population Plan of Action urged action to reduce infant mortality and attain higher average expectation of life. It recommended that life expectancy should be raised to 62 years by 1985 and 74 years by the year 2000 for the world as a whole. The Plan of Action also recommended that countries with the highest mortality levels should reduce their infant mortality rate to 120 per 1000 live births by 1985. There is little chance of achieving these hopes, United Nations estimates and projections show, if present trends continue.

It will be an important point for discussion why the rate of mortality decline slowed in the 1970s and the implications for fertility, health policies and the spread of the benefits of development.

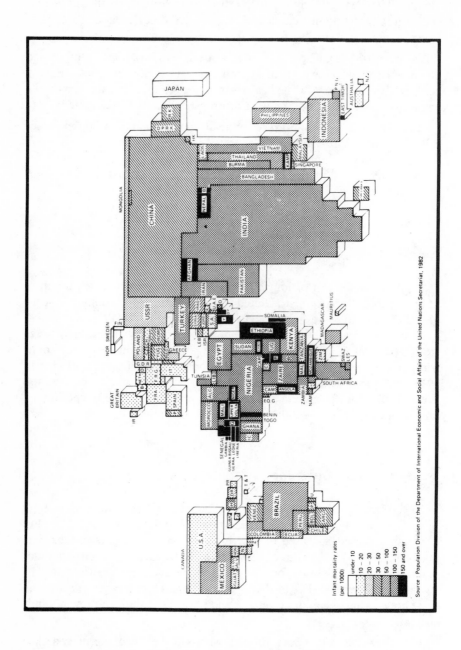

Chart 2. Estimates of Infant Mortality Rates, 1975-1980 (Sizes of countries are proportional to the estimated average annual number of births, 1975-1980.)

Since mortality reductions depend on access to health care, a point-for discussion at the Conference will be how to improve primary health care programmes. The Conference may recommend special measures to reduce inequalities in access to health care and set new targets for infant mortality and life expectancy.

POPULATION DISTRIBUTION AND MIGRATION

The promise of better economic opportunities was and is the driving force behind large-scale movements of population. People move from country-side to town, from poorer countries to richer and from labour-abundant to labour-shortage countries. The scale of migration has increased in recent years, as a result of rapid population growth. There has been an unprecedent-ed redistribution of population within developing countries from the coun-tryside to the towns and an increase in the number of migrants from the developing to the developed countries, and from one developing country to another.

Urbanization

United Nations projections show that world urban population has been growing at nearly 3 per cent per annum — much faster than the current global population growth rate of 1.7 per cent. What is most disturbing about this growth in urbanization is that it will exceed 4 per cent per annum in the de-veloping countries. The United Nations estimates that cities and towns will contain nearly half the total world population by the year 2000.[18]

Concern about urbanization arises not from numbers alone, but because a large segment of the urban population will be concentrated in giant cities of the developing countries. In 1950, Shanghai was the only city in the de-veloping countries with a population of more than 5 million. By the year 2000, there will be perhaps 45 such cities in the developing countries, mostly in Asia.[19]

Migrants to the great cities are often the young or the educated, the very people who are most valuable to the rural areas. More investment is required to support a person in the urban sector than in rural areas. If it is not availa-ble, as in most developing countries, living conditions deteriorate.

As a result, many developing countries are stimulating medium cities, regulating urban growth and creating employment opportunities in the rural areas to stem the tide of migration to the great cities.

International migration

Current international migration takes place from developing to developed countries and is mostly confined to short-stay workers; in many countries which formerly received large numbers of permanent immigrants, such as Canada, Australia and the United States, there are now strict quotas.

In Europe, nearly three-fourths of the 6.6 million foreign workers in 1973 came from outside the European Economic Community. Recently, there has been a virtual halt in recruitment of foreign workers and in many European countries some repatriation of foreign workers has taken place.[20]

The Middle East was another area of large labour migration in the 1970s. Expatriate workers constituted nearly a third of the total work force in the eight major oil-exporting countries of the Middle East.[21]

The consequence of reduced demand for foreign workers in host countries and low earnings and high unemployment in developing countries has been an unprecedented rise in undocumented migration. A recent document of the Intergovernmental Committee for Migration estimates that there are between four and five million undocumented migrants in North America, mainly in the United States. For Latin America, estimates vary from two to three million, in Europe, perhaps a million and a half. In the Middle East there may be between 350,000 and 500,000. Africa and Asia may have between them more than one million undocumented migrants.[22]

Refugees

The movement of refugees across national borders is an unplanned, abrupt and often tragic element of international migration. Since the First World War more than half of all international migration was accounted for by refugee movements. At the beginning of 1981, the number of refugees was estimated at nearly 14 million.[23] Refugee problems are found in all major regions of the Third World; in Africa alone, refugees probably number 6 million.[24]

An influx of refugees can cause serious disruption to the economy of the receiving country. When refugees arrive in large numbers in countries which are already over-burdened with the responsibility of providing the bare necessities of life to their own people, the result can only be aggravation of the problems of hunger and disease. It can create ethnic, religious, political and social problems; the presence of refugees in large numbers can heighten internal tensions and aggravate international conflicts.

International code

International migration involves a substantial proportion of the global work force, but it is being conducted with an almost complete lack of order and regulation.

The Intergovernmental Committee for Migration, which has been functioning for over two decades, is confined to 32 countries, mostly European and North and South American, and exists to provide orderly and planned migration to meet specific needs of its member countries, for refugee resettlement and for the transfer of technology. The International Labour Organisation has drafted international standards for the protection of immigrant workers and their families, but they are concerned only with host country treatment of immigrants.

An international agreement on the movement of commodities has been in existence for a long time in the form of the General Agreement on Tariffs and Trade (GATT); yet there is no international code governing the protection, treatment and security of international workers.

In 1979, the United Nations General Assembly agreed that an international convention was needed and established a working group on the subject open to all Member States. It is to be hoped that a code for ensuring humane treatment of migrants will soon emerge.

Issues for the Conference

The expert group on population distribution, migration and development which met in Hammamet, Tunisia, 21-25 March 1983, has made a number of recommendations for the consideration of the Conference. The first concerns urbanization. Since the process of urbanization is now well established in developing countries, the question before the Conference will be how to promote balanced population distribution while preserving human rights. The Conference may consider the policy recommendations of the Rome Declaration on Population and the Urban Future.[25]

A second important issue for the Conference will be protection of the human rights of international migrants, including settlers, workers, undocumented migrants and refugees, and the principles to be incorporated in a convention. Policy-making on migration is hampered by a lack of data and analysis; the Conference may consider how information on migrants may be collected for research purposes.

POPULATION, RESOURCES, ENVIRONMENT AND DEVELOPMENT

The issues raised by the interrelationships between population, resources, environment and development are complex, but not incomprehensible. Considerable research and experience over the past ten years has deepened knowledge and ability to deal with issues such as environmental pollution, the nature of ecological balance, conservation of natural resources, better management of renewable resources, and the search for alternative long-term energy resources. Though sharp differences of opinion and strong emotions still cloud the discussion, there is almost unanimous agreement that population is central to these relationships, but that population growth cannot be held solely responsible for either the deterioration of the natural environment or for depletion of the world's resources.

Carrying capacity

The primary concern is what is known as "carrying capacity": how many people can ultimately be supported by the global biological and ecological system, and at what level. But discussing global limits is not by itself sufficient for an understanding of conditions in particular countries.

Experience indicates that "carrying capacity" is a dynamic concept whose parameters are constantly changing as discoveries are made, new technologies developed and put into practice, and techniques of resource management improved.

Working on the basis of what is known now, the global projections of the Food and Agriculture Organization of the United Nations (FAO) to the year 2000 indicate that continuing present production trends would result in a slight increase in daily calorie supply per capita in developing countries.[26] Dividing the world into five regions and assuming unrestricted movement of potential surpluses within them, a joint FAO/UNFPA study of potential land supporting capacity found that all regions except southwest Asia could meet the food needs of their populations in the year 2000, assuming intermediate levels of inputs such as pesticides, fertilizers, and improved varieties of crops.[27]

However, when the analysis assumed food movements only within and not between countries, it was found that with low levels of inputs 65 developing countries would have between them in the year 2000 a population of 441 million in excess of their domestic food supply. Of the "excess" population, 55 per cent would be in Africa. Even with high levels of inputs, there would still be an excess of population over food capacity of 47 million in 19 countries. Yet by the year 2000 the population of the world will be only 6.1 billion. It will probably continue to rise for another century until it eventually stabilizes at about 10.2 billion. The long-term implications for food supply can be imagined.

The question of food supply is further complicated by the impact of increasing numbers of people on the environment. For example, as more and more land is brought under cultivation, and demand for fuelwood and timber rises, essential tree cover is removed. The result is erosion, flooding and silting which lead to deterioration of the soil and reduced agricultural productivity.

Imbalances between food and population growth imply continuing widespread malnourishment in developing countries. This in its turn means high mortality and shortened lifespans. The response, as all the evidence shows, is continued high birth rates. Any attempt to bring down birth rates will be defeated if poverty and malnourishment continue to exist on a large scale in developing countries.

Maintaining the balance

It may not be necessary to resort to drastic measures to maintain the balance between population, resources and the environment. Japan and Singapore, for example, have overcome their resource shortages by developing the ability to compete in world markets, thus improving national income and stimulating declines in population growth. Though this option is not open to most developing countries at their present stage of development, China and India provide good examples of planning which has made it possible for food supply to remain ahead of population growth. While there is grave concern for the environment in certain threatened areas, such as the hill region of Nepal, improved environmental management can help restore the balance threatened by human depredations.

Issues for the Conference

The World Population Plan of Action explicitly recognized the relationship between population and development. It also recognized that population is critical to the solution of problems of resources and environment. A large number of questions arise from the interrelationships between population, resources, environment and development, but the Conference will concentrate on those which directly concern population. First, the use of technology in balancing population with resources and environment and in promoting development: available technology determines resource use and employment patterns which are critical to the solutions of some of the existing problems in the developing countries. Improved technology is also an instrument of modernization, a condition favouring fertility declines.

A second issue for discussion at the Conference will be the relationships between population, poverty and environmental degradation. Some studies indicate that poverty, more than population pressure, leads to the deterioration of the environment. The Conference may discuss these relationships, recommend areas for further research and suggest policy measures.

The question of what mix of socio-economic policy will have the greatest impact on population growth will form a third area of discussion at the Conference. Suggestions may be expected on how social measures which help to lower fertility and mortality, such as universal education, easy access to health and improvement in the status of women, may be incorporated in development programmes.

1984 AND BEYOND

The International Conference on Population will provide the first opportunity to review the World Population Plan of Action, evaluate the experience of governments and the United Nations system in the management of population programmes, and suggest how to further the objectives of the Plan. The Plan suggested targets for population growth, mortality and life expectancy, and measures to conserve resources, regulate migration and improve education, nutrition, health and the status of women. Though achievement has often fallen short of the target, it is impressive when set against the problems which have had to be overcome.

During the last thirty years the world has seen the highest rates of population growth in human history, caused by an imbalance between birth and death rates. The imbalance started a chain of effects on living conditions, on movement and distribution of populations, on natural resources and on the environment, which have been of increasing concern to governments and the international community.

The policies and programmes of the various governments, supported by the United Nations system and the community of nations, have gone a long way towards correcting the imbalance. A rapid decline in fertility has begun in countries where nearly two-thirds of the developing world's population reside. A majority of governments now perceive lower fertility as essential for national development.

Governments also see the necessity to lower mortality rates still further, relieve the pressure on the largest cities, conserve resources, develop alternative sources of energy and at the same time preserve the quality of the environment.

All these issues will come before the International Conference on Population next year. At that time the international community will have an opportunity to study progress towards the targets of the World Population Plan of Action and if necessary adopt new ones. The Conference will probably suggest policies on fertility, mortality and life expectancy which governments may adopt and make recommendations about further international support for population programmes.

In the last analysis, all the experience of the last thirty years of unprecedented population growth, all attempts to change its course and mitigate its effects, all the complexities of population can be reduced to the results of decisions taken by individual men and women. It was a cornerstone of the World Population Plan of Action that men and women had the right freely and responsibly to decide the number and spacing of their children and the right to the information and the means to do so. It is a principle which demands respect from the practical and the moral standpoint.

By stating this principle, the Plan of Action did not intend to deny governments a part in the population process. On the contrary, it acknowledges governments' responsibility to provide people with the means to make effective decisions on family size. Government interventions to improve health standards, education, employment opportunities and the status of women can have considerable effects on decisions about family size and migration. It is equally clear that where these responsibilities are neglected or cannot be fulfilled, the result is damaging both to individual lives and to prospects for balanced development.

REFERENCES

1. *World Population Prospects as Assessed in 1980* (United Nations publication, Sales No.E.81.XIII.8), New York, 1981. *Demographic Indicators of Countries: Estimates and Projections as Assessed in 1980* (United Nations publication, Sales No.E.82.XIII.5), New York, 1982.
2. United Nations Secretariat, "Long-range Global Population Projections, as Assessed in 1980", *Population Bulletin of the United Nations*, No.14 — 1982 (United Nations publication, Sales No.E.82.XIII.6), New York, 1983.
3. Noreen Goldman and John Hobcraft, "Birth Histories", *Comparative Studies*, No.17, June 1982 (London: World Fertility Survey). Roushdi A. Henin, Ailsa Korten and Linda H. Warner, "Evaluation of Birth Histories: A Case Study of Kenya", *Scientific Reports*, No.36, October 1982 (London: World Fertility Survey).
4. *Demographic Indicators of Countries. . . .*
5. *World Population Prospects. . . .*
6. *Ibid.*
7. Goldman and Hobcraft, *op. cit.*; Henin, Korten and Warner, *op. cit.*
8. Goldman and Hobcraft, *op. cit.*, p.17.
9. Robert E. Lightbourne and Alphonse L. Macdonald, "Family Size Preferences", *Comparative Studies*, No.14, November 1982 (London: World Fertility Survey).
10. *Ibid.*
11. *World Population Prospects. . . .*
12. *Ibid.*
13. *Ibid.*
14. United Nations Secretariat, "Infant Mortality: World Estimates and Projections, 1950-2025", *Population Bulletin of the United Nations*, No.14 — 1982 (United Nations publication, Sales No.E.82.XIII.6), New York, 1983.
15. *Ibid.*
16. *Ibid.*
17. Jacques Vallin, "Socio-economic Determinants of Mortality in Industrialized Countries", *Population Bulletin of the United Nations*, No.13 — 1980 (United Nations publication, Sales No.E.81.XIII.4), New York, 1981.
18. *Patterns of Urban and Rural Population Growth* (United Nations publication, Sales No.E.79.XIII.9), New York, 1980.
19. *Ibid.*
20. *International Migration Policies and Programmes: A World Survey* (United Nations publication, Sales No.E.82.XIII.4), New York, 1982, p.20.

21. *Ibid.*

22. Intergovernmental Committee for Migration, "Worldwide Situation and Problems of Undocumented Migration, and the Role of Planned Migration of Qualified Personnel from Developed to Developing Countries" (IESA/P/ICP.1984/EG.II/14), paper presented to the Expert Group Meeting on Population Distribution, Migration and Development, Hammamet, Tunisia, 21-25 March 1983.

23. *International Migration Policies* . . . , p.84.

24. *Ibid.*

25. Philip M Hauser, Robert W. Gardner, Aprodicio A. Laquian and Salah El-Shakhs, *Population and the Urban Future* (Albany: State University of New York Press, 1982).

26. Food and Agriculture Organization of the United Nations, *Agriculture: Toward 2000*, Rome, 1981.

27. G.M. Higgins, A.H. Kassam, L. Naiken, M. Shah and R. Calderoni, "Can the Land Support the Population?", *Populi, Journal of the United Nations Fund for Population Activities*, vol.9, No.3, 1982, pp.24-30.

The State of
World Population 1984

POPULATION AND THE QUALITY OF LIFE

The World Population Plan of Action states that "the principal aim of social, economic and cultural development, of which population goals and policies are integral parts, is to improve levels of living and the quality of life of the people".[1] This will be an important concern at the International Conference on Population to be held in Mexico City in August 1984.

From 1980 to 1982 the economies of the developing countries grew at 1.9 per cent annually while population grew at 2.02 per cent.[2] In the poorest nations, per capita income rose only about one per cent a year between 1960 and 1981.[3] The reduction in international aid during the economic recession, slackening demand and falling prices for their exports, the high cost of borrowing and the debt repayment crisis have all contributed to slower economic growth; but even a high growth rate of 5 to 6 per cent between 1975 and 2000 would still leave over 600 million persons below the poverty line in the developing countries in the year 2000.[4]

The combination of rapid population growth, slowly growing income and inadequate technology lead to over-exploitation of land resources for food and fuel. The result is a deteriorating human and natural environment.

These are compelling reasons for a re-examination of the relationship between population and quality of life. It is necessary now to identify factors which will contribute to improvement of the quality of life despite probable low growth in income. The international community will then be able to re-direct development policies and programmes and select specific targets for population, both to improve the quality of life and alleviate poverty.

Demographic factors in the quality of life

In traditional economics, income or output per capita is taken as an indicator of the quality of life. In 1981, the per capita income of the richest country was nearly 220 times the per capita income of the poorest country.[5] Such low levels of income will barely provide the minimum needs of life. Under present growth trends, international disparities will almost certainly widen. At present growth rates, it will take 70 to 90 years for the poorest countries to double their per capita income; even this will only slightly improve their standards of living. Meanwhile, their populations will double in thirty-five years or even less.

The long-run objective of development will continue to be the growth of per capita income in the developing countries, as the only means to improve living conditions and reduce international disparities in income and wealth. In the meantime, immediate and short-term measures are necessary to improve the quality of life independent of a rise in per capita income.

It is difficult to describe what constitutes the quality of life. The ability to acquire material goods is an important component, but it should also include cultural, social and intellectual elements. As early as 1954, a United Nations Committee of Experts said that "there is no single index of the level of living as a whole that can be applied internationally. . . . The problem of levels of living must be approached in a pluralistic manner by analysis of various components."[6] It is now recognized that demographic factors are important because people are both the means and the object of improvement in the quality of life.

The demographic variables associated with a better quality of life are: (1) longer life expectancy, (2) lower mortality rates for all age groups of the population, (3) lower morbidity rates and (4) lower fertility rates. At the International Conference on Population, considerable attention can be expected, firstly to current positions and trends of these indicators, and secondly to measures which might modify them in order to improve the quality of life for the people of the developing countries.

The World Population Plan of Action recommended the integration of demographic and economic variables in development planning. Though it is widely recognized that demographic variables underlie the broader economic analysis, they are not normally treated as part and parcel of the economic system. The result is that even when demographic targets are laid down they are often not met, because demographic policies and programmes are not integrated with general development programmes. This is probably the result of failure to appreciate the significance of demographic targets in improving social and economic welfare. The integration of population with development will therefore be a central issue of the 1980s; the extent of its success will determine what happens to population trends and quality of life.

Before examining policies and programmes to improve demographic conditions, it is necessary to examine their current status in the developing countries by comparison with the developed countries.

Life expectancy

Children born in a developed country in 1950 had a life expectancy on average of 65 years. For a child born today it is 73.[7] In contrast, life expectancy in a developing country in 1950 was only 41 years; this has now risen to an average of 56.6,[8] an improvement of 40 per cent. While this is a remarkable achievement, United Nations projections indicate that average life expectancy will rise only to 61.8 years for the developing countries as a group by the year 2000.[9] The World Population Plan of Action of 1974 recommended the attainment of an average expectation of life of 62 years by 1985 and 74 years by the year 2000 for the world as a whole.[10] (See Table 1.)

Table 1. Estimated and projected life expectancy at birth, major regions

Region	1950-55	1980-85	1995-2000
World	45.8	58.9	63.5
Developed countries	65.1	73.0	75.4
Developing countries	41.0	56.6	61.8
Africa	37.5	49.7	55.7
Eastern Africa	36.6	48.8	55.0
Middle Africa	35.9	47.5	53.6
Northern Africa	41.2	55.9	63.0
Southern Africa	41.1	53.0	59.0
Western Africa	35.2	46.8	53.0
Latin America	51.0	64.1	68.3
Caribbean	51.9	64.0	67.1
Central America	49.3	65.0	69.5
Temperate South America	60.3	69.0	71.6
Tropical South America	49.9	62.9	67.4
Northern America	69.0	74.1	76.2
Asia	41.2	57.9	63.7
East Asia	42.5	68.0	71.4
South Asia	40.1	53.6	59.8
Western Asia	45.0	60.6	66.9
Europe	65.3	73.2	75.4
Eastern Europe	63.1	71.7	74.4
Oceania	61.0	67.6	71.6

Source: See reference 7.

Failure to reach the 1985 target for life expectancy is mainly attributable to conditions in Africa and South Asia. In both these regions, life expectancies have risen almost by one-third between 1950 and 1985, but because of their extremely low levels in the early 1950s, they are still considerably below the recommended levels. Life expectancy in Africa was 37.5 years in 1950-1955; it has risen only to 49.7 years for 1980-1985.[11] United Nations projections based on present trends and anticipated changes indicate that it will still be only about 56 years by the year 2000.[12]

In the African region, only Northern Africa shows improvement in levels of life expectancy. Average life expectancy has reached 56 years during 1980-1985 and it is expected to rise to 63 by the year 2000.[13] Countries of Western and Middle Africa have the lowest life expectancies; they are expected to reach only 53 years even by the year 2000.[14]

Life expectancy is low in South Asia, which includes the Indian sub-continent and the adjacent countries. The countries of this region contain about one-third of the total population of the developing countries.

Most progress has been achieved in life expectancy in Latin America and East Asia where it already exceeds 62 years. In East Asia, China has made impressive gains in average length of life, where it is estimated at 67.4 years for the period 1980-1985.[15]

Mortality rates

Closely related and determining life expectancy is the pattern of mortality. There are marked differences in mortality patterns between the developed and developing countries. In the former, there is a sharp drop in death rate from the first year, while in the developing countries high death rates persist throughout early childhood.

The crude death rate for the world as a whole declined from an annual average of 19.7 per 1000 population during 1950-1955 to 10.6 per 1000 during 1980-1985 and is projected to fall to 9.1 per 1000 by 1995-2000.[16] For the developing countries, the average annual crude death rate declined from 24.4 per 1000 during 1950-1955 to 11.0 per 1000 in 1980-1985 and is projected to decline to 9 per 1000 by 1995-2000.[17] The death rate in the developed countries has remained stable between 9 and 10 per 1000 for a number of years. Differences in rates between countries in this group are negligible.[18] For developing countries, on the other hand, there are wide variations between regions, and between countries within a region, which the average figures do not show.

The close relationship between life expectancy and mortality rates suggests that the differences in regional levels of mortality would be similar to differences in life expectancy. Africa (excluding Northern Africa) and South Asia exhibited the highest mortality levels in 1950, and in spite of substantial declines, their mortality rates are still higher than in other regions of the developing world. In a number of African countries, average annual death rates ranged between 30 and 35 per 1000 population during 1950-1955 and are estimated at between 20 and 25 per 1000 during 1980-1985.[19] The little evidence available indicates that overall mortality has been declining among developing countries, though at varying rates. The high mortality countries have experienced the slowest rates of mortality decline; thus the gap between high-mortality and low-mortality countries persists.

Principal among the varied components of high mortality in the developing countries is high infant mortality. In fact, infant mortality is considered an important indicator of demographic welfare, since it reflects best the prevailing economic and social conditions of a country. Infant mortality rates are very high in African countries and especially in tropical regions of sub-

Saharan Africa, the most recent estimates exceeding 200 per 1000 live births. That is to say that more than one out of five babies die before their first birthday.[20] Infant mortality rates are also high in South Asia, particularly in the countries of the sub-continent (excluding Sri Lanka) and are declining much more slowly than elsewhere in Asia. Countries of Temperate South America and East Asia have the lowest infant mortality rates among developing countries, below 50 per 1000 live births in 1980.[21]

Mortality rates also vary considerably between the sexes, social and ethnic groups, and across occupational categories. For instance, the World Health Organization estimated that some 50,000 maternal deaths occurred in Africa, 20 per cent of the world total.[22] In the developing countries, there are also marked differences between urban and rural mortality rates. All these differences are closely linked to social and economic policy and have important implications for improving the quality of life of the population.

Morbidity patterns and causes of death

Morbidity patterns and causes of death in developing countries provide important information on the health of their populations and on the nature of health care systems. They also provide insights into the state of nutrition, sanitary and living conditions and the extent of preventive public health measures. An analysis of the causes of death indicates the contributions of different factors to overall mortality and helps in designing health interventions to reduce it.

Paucity of data in the developing countries prevents such a detailed analysis. The limited information available for a few of the developing countries whose mortality rates are most similar to the mortality rates of developed countries indicate that their patterns of morbidity and causes of death have also become similar. But these are hardly typical of general conditions in developing countries. Using all the information available, the World Health Organization has estimated the distribution of causes of death around 1980 for the developed and developing countries separately[23] (see Figure 1).

These estimates show marked differences between the developed and developing countries. Circulatory diseases (A80-88) and neoplasms (A45-61) account for 48 per cent and 19 per cent respectively of the deaths in developed countries, but for only 16 per cent and 6 per cent respectively among the developing countries. On the other hand, in developing countries influenza, pneumonia and bronchitis (A90-93) account for twice the total percentage of deaths from all respiratory diseases in developed countries. Besides, diseases of infancy, diarrhoeal diseases and other infectious and parasitic diseases account for a quarter of all deaths in developing countries.

There are again marked differences in morbidity patterns between the regions of the developing world, the pattern and the underlying factors in

a) DEVELOPED COUNTRIES

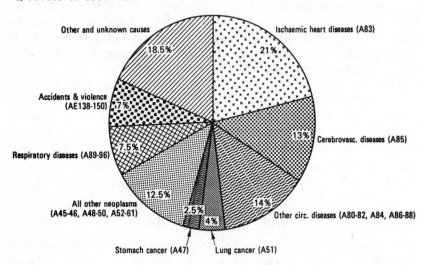

Other and unknown causes

18.5%

Ischaemic heart diseases (A83)

21%

Accidents & violence
(AE138-150) 7%

Respiratory diseases (A89-96) 7.5%

13% Cerebrovasc. diseases (A85)

All other neoplasms
(A45-46, A48-50, A52-61)

12.5%

2.5%

4%

14% Other circ. diseases (A80-82, A84, A86-88)

Stomach cancer (A47)   Lung cancer (A51)

b) LESS DEVELOPED COUNTRIES

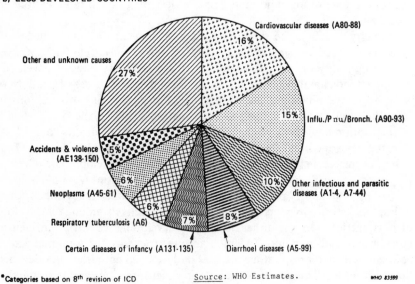

Cardiovascular diseases (A80-88)

16%

Other and unknown causes

27%

15% Influ./Pnu./Bronch. (A90-93)

Accidents & violence
(AE138-150) 5%

6%

10% Other infectious and parasitic
diseases (A1-4, A7-44)

Neoplasms (A45-61)

6%

7%

8%

Respiratory tuberculosis (A6)

Certain diseases of infancy (A131-135)   Diarrhoel diseases (A5-99)

*Categories based on 8th revision of ICD   Source: WHO Estimates.   WHO 83599

Figure 1. Estimated distribution of causes of death around 1980, developed countries and less developed countries

Africa, for example, being quite different from those of Latin America. However, lack of information prevents detailed analysis of the differences.

The pattern of morbidity and causes of mortality in Zambia illustrate the nature of some of the special problems confronting Africa.[24] Even the Zambian situation may not be fully representative of conditions prevailing in the countries of Western and Central Africa. Zambia, one of the group of middle income economies, has achieved a life expectancy of about 50 years and has brought down the death rate from 26 per 1000 population in the early 1950s to about 15 per 1000 at present.[25] Table 2 provides some data on the causes of mortality and morbidity during 1979. Measles, malnutrition and anaemias, pneumonia, malaria and diarrhoea were among the leading causes of mortality among patients admitted to health centres. They accounted for over 70 per cent of the deaths and over 40 per cent of the in-patients in hospitals.

Table 2. Principal causes of mortality and morbidity in Zambia,
as recorded by the health centres, 1979

Diagnosis	Mortality (percentage of total deaths)	In-patients (percentage of total admissions)
Measles	19.9	6.9
Malnutrition and anaemias	15.5	4.4
Pneumonia	14.1	5.4
Malaria	11.3	19.5
Diarrhoea	9.9	7.7
Upper respiratory tract infections	2.4	6.3
Other abdominal cases	2.1	4.8
Injuries	1.1	5.4
Other pulmonary cases	0.8	1.8
Jaundice	0.8	0.3
Total	77.9	62.5

Source: Ministry of Health, Planning Unit, *Health by the People: Implementing Primary Health Care in Zambia* (Lusaka: January, 1981).

Fertility

Fertility rates influence the quality of life in a number of ways. The rate of population growth is determined by fertility rates in combination with mortality rates. Reduction of mortality is an important contributing factor to an improvement in the quality of life, but if it is not accompanied by reductions in fertility rates, its effects will be neutralized by population growth. Secondly, high fertility rates affect the status of women, their participation in the labour force, the conditions of maternal and child health and even the opportunities for children's schooling. Studies indicate that a reduction in fertility is also conducive to lower pre-natal and post-natal mortality rates. Smaller family size not only raises per capita income and consumption level of the family, but also creates the pre-conditions for the younger generation to rise in the world.

United Nations estimates and projections indicate a global decline of 22 per cent in the average number of children born to a woman over the period 1970-1975 to 1980-1985, from 4.5 to 3.6. During the same period, the decline in the developing countries was 26 per cent, from 5.5 to 4.1 children.[26] Much of this decline arises from a drastic reduction of fertility in China, amounting to 54 per cent, but 26 other developing countries with a combined population of more than 1 billion also experienced fertility declines in excess of 20 per cent.[27] However, fertility has not declined in Africa as a whole and has in fact risen in some countries. (See Table 3.)

The average number of children born to a woman in Africa during the period 1970-1975 to 1980-1985 is estimated to have declined by only 0.9 per cent, from 6.49 children to 6.43 children, and this is solely due to the decline observed in Northern and Southern Africa.[28] In all other parts of Africa, fertility rates have risen.

In Latin America, the countries of Central America and the Caribbean have experienced the largest decline, over 25 per cent, during the same period. Apart from China, other East Asian countries show fertility declines of about one-third. South Asia, which includes India and other countries of the sub-continent, indicate fertility declines of 18 per cent.

The differences in the rates of fertility decline have important implications for global and regional trends in population growth. During the thirty-year period 1950-1955 to 1980-1985, the global birth rate declined by 28 per cent and the global death rate by 46 per cent. During the same period, the declines in developing countries were 31 per cent and 55 per cent respectively. In the developing countries during the period 1970-1975 to 1980-1985, birth rates declined by 16.5 per cent and death rates by 21 per cent. These figures suggest that there has been a deceleration in the rate of decline of mortality while birth rates are declining more quickly than before.

Integration of population with development

World population is estimated at 4.76 billion in 1984, 770 million more than the population of 1974.[29] By the year 2000, total global population is projected to reach 6.13 billion.[30] These projections assume a declining rate of population growth, falling from an annual rate of increase of 1.72 per cent in 1980 to 1.46 per cent in the year 2000.[31]

However, the global growth rate conceals wide diversity between rates for developed and developing countries. In the former, growth is projected to decline from an annual rate of 0.69 per cent in 1980 to 0.49 per cent in the

Table 3. United Nations estimates and projections of crude birth rate and total fertility rate for major regions and sub-regions (1970-75, 1975-80, 1980-85), medium variant

Major regions and subregions	Crude birth rate				Total fertility rate			
	1970-75	1975-80	1980-85	per cent change	1970-75	1975-80	1980-85	per cent change
World	32.7	28.9	27.3	-16.5	4.53	3.90	3.55	-21.6
More Developed Countries a/	17.0	15.8	15.5	- 8.8	2.17	2.02	1.98	- 8.8
Less Developed Countries b/	38.7	33.5	31.2	-19.4	5.53	4.63	4.09	-26.0
Africa	47.0	46.9	46.4	- 1.3	6.49	6.46	6.43	- 0.9
Eastern Africa	49.5	49.4	49.1	- 0.8	6.75	6.80	6.79	0.6
Middle Africa	45.6	45.3	44.9	- 1.5	6.00	6.01	6.03	0.5
Northern Africa	43.3	43.8	41.9	- 3.2	6.29	6.16	6.01	- 4.4
Southern Africa	40.3	39.1	39.6	- 1.7	5.43	5.20	5.21	- 4.0
Western Africa	49.7	49.4	49.3	- 0.8	6.84	6.85	6.86	0.3
Americas								
Latin America	35.4	33.3	31.8	-10.2	5.02	4.51	4.12	-17.9
Caribbean	32.3	27.4	27.1	-16.1	4.54	3.64	3.36	-26.0
Central America	42.7	38.4	35.1	-17.8	6.33	5.47	4.76	-24.8
Temperate South America	23.9	24.7	24.3	1.7	3.18	3.26	3.21	0.9
Tropical South America	35.2	33.7	32.4	- 8.0	4.98	4.51	4.13	-17.1
Northern America								
Northern America	16.5	16.3	16.0	- 3.0	1.95	1.90	1.85	- 5.1
Asia								
East Asia	32.4	21.6	18.2	-43.8	4.66	2.96	2.30	-50.6
China	34.1	22.0	18.5	-45.8	5.09	3.07	2.33	-54.2
Japan	19.2	15.1	12.4	-35.4	2.08	1.82	1.71	-17.8
Other East Asia	30.3	27.1	23.8	-21.4	4.29	3.62	2.91	-32.2
South Asia	40.6	37.7	34.9	-14.0	5.74	5.22	4.65	-19.0
Southeastern Asia	38.8	35.7	31.7	-18.3	5.37	4.84	4.11	-23.5
Southern Asia	41.3	38.3	35.8	-13.3	5.87	5.32	4.78	-18.6
Western Asia	40.7	39.6	37.8	- 7.1	5.94	5.73	5.46	- 8.1
Europe	16.1	14.4	14.0	-13.0	2.16	1.95	1.90	-12.0
Eastern Europe	16.6	17.5	16.4	- 1.2	2.20	2.22	2.17	- 1.4
Northern Europe	15.9	12.5	12.8	-19.5	2.05	1.76	1.78	-13.2
Southern Europe	17.7	16.1	15.4	-13.0	2.47	2.22	2.12	-14.2
Western Europe	14.6	11.8	11.7	-19.9	1.89	1.61	1.58	-16.4
Oceania	24.8	21.9	21.1	-14.9	3.15	2.82	2.71	-14.0
Union of Soviet Socialist Republics								
USSR	17.8	18.3	18.8	5.6	2.42	2.37	2.36	- 2.5

a/ More Developed Countries include Europe, Northern America, Australia, Japan, New Zealand and USSR.

b/ Developing Countries include Africa, Asia, Latin America, and Oceania excluding Australia, Japan and New Zealand.

year 2000, while in the developing countries, the decline would be from 2.08 per cent to 1.71 per cent.[32] By the year 2000, four-fifths of world population will be living in developing countries.

United Nations estimates for economic growth show that total output grew at an annual average rate of 6.0 per cent during 1960-1970 and at 5.2 per cent during 1970-1980 for the developing market countries, compared to 4.9

per cent and 3.1 per cent respectively for the developed market economies.[33] But because of rapid population growth, per capita incomes in the developing countries grew more slowly than in the developed countries, at around 2.6 per cent per annum, widening the international disparity in income and wealth.[34] The relative income gap, expressed as a ratio of the per capita output of the developed market economies to that of developing market economies remains almost the same, 11.5:1 in 1960 and 11.8:1 in 1980; but if only the petroleum importing low-income countries are considered, the ratio rises from 27.3:1 in 1960 to 40.6:1 in 1980. For the least developed countries, this ratio has risen from 25.1:1 to 41.2:1 during the same period.[35] Even using the most optimistic projections of output for the developing countries, a United Nations Industrial Development Organization (UNIDO) study indicates that the gap in per capita income levels between the developing and developed countries would close only slightly.[36]

The UNIDO study assumed a gross domestic product growth rate of 7.4 per cent per annum during 1980-1990 (higher than the 7.0 per cent assumed in the Third International Development Decade Strategy), 8.2 per cent during 1990-2000 and thereafter 6.0 per cent till the year 2025.[37] The output growth rate assumed for the industrialized countries during the same period lies between 3.7 and 4.0 per cent per annum. The UNIDO study summarizes its finding thus:[38]

"Overall it can be seen that the developing countries, which in 1980 had a GDP per capita of just over 10 per cent of that of the developed countries, will have in the year 2025 a figure that is still less than 19 per cent of that of the developed countries. *Thus the high growth rates of GDP, which are in this scenario, barely compensate for population growth.* Indeed, if the individual developing regions are examined, it can be seen that the relative position of Africa cannot be expected to improve, and the figure for Asia in 2025 is barely higher than that for Africa. Only Latin America and the Middle East make substantial progress, but even by the year 2025, they will have GDP per capita figures that are just over one-half and one-third respectively that of the developed countries."

Given the past performance of the developing countries and the current global situation it is unlikely that the growth rates in the UNIDO model could ever be realized. On the other hand, projections made by the United Nations on the assumption that the recent trends would continue, indicate that annual growth rates of production between 1980 and 2000 would average only 4.8 per cent for the developing market economies and 2.6 per cent for the developed market economies.[39] These projected growth rates carry serious implications for the quality of life and the nature of development in many developing countries.

Africa and South Asia have the lowest life expectancies, highest mortality rates and some of the highest birth rates. These two regions between them will account for about 47 per cent of the total population of developing countries in the year 2000. During the period 1974-1984, population growth in Africa has averaged 3.0 per cent per annum while total output has grown at a rate of less than 1.5 per cent per annum, resulting in a decline in per capita income. The annual population growth rate for Africa will exceed 3 per cent for the rest of this century, and if the economies of the developing countries as a group could grow at only 4.8 per cent per annum, the prospects of raising per capita income in Africa and other least developed countries appear rather bleak.

It is in this context that population policy assumes the greatest significance. Is it possible to implement policies and programmes which can lengthen life expectancy, reduce mortality rates and lower fertility rates? If these policies are integrated with development programmes, will they not at least achieve an improvement in the demographic components of the quality of life?

A number of low-income and lower middle income countries such as China, Colombia, Costa Rica, Cuba, Jamaica, the Philippines, Sri Lanka and Thailand have achieved life expectancies exceeding 60 years, low infant and general mortality rates and substantial reductions in birth rates. A number of common elements can be discerned in the policies and programmes of all these countries. The most important appear to be related to (1) health, (2) family planning and (3) education.

Thailand is typical of this group of countries, where integration of population policy with development programmes has produced impressive gains in the demographic factors of quality of life. The annual average life expectancy rose from 47 years during 1950-1955 to 62.7 years during 1980-1985 and is projected to reach 66.8 years by 1995-2000.[40] During the same period, infant mortality and crude death rate declined from 132 per 1000 live births and 19.2 per 1000 population to 51 per 1000 live births and 7.7 per 1000 population.[41] In the same time span, the birth rate declined by nearly 40 per cent, from 46.6 to 28.6 per 1000.[42]

Thailand achieved these results by extending health care, family planning and education to rural areas and making them easily accessible to the majority of the population.

Health. There are nearly 2000 midwifery centres and over 4000 village health centres staffed with 220,000 village health communicators, besides traditional *tambon* (village) doctors and birth attendants.[43] These achievements have been made without any substantial increase in central government health expenditures, the per capita annual expenditure on health being only US$4.0 at 1975 prices. Many developing countries have spent more with less result.[44] In many of them health personnel and health expenditures are concentrated in urban areas where only 10 to 20 per cent of the population live, while health care is not available to rural populations.

Family planning. The decline in birth rate in Thailand is closely related to the spread of contraception. Among currently married women aged 15-49 years, 56 per cent were using contraception according to the 1981 Contraceptive Prevalence Survey.[45] In 1969-1970, before the government family planning programme began, a survey found that only 15 per cent of currently married women were practising contraception. The birth rate at that time was over 40 per 1000 population.[46] The Government of Thailand's goal is to reduce the population growth rate to 1.0 per cent by 1991.[47]

Education. Though health and family planning programmes directly influence mortality and fertility rates, the indirect effect of education on these programmes should not be overlooked. In fact, it is a moot question whether these programmes can succeed without a high level of literacy among the population. Various studies have shown that infant and child mortality rates and birth rates are inversely related to the level of education of the mother. In Thailand, 96 per cent of the relevant age group were enrolled in primary school in 1980 compared to 83 per cent in 1960; 86 per cent of the total population were literate compared to 68 per cent in 1960.[48] Such levels of enrollment were made possible by locating schools near all population concentrations. As with health, they were achieved in Thailand with only moderate expenditure.

Reduction of mortality and fertility rates in the other countries mentioned earlier were brought about by similar policies and programmes. The incorporation of health, family planning and education policies into overall economic and social policies and programmes will go a long way towards reducing mortality and fertility rates and prolonging life.

Because patterns of morbidity and causes of death vary considerably between regions and countries, in working out detailed programmes it is necessary to consider local conditions.

For example, a high proportion of deaths in Africa occur from nutrition-related diseases. Without an improvement in food consumption, it will not be possible to eliminate nutrition-related mortality and morbidity in this region. The per capita food output in Africa has been declining during the past decade; given the high rate of population growth (over 3 per cent) only a substantial rise in food output can reverse the trend. It will call for heavy investment in agriculture and irrigation, and for changes in technology and cropping patterns.

On the other hand, deaths from malaria, infectious and parasitic diseases could be eliminated with appropriate public health and sanitation programmes. It is estimated that at least one million children die of malaria each year in tropical Africa.[49] An insecticide spraying project in Kenya carried out during 1972-1976 in an area of 17,000 inhabitants helped reduce the crude death rate from 23.9 per 1000 to 13.5 per 1000. The infant mortality rate was reduced from 157 per 1000 live births to 93 per 1000.[50] In a nearby area where no spraying was undertaken, death rates remained the same. Such experiments clearly show how death rates can be significantly reduced even by simple measures.

Population, resources and environment

The Report of the Preparatory Committee for the International Conference on Population states that "to achieve the goals of development, the formulation of national population goals and policies must take into account the need to contribute to an economic development which is environmentally sustainable over the long-run and which protects the ecological balance".[51]

An increase in life expectancy and improvement in the general health of the population cannot be sustained for long without an improvement in standards of living. It is the struggle to survive even in abject poverty that has made the ecological balance a razor's edge. Three factors, nutrition, energy and shelter — essential ingredients of the quality of life — have significant environmental impacts. Since natural resources are part of the environment, the rate and manner of their utilization will determine how the ecological balance is maintained. All indications are that this will be a crucial issue if investment and technology are not provided to the developing countries to meet their food, fuel and housing needs.

An adequate calorie intake is an important component of the quality of life. While growth of total food output exceeded total population growth during 1960-1980 in the developing countries, there were many countries where it did not. This was particularly so in Africa where population growth rate was at least twice the growth rate of food output. FAO estimates that cereal self-sufficiency in the developing countries (excluding China) would decline from 92 per cent for 1975-1979 to 83 per cent in 2000; to meet this shortage, cereal imports would have to rise from approximately 100 million tons in 1981 to nearly a quarter billion tons in the year 2000.[52] If imports on this scale fail to materialize, the number of undernourished persons is projected to increase from an average 435 million during 1974-1975 to nearly 700 million in the year 2000.[53]

The food-population imbalance largely arises from low agricultural productivity in the developing countries. In the past, growth of food output kept pace with or exceeded population growth mainly because of an expansion in the area under cultivation. Between 1860 and 1920, arable land area increased at the rate of 0.77 hectares per additional person. Between 1920 and 1978, this figure declined to 0.17 hectares per additional person.[54] Though there are large areas of unused land in Africa, much is unsuitable for farming or grazing because of climatic, soil and other ecological factors. Extension of cultivation to such areas often results in an increase in desertification and a decrease in soil nutrients.

Another factor tilting the ecological balance is the failing supply of energy in the developing countries. In many developing countries, rural populations depend on local wood for their energy needs and as supplies shrink, its collection has become more and more time-consuming. This is now considered an important factor in deforestation in the developing countries with drastic consequences for the future.

Finally, the inadequacy of housing, and the lack of basic amenities such as drinking water and sanitation not only affect the quality of life but also the rates of morbidity and mortality. An improvement in quality of life requires not only population policies, but also programmes to improve nutritional intake, new and renewable sources of energy and better living conditions.

FACING THE FUTURE

In about seventeen years' time, over six billion people will enter a new century. The quality of life for them and their successors will be determined by the policies, actions and programmes begun during the rest of this decade. The guidelines adopted and decisions taken at the International Conference on Population will shape the nature and the extent of commitment to population programmes.

Population policy can succeed only if it is conceived as part of social policy. Individuals and couples will accept population programmes if they perceive the benefits to them and to their families. Nations will pursue population programmes if they are seen to lead to desired social goals and their absence to irrecoverable economic costs.

The United Nations projections indicate that if population growth continues under the assumptions made for the "medium variant", world population will be 8177 million in the year 2025.[55] On the other hand, if fertility were to follow the assumptions for the "low variant", total world population in the year 2025 would be only 7278 million, lower by 900 million.[56] The low variant assumes that the annual rate of population growth could be reduced from 1.77 per cent in 1980 to 1.29 per cent by the year 2000 instead of 1.52 per cent as the medium variant assumes.[57] This is not an insurmountable task; by doing so, the total global population in the year 2025 will be less by a number almost equal to the population of China in 1980.

It is important that the International Conference on Population recognize and identify those demographic factors which are crucial for an improvement in the quality of life. Since life expectancy and mortality rates are important indicators of the quality of life, goals and targets should be specified for each region taking into account regional conditions and the capabilities of countries within each region.

The Preparatory Committee recommended the achievement of a life expectancy of at least 60 years and an infant mortality rate of less than 70 per 1000 live births by the year 2000 for countries with higher mortality levels.[58]

The Committee also recommends the reduction of maternal mortality by at least 50 per cent in those countries where it exceeds 100 maternal deaths per 100,000 births.[59] Population growth rate and family planning targets are equally necessary to fulfil the goal of low variant population level by the year 2025. Government commitment, with people's participation, can make this an attainable goal.

REFERENCES

1. *Report of the United Nations World Population Conference, 1974, Bucharest, 19-30 August 1974 (United Nations publication, Sales No.E.75.XIII.3), part one, Chap. 1, para. 14(a).*
2. World Bank, *World Development Report 1983* (New York: Oxford University Press, 1983), p.7, Table 2.1.
3. *Ibid.*, p.148, Table 1.
4. *Ibid.*, p.39.
5. *Ibid.*, p.148, Table 1.
6. United Nations, "Report on International Definition and Measurement of Standards and Levels of Living", New York, 1954.
7. United Nations, "Demographic Indicators by Countries as Assessed in 1982" (computer printout), 19 December 1983.
8. *Ibid.*
9. *Ibid.*
10. *Report of the United Nations World Population Conference . . . ,* para. 22.
11. United Nations, "Demographic Indicators by Countries . . . ".
12. *Ibid.*
13. *Ibid.*
14. *Ibid.*
15. *Ibid.*
16. *Ibid.*
17. *Ibid.*
18. *Ibid.*
19. *Ibid.*
20. United Nations, "World Population Trends and Policies, 1983 Monitoring Report" (Population Division Working Paper, IESA/P/WP.82 and Add.1), New York, 9 December 1983, p.234.
21. *Ibid.*, pp.235-241.
22. *Ibid.*, p.276.
23. *Ibid.*, pp.272-290.
24. United Nations Fund for Population Activities, "Zambia, Report of Mission on Needs Assessment for Population Assistance" (Report Number 63), New York, November 1983, pp.27-34.
25. United Nations, "Demographic Indicators by Countries . . . ".
26. United Nations, "World Population Trends and Policies . . . ", p.62.
27. *Ibid.*
28. *Ibid.*
29. United Nations, Economic and Social Council, "Report of the Preparatory Committee for the International Conference on Population, 1984" (E/1984/28/Add.l), 28 March 1984, para. 3(a).

30. United Nations, "Demographic Indicators by Countries . . . ".
31. *Ibid.*
32. *Ibid.*
33. United Nations, General Assembly, "Over-all socio-economic perspective of the world economy to the year 2000 (preliminary draft), Report of the Secretary-General" (A/37/211), May 1982, Annex p.46.
34. *Ibid.*
35. United Nations, "World Population Trends and Policies . . . ", p.522.
36. *Ibid.*, p.473.
37. *Ibid.*, p.471.
38. *Ibid.*
39. United Nations, General Assembly, "Over-all socio-economic perspective . . . ".
40. United Nations, "Demographic Indicators by Countries . . . ".
41. *Ibid.*
42. *Ibid.*
43. United Nations Fund for Population Activities, "Thailand, Report of Second Mission on Needs Assessment for Population Assistance" (Report Number 55), New York, May 1983, pp.33-35.
44. World Bank, *World Development Report 1983* . . . , Table 26.
45. United Nations Fund for Population Activities, "Thailand, . . . ", p.36.
46. *Ibid.*, p.36, footnote 29.
47. *Ibid.*, p.35.
48. World Bank, *World Development Report 1983* . . . , p.196.
49. United Nations, "World Population Trends and Policies . . . ", p.276.
50. *Ibid.*
51. United Nations, Economic and Social Council, "Report of the Preparatory Committee . . . ", para.8.
52. United Nations, "World Population Trends and Policies . . . ", p.423.
53. *Ibid.*
54. *Ibid.*, p.426.
55. United Nations, "Demographic Indicators by Countries . . . ".
56. *Ibid.*
57. *Ibid.*
58. United Nations, Economic and Social Council, "Report of the Preparatory Committee . . . ", recommendation 9.
59. *Ibid.*, recommendation 10.

SELECTED
STATEMENTS

Editors' note: Because of their focus on the particular population situations of various major regions of the world or other matters not addressed at length in the main body of the present volume, a few selected statements of the Executive Director are here reprinted. Demographic and other figures, which were based on the most current estimates and projections available at the time each statement was given, have been retained as originally presented.

THE WORLD POPULATION CRISIS

Statement to the National Press Club, Washington, D.C., 15 January 1980.

The word "population" invariably brings to one's mind varied images, problems and solutions. Most of us nurture, without even realizing it, our own preconceived notions about the nature and extent of population problems, and our own ideas about how to solve them. However, on closer examination, one often finds that most of these ideas are based on a lack of understanding of the real situation. Some of these have gained wide popular acceptance and have assumed the status of population myths, so much so that many people accept these as if they were universal truths.

The first myth is the belief that over-population is the major cause of poverty. A corollary of this is that control of population will lead to the eradication of poverty. This kind of reasoning fails to understand not only the nature of poverty and measures needed to eliminate it, but also the consequences of poverty and population variables. Poverty leads to malnutrition, ill health and lack of education, which in turn perpetuate high death and birth rates. In most situations, poverty and population constitute a vicious circle, thus reinforcing their impact on each other.

The second myth is the belief that population problems exist only in developing countries. One or more population problems have existed at all times in all countries, their nature varying from situation to situation or country to country. Population problems will continue to arise in the future as well. The developed countries equally face various factors relating to population, such as aging, slower growth rates of population and labour force, or the problems associated with the social and economic adjustments of increasing numbers of teenage mothers. In a few countries, the population growth rate has fallen below the growth rate required to maintain a constant level of population and, hence, the size of their populations has started to decline. Some of these countries have now initiated pro-natalist policies for raising birth rates, which may lead to the reversal of such population trends in these countries.

The third myth that is widely believed, without much examination, is that population programmes should be regarded exclusively as family planning programmes. Obviously this is rooted in the belief that the only population problem one faces is the problem of over-population, which could be tackled by curbing population growth. In fact, population problems and programmes cover a wide range of issues, such as size, growth, distribution, composition, structure, mortality, fertility, migration and many other variables. The need to reduce the birth rate is only one component although an important one for most of the populations of the developing world.

The population problems of developing countries have received greater attention not because there has been an increase in their birth rates but because of acceleration in their population growth rates due to dramatic declines in death rates brought about by improvements in health measures and the great progress in medical technology which has taken place since the 1940s.

Whatever be the myths on population, a recent fact that has emerged and which is worthy of our attention relates to the unprecedented decline experienced in birth rates in a number of developing countries and for the developing countries as a group, especially since the 1960s. This has been hailed as the beginning of the third wave of fertility transitions in the world. The first took place in Western Europe and North America in the 19th century; the second in Eastern and Southern Europe and Japan after 1945, when fertility rates turned sharply downwards. This downward trend in birth rates marks the end of an unchanging pattern which has existed for centuries, since sharply rising population growth rates have been a fact throughout the modern historical era.

The significance of this reversal of the trend in birth rates can be fully understood only if one examines its consequences for total world population. It took one hundred and thirty years, from 1800 to 1930, for world population to double from 1 billion to 2 billion. But, it took only 45 years for the population to double again and to reach 4 billion in 1975. However, because of a decline in growth rates, the next doubling of population is likely to take around 40 years, thus reversing the observed trend in the time span required for this purpose.

The decline in birth rates is almost becoming a universal phenomenon. There have been substantial declines in the geographic regions of the Caribbean, Temperate South America, and East Asia, in such countries as Colombia, Costa Rica, Malaysia, Mauritius, Singapore and Sri Lanka.

The causes for the sudden reversal of trends in birth rates are still being debated among population experts. In addition to family planning, factors such as education of women, greater participation of women in nontraditional roles of economic activity, greater access to health care and the subsequent decline in infant and child death rates have all been found to influence the level of birth rates and have played a part in their decline. Given the multiplicity of the factors involved and the complex nature of the interrelationships, it is not possible to isolate the contribution of each of these factors to the decline in birth rates. One should not in these matters pose a question and answer it in terms of either/or because life is, after all, based on the balancing of a number of forces.

An improvement in the quality of life is considered essential in bringing about this decline in birth rates in the developing countries. It appears that the most important policy measures which can improve the quality of life are education, especially education of women, and the development of a more accessible health care system leading to a decline in infant and child mortality rates. Data from the World Fertility Survey and from other sources indicate that the number of children born to a married woman declines directly with the level of her education.

The provision of access and better utilization of health care systems will lead to a decline in infant and child mortality rates, assuring a greater survival rate for children which, in turn, also will result in a decline in birth rates. Herein lies an important population paradox: the higher the mortality rates, the higher the birth rates, which in turn continue to perpetuate higher mortality rates and so on. On the other hand, a lowering of the death rates eventually will result in a lowering of birth rates also. An examination of different developing countries indicates that the levels of social and economic development vary considerably, which is reflected in the uneven changes in the birth rates.

While the reversal of the trend in birth rates marks the beginning of a new epoch in the history of world population, it is essential in order to avoid falling into a state of complacency to point out certain caveats to this situation. First, the pattern of decline noted has been very uneven among countries and regions. Second, which is even more important, the decline in birth rates, however significant it might be, should not obscure the reality that it is occurring at an already very high level. This has important implications in terms of employment, provision of basic needs and the carrying capacity of the global system.

But even with a lower growth rate of population during the coming two decades, these problems will multiply manifold by the year 2000. This is reflected in the growth in terms of population size of a number of countries. We have already entered an era of population "giantism" and, by 2000, a number of countries will have to deal with three or more times the size of populations they had in 1950. For instance, in 1950 only four countries (China, India, the United States and the USSR) had populations exceeding 100 million, but by the year 2000 the number of countries is expected to increase to 11. Not only that. By 2000 China and India alone will have combined populations close to 2 billion, whereas the total world population of 1950 was only 2.5 billion.

However, these facts should not be allowed to push us into a pessimistic position, but help us to anticipate the problems and face reality boldly so that the increased demands on the planet's resources in the not-so-distant future will already have been taken into account in shaping government policy and planning programmes of development.

While the total world population is expected to increase from 4.3 billion in 1980 to 6.2 billion by 2000, the total labour force is projected to increase from 1.8 billion to 2.6 billion during the same period. To get an idea of the complex problems involved in generating employment in the developing countries it may be pointed out that the additional number of jobs to be created in the developing countries between now and 2000 will have to equal at least the total number of jobs that exist today in the developed countries. In fact, if the people in the developing countries are to better their living conditions, the number of jobs to be created will have to exceed the additions to the labour force to take into account the backlog of the unemployed and underemployed. These facts will require a rethinking of the modes of employment creation and in promoting appropriate technology.

Besides employment, the increase in total world population by 2000 will also call for new approaches to policy formulation in the area of food production, in providing access to education and health, provision of shelter, approaches to national and international migration and the issues of exploding cities.

An important factor which has a direct bearing on mortality as well as the levels of health care and nutrition in the developing world is the supply of food. The growth of the population and its regional distribution between

1930 and 1975 has already brought about a major transformation in the world food economy. While world grain output nearly doubled between 1950 and 1975, per capita grain production increased by only one-third during the same period. Regions which were net exporters of grain during the 1930s have become net importers of grain in the 1970s, partly reflecting those changes. Food has become such an important item in the world that its possession is considered important as an instrument of foreign policy. Given the constraints imposed by a paucity of investible resources on increasing the growth of grain production in a number of countries, this role of food is likely to gain even more importance by 2000.

Access to education and health care are closely interrelated. Education leads to better utilization of health care. I mentioned earlier that birth rates decline with rising levels of education of women, and also with declines in infant mortality rates. On the basis of projections made by UNESCO, it is projected that by the year 2000, even though literacy rates are expected to improve considerably, the absolute number of illiterates will be larger than in 1980. Some recent studies have also indicated that the mortality declines experienced during the last quarter-century are tapering off. It is contended that the benefits from preventive measures such as inoculations and the elimination of communicable diseases have already been reaped, and further declines in mortality could take place only with a substantial expansion of medical care and the provision of curative facilities. Such a change in the character of health care facilities would be possible only if a substantial increase in investment is undertaken in this field.

The greatest impact of population growth between now and 2000 will be reflected in the growth of urbanization, created not only by the natural increase in urban population but largely contributed to by massive migrations of population to these areas in search of employment. The projected rates of growth of cities indicate that some are likely to reach proportions which are totally unfamiliar to town planners.

Latest United Nations estimates suggest that world urban population has doubled since 1950 and may well double again before the end of the century. About two-thirds of the population of the developed countries live today in urban areas, and this proportion is likely to increase to three-quarters by the year 2000. While only about one-third of the population lives today in urban areas in the developing countries, this proportion is likely to increase to nearly one-half by 2000.

There were only six cities with populations of 5 million and over in 1950 and their combined population was only 42 million. This number has already risen to 26 cities in 1980 with a combined population of 252 million. It is projected that by 2000 this number will increase to 59 with an estimated population of nearly 650 million. Projections for a few major cities indicate the magnitude of these changes.

Tokyo-Yokohama, with nearly 20 million in 1980, may have 26 million in the year 2000.

Greater Cairo is projected to increase from 8 million in 1980 to 16 million by 2000.

Mexico City metropolitan area, with 14 million in 1980, may have 32 million by 2000.

Such unprecedented expansion of cities will have far-reaching consequences. This is already becoming apparent even by merely looking around us. Most of us — at least most of us who are present here — live in large and growing urban agglomerations. There is not only an explosion of population in these areas but at the same time they are also experiencing an implosion. The city centres are unable to handle such large numbers of people and urban facilities are on the verge of collapse in some of these urban areas. In fact, the problems created by the failure of the transportation systems, the cost of housing and higher wage costs are leading to a relocation of offices and firms away from such city centres, which will in turn only increase the difficulties already faced by such areas.

It is widely recognized now that national policies and programmes specially geared to the managing of problems of crowded cities and which reverse the flow of population, not by compulsion but by developing "growth poles", are a necessity to deal with these problems of metropolitan growth. The development of underpopulated regions by providing social overhead facilities such as education, health, transportation, housing, water, irrigation and, above all, employment opportunities to attract settlers is becoming an important policy instrument to divert the influx from the metropolitan centres. However, this policy has failed to "take off" due to the high cost of investment involved.

While foreign aid has played a crucial catalytic role in development efforts, its volume has always been marginal, never exceeding ten per cent of total resources committed by the developing countries themselves either to overall development or to population programmes. Nonetheless, it has been instrumental in influencing and changing government policy with regard to population programmes. In the mid-1950s only one country, that is India, had a population policy. In 1980, almost all developing countries have formulated population policies of one form or another. Foreign aid still continues to be essential in providing the badly-needed technology and expertise for undertaking developmental programmes.

UNFPA, in collaboration with the Inter-Parliamentary Union, organized a Conference of Parliamentarians on Population and Development in Sri Lanka in August 1979. The Conference called for an increase in international population assistance from all channels to $1 billion annually by 1984. The total amount of foreign assistance, multilateral as well as bilateral, for population programmes is now no more than $400 million a year, which I hardly need point out to journalists familiar with the figures, is less than one-tenth of one per cent of what the world spends on armaments annually. Perhaps the disturbing global events taking place around us with increasing frequency will help us to realize that more money, effort and understanding given to bringing about much needed social change, to making people's lives worth living, may reduce the need for such massive military budgets.

People in the developing world, by and large, have shown their awareness and responsibility in bringing about a decline in fertility. It is now up to us all to respond with a similar depth and breadth of understanding. Because population growth projections are known to be less critical than had been suggested by alarmist forecasts, there has been a tendency to swing to the other end of the pendulum and imagine that population is a problem of the past.

Whatever is happening to birth rates and world population growth rates, the latest United Nations projections of world population indicate that by the year 2000 at least 2 billion individuals will be added to the already existing figure of 4.3 billion. This addition is likely to worsen the already existing imbalance between poverty for most and affluence for a few. Thus, it would be a serious error of judgement to conclude from the above trends in birth rate decline that the "population problem" has now been solved.

Despite the fall in fertility, population growth and distribution remain with us as urgent concerns. What has changed is our perception of the nature of those concerns and the need to respond to that new understanding of population with new assessments of the magnitudes of international co-operation and a renewed commitment to take adequate action now to prevent the problem of poverty from overwhelming us in the future.

POPULATION IN ASIA: THE CRESTING WAVE

Statement at the Third Asian and Pacific Population Conference, Colombo, Sri Lanka, 20 September 1982.

Since 1951, when India began the world's first national family planning programme, the nations of Asia have become the world's leaders in population activities. The Asian regional population conference has come to symbolize this leadership. The first conference in 1963 foreshadowed the United Nations' active involvement in population programmes. In 1972 the second conference showed the way to the international consensus reached at the World Population Conference in 1974. This conference will be no less important in setting the scene for the next global meeting in 1984.

It may help to define the issues which will concern us now and at the world meeting in 1984 if we look back over the decade since the last regional conference. Ten years ago I noted the "phenomenal recognition" which Asian governments had given to population. Birth rates were already beginning to decline. During the last ten years, the rate of decline has accelerated, and is now a well established trend. Asia first adopted regional targets for slower population growth as long ago as 1975. Last year the Asian Conference of Parliamentarians on Population and Development in Beijing adopted a target of one per cent annual growth for the region as a whole by the end of the century.

The commitment of Asian governments to bringing about slower population growth has been an important contribution to this trend. Intensified national family planning programmes have brought education and the possibility of choice within the reach of the ordinary man and woman. In the process of developing and managing these programmes, Asian nations have broadened and deepened their understanding of the interaction between population and other aspects of development.

In particular, the connection between population growth and social development has been demonstrated conclusively. A new chapter has been added to the theory of demographic transition. We are now aware that even poor and rural populations, traditionally among the most conservative groups, will change their fertility behaviour under the right conditions. The transition from large to small families depends not on money incomes alone, but also on the level of social development, that is to say, on adequate nutrition, health, education, housing and employment, with particular attention to the needs of women. We may not yet be in a position to define its elements precisely, but we can perceive that a threshold of transition has been reached in many parts of Asia. Beyond this threshold, perceptions favour the smaller family and there is an active or latent demand for the means of limiting family size. Before the threshold has been reached, attempts to change perceptions have little to build on and are unlikely to be effective.

But the last decade has also taught us that the problems of growth do not disappear when the rate of growth goes down. During the 1970s, though growth declined as a percentage of the population, it was calculated on an ever-increasing base, so that the numbers added each year were greater than the year before.

We need only look at the demographic projections for Asia to know that growth must continue to be taken seriously. The United Nations' figures suggest that growth will continue in the region until the end of the twenty-first century. Asia's population will then be nearly six billion, compared with about 2.5 billion today. This projection assumes a continuing rate of decline which can only be achieved by constant attention to population factors. Without this attention, the time of stabilization will be postponed and the eventual numbers will be bigger.

Growth will not be evenly spread through the region. While numbers in East Asia, which includes China, will grow relatively slowly, South Asia, including the Indian subcontinent, is projected to rise from 1.4 billion in 1980 to 4.1 billion before stabilizing. In absolute terms, the numbers of people added yearly are beginning to go down in East Asia, while in the remainder of the region annual additions will continue to increase at least until 1995. Though spectacular progress has been made in lowering birth rates, particularly in East Asia, and substantial gains made elsewhere, some countries in the region have maintained a virtually unchanged growth rate since the 1960s. In part this is the result of successful public health measures which have cut both birth and death rates, but several governments in the region still see their birth rates as unsatisfactorily high.

Birth rates vary within countries as well as between them, calling for special emphasis in population programmes on areas of high growth. Since the highest birth rates are commonly found in the rural areas and among the poorest people, the population groups which are hardest to reach, further extension and sophistication of the methods of delivery of family planning and other elements of the social development package will be needed. The mechanisms to produce the right conditions for slower growth are complex. Their success depends on the active involvement of the community, supported by the official network of service providers and administrators. Gaining and maintaining access to the rural community demands time, skills and money, and to ensure that the demands are met will require a national commitment at all levels and from all sectors, including some not traditionally associated with population programmes.

Mortality, particularly infant mortality, remains a pressing concern in many Asian countries. Apart from avoiding countless personal tragedies and the needless waste of human life, lowering infant mortality has a long-term effect on birth rates. Low rates of maternal mortality are an equally essential basic aim of population and development programmes. In both cases, spacing childbirth has a beneficial effect, allowing children the care they need in early life and permitting mothers to recover fully from the effects of pregnancy and birth.

After growth itself, the question of migration to the cities became the biggest population issue for Asian nations in the 1970s, and the most important they will have to face in the years ahead. It has been calculated that the largest cities will grow at four times the over-all rate. In most parts of Asia, where the basis of the modern city was laid down in the 19th century, this may represent an intolerable strain on systems which are already overloaded.

Cities represent a great national resource in which the concentration of people produces ideas, inventions, the equipment for survival and further development. Like population growth itself, however, over-rapid urban growth may overwhelm the ability to support it. We still do not know the

dynamics of urban growth sufficiently well to be able to manage it effectively. But there are some pointers. It is clear, for example, that the "push factor" driving people from the rural areas may be as important as the "pull
factor" drawing them to the cities. In this case, concern for the needs of the
rural sector can have an important effect on migration.

To help further understanding and awareness of the process of urbanization, UNFPA sponsored a conference on Population and the Urban Future.
The "Rome Declaration" adopted by the conference recognizes that the city
has been "the engine of development and the forge of human creative
energies". But, as the Declaration points out, if urbanization is to be harnessed
to achieve mankind's goals, it must take place under planned and orderly
conditions. This is the challenge facing Asia today — as urban numbers increase, perhaps reaching 40 per cent of the total by the end of the century,
governments and communities must seek to liberate their energy in construc-
tive and peaceful ways.

Other migration issues, notably movement of workers between countries,
assumed growing importance for Asian economies in the 1970s. Little effective research has yet been done into the effects of this sort of migration either
on the sending or on the receiving countries. As the flow of people and money
increases, better understanding will become essential.

As the century nears its end, Asian countries will become aware of a sub-
tle but important shift in the makeup of their populations. Increased life expectancy and lower fertility are combining to produce a growing proportion
of elderly people. Asia may expect that 8.5 per cent of her population will
be over sixty by the end of the century. In absolute numbers, this means
perhaps 300 million people. In our traditional Asian societies the old had
an honoured place as repositories of wisdom, of experience and of history.
They helped hold together both family and society. In the rapidly changing
conditions of Asia today, an increase in the number of elderly people may
also contribute to continuity and stability, providing that we are able to maintain the structures and values which ensure that their position is both
honoured and secure.

During the 1970s Asian nations became fully aware of the complex causes
of growth, movement and the changing structure of populations, and their
effects on the other sectors of development. Much progress has been made
in dovetailing population and other development programmes, but population factors have not yet successfully been made part of the development
planning process. Vital statistics and population data in Asian countries
generally are more readily available and are of higher quality today than ever
before. What is needed now are techniques of processing population information and merging it with data in other areas to produce a rounded picture
of the development process. At the policy level the high priority which population issues claim is still not reflected in the machinery of government. At

the practical level, there is still a real need for additional training in managerial skills to carry out integration of programmes on the ground. It should be made clear at all levels that population has a pre-emptive claim on national attention and resources.

This question of integration is particularly important when we consider the interrelationship of population, natural resources and the environment. All planning, all our thoughts and dreams for the future, are based on the assumption that development activities will not irrevocably upset the balance of the ecosystem which sustains us. In order to justify the assumption, positive steps are needed to protect the environment.

Population growth does not by itself present a threat to the environment and the natural resource base. But irreparable damage becomes a real possibility unless ways can be found to meet the needs of growing populations for water, food, fuel and building materials. We are working towards a better understanding of the effects not only of population growth, but of industrial and agricultural development, and of the eventual costs and benefits of taking steps against environmental damage. Commitment to improving that understanding and acting upon it should be a priority for Asian countries.

The extension and intensification of population programmes have produced an explosion in demand for financial resources, technology and human skills. To supply them will call for an international effort even bigger than we have seen so far.

To take the question of financial resources first. The share of national resources devoted to population has increased absolutely and as a proportion of development budgets in nearly every Asian country. To give only two examples from many, the percentage rise in government expenditure in 1976-1980 as compared with the previous quinquennium was nearly 200 per cent in Indonesia and 250 per cent in Thailand. Although international assistance has also increased, countries on the average spend on population four times as much from local revenues as they receive from UNFPA, the biggest multilateral source of international population assistance.

It is clear that additional resources for population programmes will largely come from governments themselves. International assistance in recent years has first plateaued and now dropped in real value, eroded by global recession, inflation and fluctuating exchange rates. In June, UNFPA's Governing Council expressed its "grave concern" about falling real amounts of contributions to UNFPA and called on all countries to increase their contributions.

However, in the new and financially constrained atmosphere of the international economy, we cannot rely on substantial increases in international funding to support population programmes. UNFPA among other international agencies is re-examining its capabilities in order both to extract the maximum value from the international resources available and to help governments liberate the potential of presently unused or underused national resources.

The expertise acquired by Asian nations in the development of programmes may be of great value to other countries. UNFPA is helping the cross-fertilization of ideas and techniques by means of training, of study tours and visits by experts from other countries in the region. This kind of technical co-operation between developing countries can only increase self-reliance and encourage the development of specifically Asian solutions to Asian problems.

As far as we may increase and stretch our assistance, it is still true that UNFPA and the other international agencies cannot supply more than a small proportion of the resources needed for development. We can, however, act as a catalyst in the development of ideas and approaches to development problems and thus through small inputs produce larger results. Our approach to international assistance will concentrate even more than in the past on supporting projects which will develop their own momentum and stimulate the community both by education and example.

The countries of Asia have shown the world how problems of population may successfully be confronted. As population continues to grow, the confrontation will become more intense. More attention to population problems will be required through the coming years. The sense of urgency which has stimulated us over the last decades should not be allowed to fade. As we have learned, population growth is less like a bomb than a slowly building wave. Riding on its crest, we can sense its power. It may be a destructive force, but it may equally be channeled into productive courses which will ensure, as the World Population Plan of Action puts it, that "the future of mankind is infinitely bright".

The Plan of Action adopted eight years ago will be part of the agenda for the international conference to take place in 1984. We shall have an opportunity at that time to assess our progress and determine our future course. Your discussions at this conference will be of immeasurable service to the global community. In its breadth and depth the experience of Asia is unique and may serve as a guide for the world.

POPULATION PROBLEMS
AND INTERNATIONAL CO-OPERATION

Statement at a Meeting of the Scientific Council of the Moscow State University, Moscow, Union of Soviet Socialist Republics, 29 September 1982.

Never before have the dynamics of population assumed greater significance than at the present time. They have not only led to a re-examination of traditional explanations for demographic transition, but have also questioned the conventional thinking on the interrelationships between population and development. These elaborations in the fields of demography and economics have profound practical implications for the currently less developed countries.

The third quarter of this century witnessed an unprecedented acceleration in the growth of world population, with nearly one and a half billion people being added during the short span of 25 years, reaching a present total of 4.6 billion. Towards the end of this period, however, definite evidence became available that the annual rate of population growth had declined from 2 per cent at the beginning to 1.7 per cent at present. This decline is now projected to reach 1.5 per cent by the year 2000. This development, however significant, does not yet reduce the magnitude of population problems. Nearly 1.5 billion people will still be added to the world's total population before the end of the century, nine-tenths of which will be in the developing countries.

The developing countries will be faced with population growth rates in the 1980s of around 2 per cent a year. According to United Nations projections, the share of the total world population living in the developing countries would rise from 74 per cent at present to 80 per cent by the year 2000. A striking feature of prospective future population growth is that the largest increases in population will occur in the poorest countries and regions of the world which have also experienced the largest increases in recent decades.

In the next decade or two, the changes in population size, growth, structure and distribution will have far-reaching implications for global political, economic, and social order as well as the living conditions of people throughout the world. Population changes are taking place within much shorter timespans than previously experienced and existing institutions will come under considerable stress in trying to cope with the dynamics of population trends. The International Development Strategy for the Third United Nations Development Decade, adopted by the General Assembly in December 1980 as well as other reviews, studies and strategies, have recently identified population, along with resources and environment, as three vitally important areas of concern to mankind in the remaining years of this century and beyond.

Future population growth will have far-reaching consequences for the global balance between population and resources. A continued growth of population will result in increasing demand for food, fuel, housing, education, health care, and other necessities of life. The additional demand will most certainly affect the availability of resources and the viability of the environment.

The various forces generated by population growth, the imbalance of resources and the lack of gainful employment opportunities will undoubtedly affect economic and social stability. In many developing countries, population pressures have been particularly acute in the cities, where increasing migration from the rural areas has generated social problems of a severe nature.

The vital role that population factors will play in the future requires increased efforts at the national and international levels to deal with population-related problems. Recent projections prepared by the United Nations indicate that world population may become stabilized between the latter part of the twenty-first and the first half of the twenty-second century, but only if the current level of population activities in various parts of the world can be maintained. Because it takes time for population measures to have an effect on social and economic conditions, it is important that the momentum which has been built up over the years in population programmes and assistance to developing countries be sustained and reinforced.

Linkages between population and development

Let us examine the changing perceptions of the processes of development, of population, and of the linkages between the two. From the mid-1940s until the latter part of the 1960s, development economists were relatively optimistic concerning future possibilities for continued development in the Third World. They perceived development to be a gradual but a continuous and cumulative process which could effectively rely on marginal adjustments in its spread among groups within nations, as well as across the boundaries between and among nations.

The view that developed countries may have in regard to population may not exactly match that of the developing countries, and the view would be clearer, if we try to imagine ourselves as a group looking at the 130 or so developing countries and territories with which UNFPA is involved. In the course of the last three decades, the concept of population and development has been modified considerably. Initially, in the 1950s the concept was that industrialization was the key to development. In the 1960s and 1970s, views on development began to change, emphasizing more and more the provision of basic needs and the quality of life for people in the developing countries. Similarly, at the initial stage of the involvement of the United Nations in population programmes, the drive was to assist countries purely in the field of family planning with the hope that this would result in a diminution of the population growth rate and thus contribute towards improving economic development. So the intimate linkage was defined from the beginning in terms of economic growth rate and population growth rate, or, at the very least, the population growth rate was seen as a factor in hampering the rate of economic growth in developing countries.

Since the adoption of the World Population Plan of Action at Bucharest in 1974, the emphasis has swung to aspects of human welfare, the quality of life, and the humane aspects of economic development. This means that all population programmes, while strategically important in terms of economic development, must be modified so that the individual's potential is given the opportunity to develop fully. In this way, the concept of population programmes aiming at individual development is linked to the total development effort.

The political forum of the Bucharest Conference — the first of its kind — served to direct attention to, and interest in, a broader, less simplistic, more sophisticated view of the mutual interrelationships between population and development factors. The World Population Plan of Action firmly established population as an important element in international strategies to promote development and to improve the quality of life, and set as an important goal the expansion and deepening of the capacity of countries to deal effectively with their national and subnational population problems.

The Bucharest Conference, while clearly recognizing that population policies, and in particular the policies for moderating fertility and population growth alone, could not solve the problems of development, noted that such policies, in conjunction with an intensified development effort, could make a significant contribution to their solution. Population policies were stressed to be an integral part of, but never a substitute for, development policies. Therefore, it was emphasized that policies and programmes designed to influence population trends, composition and distribution should go hand in hand with socio-economic development policies.

In this framework, the approach to population issues becomes much more complex and broader. Rather than looking at population in the aggregate, attention is directed to the components of the population. Population growth, assumed to have been independent of socio-economic development and change, is now seen as intimately and mutually related. Population, once viewed as exogenous by development planners, is now seen as endogenous. The maturation and sophistication of population thinking has put an end to simplistic models of population change. UNFPA, from its inception, has acted upon this broader view of population concerns.

The vital conditions for solving the problems generated by rapid change in the size of populations of developing countries are social and economic development, intensive accumulation of resources for building up the national economy and securing the most rapid rates of economic growth. These can be achieved only through effective utilization of manpower and material resources available within each country. In the long run, industrialization must go hand in hand with social and cultural development.

The success of family planning in bringing down the birth rates and harmonizing population growth with the rate of economic growth depends directly upon a country's social and economic development. Measures to spread the practice of family planning can be effective only when a population is prepared for the concept of "conscious parenthood" by social, economic and cultural development. For this to happen, it is necessary to recognize the true status of women in society by providing them with opportunities to work and incorporating them in the productive decision-making apparatus of the household and the society.

Thus having re-established the linkage, and the need for greater attention to the population and development interface, we find ourselves today standing at a very broad frontier. For, having identified the need to integrate population factors into development planning, we find that there is still much territory to be explored to bring this idea to its full fruition and implementation.

Basic data collection

First and foremost, all countries need data on population structure and its changes in order to plan effectively. As recently as the early 1970s, 36 countries had not taken a modern census. The situation was particularly critical in Africa where up to that point 21 countries had never conducted a census. Through its support of the African Census Programme, UNFPA has been able to change that situation dramatically, so that today all but three countries on that continent have conducted a census in the last ten years. Data on the present structure of the population—age, sex, urban/rural residence, and other demographic data—are now available for planning purposes, as well as information on the elements of population change—fertility, mortality and migration.

It is important to note the emergence of scientific research on population issues especially in large countries such as India and China. It is only with a proper scientific assessment of demographic trends and their relationships with other socio-economic phenomena, based on accurate statistics, that action-oriented population programmes can be developed, sustained and strengthened. In this connection, more reliable estimates of the population of China will soon be available as a result of the population census, now under way, which is being partly supported by UNFPA.

Population and development research

While action cannot always await the findings of research, there is a continuous need to learn more about the dynamics of population change so that countries will be in a better position to plan programmes and policies. Adequate solutions to population problems can emanate only from adequate demographic analysis and population studies.

The need for demographers in developing countries has been partially met by national institutions and the United Nations Regional Demographic Centres. But the integration of population with development planning is still an area of study that continues to need attention. It is a significant contribution in meeting this need that the Moscow State University in co-operation with the United Nations has developed in its Faculty of Economics an Interregional Training and Research Programme in Population and Development.

It is appropriate that the Soviet Union, with its tradition of comprehensive planning for socio-economic development, has chosen to share its experience with interested developing countries through this Programme. Under its auspices, approximately one hundred individuals from 35 developing countries have been trained during 1977-1981 in the complex issues of integrating population and development. There is no doubt that many of the research findings that will continue to emerge from this Programme will strengthen the formulation of population and development policies in the developing countries.

The interdisciplinary character of the course and its empirical content are distinctive. And, the continued high rate of nominations of individuals by governments of developing countries to the training programme is evidence of its wide acceptance, and a general recognition of its practical value. The United Nations system, to fulfill the provisions of the World Population Plan of Action, is committed to supporting research and training programmes as have been established in this University.

Policy formulation

Data gathering, processing, analysis and research to inform the policy makers necessitate the development of high-level units within governments to make use of what has been learned most effectively. Increasing attention is being paid by governments to the development of national population councils and/or population planning units within national planning offices to assume responsibility for co-ordinating and facilitating these myriad activities, and for translating them into policies. For example, UNFPA is assisting the Government of Sri Lanka, at its request, in the development of such a unit. At the regional level, we are also assisting the League of Arab States to accomplish a similar task for its constituencies.

Family planning

Although, as we have previously noted, the field of population is much broader than family planning, family planning is nonetheless essential to assist families in achieving the number and spacing of children that they desire.

Thus, close to fifty per cent of all UNFPA funds have been allocated to this important area. In addition to providing support to existing country programmes, the Fund has also made particular efforts at the country, regional and global levels to improve the delivery of services through new approaches. Attention is being directed to primary health care, community-based programmes, and integrated health and family planning programmes. For example, the Fund is assisting the National Family Planning Board in Malaysia to further strengthen the service capabilities, as well as to develop practical mechanisms to integrate family planning into national development efforts.

Communication and education

For programme activities to succeed, they must be responsive to the needs of the people and must have their understanding and support. This is true for census activities, for migration programmes, and for family planning programmes as well. To this end, therefore, the Fund has supported programmes of population education for the schools in Mexico, communication support activities for census operations in Afghanistan, a population and development feature service of the Press Foundation of Asia, to name but a few communication and education activities which have been designed to contribute to development.

Training

The success of all of these programmes requires well-trained personnel at the national and subnational level. And the UNFPA has invested considerable sums in assisting the nations of the developing world to become self-reliant in their population activities. At the regional and also at the national levels, training programmes for nurse/midwives, educational planners, development specialists—the list could be extended beyond the time available to us today—have been undertaken, pointing to that day some time in the future when the developing nations will need only financial support to meet their population needs and to achieve their demographic transition. The Fund is supporting an integrated programme of training on population and development in Egypt. The programme involves the training of central co-ordinators, regional co-ordinators, village co-ordinators and extension workers at the community level.

Population Challenges of the Future

The challenges of future population programming are serious and wide-ranging. The mandate of UNFPA and a flexible interpretation of it should permit the United Nations to respond to changing population issues and needs. What are some of the major population challenges of the future?

Population migration

An important aspect of population growth in the less developed countries has been the inability of employment opportunities to keep pace with population growth. This has turned out to be one of the most intractable problems of development in these countries in the past, leading to considerable internal migration of populations, as well as international migration between countries and regions. Within the developing countries themselves, labour migration and the movement of population have been from rural areas to mainly urban areas. This has led to unprecedented growth in urbanization in many less developed countries.

Apart from internal migration, there has been an increase in international migration of skilled and unskilled labour from the less developed countries. Such migration has become, for some countries, a major element in their population trends. The nature and extent of migration between countries is generally determined by income differentials, but the number of immigrants is often restricted by the recipient countries. In spite of such restrictions, it seems clear from an examination of available data on international migration that it does reflect a salient population trend in various regions of the world.

International migration of workers across national boundaries acquired a new character in the 1970s. Such labour movements have involved all the major continents and have been between Latin America and North America, within Europe, and to Europe and to the oil-exporting nations from North Africa and Asia. A combination of "pull" factors abroad and "push" factors at home has made the developing countries seek out economic opportunities across their national boundaries. These trends are likely to continue well into the future, portending a new wave in international labour migration. Given the somewhat unique set of factors influencing these migration trends, problems of economic and cultural assimilation of these migrants at destination have become more difficult.

Urbanization

The expected growth in urbanization in the less developed countries largely reflects population growth between now and the year 2000. It is the result not only of the natural increase in urban population but also of massive migrations of population to these areas in search of employment. It is estimated that the largest cities will grow more rapidly than the smaller cities and some of these are likely to reach proportions which are totally unfamiliar at this time to town planners. In 1950, only four of the fifteen largest cities were in the less developed countries, but this number rose to seven by 1975. It is projected that twelve of the fifteen largest cities will be in the less developed countries by the year 2000.

In 1950, there were only six cities with populations of five million and more and their combined population was only 47 million. By 1980, there were already 26 cities with a combined population of 252 million. By the year 2000, it is expected that this number will increase to approximately 60 cities of more than five million each, with an estimated population of nearly 650 million, of which 45 will be in the developing world.

The growth of urbanization in the less developed countries reflects as much the lack of rural development as the growth of industry and employment opportunities in the urban agglomerations. Thus, the problems of the urban future and the growth of metropolitan areas in the less developed countries are equally a problem of "total" development of the country like any other population or socio-economic problem. The solution to the urban problem lies as much in the rural areas as in the cities themselves. Only a contented countryside can provide a lasting solution to the ills afflicting the urban world.

Aging of population

A population issue that is already important in developed countries and is likely to become significant in developing countries is the aging of human population. As a consequence of declining fertility and mortality, the average age of population has been on the increase for some time in the developed countries. One of the important manifestations of this trend is the accelerated growth of population which is "older", that is, 65 and over. The current estimate of "older" population is put at roughly 128 million people or over 11 per cent of the population in the developed countries. While only four per cent of the population of developing countries is similarly aged, the absolute number of older persons is already higher (132 million) in the latter. Between 1980 and the year 2000, the developing countries are expected to experience an 80 per cent increase in the number of older people in their population as against only a 30 per cent increase in the developed countries. This rise in the absolute size of the older population augurs a predictable increase in social concern for the medical, housing, economic and social services problems of the aged in both developed and developing countries.

Integration of population with development planning

Another challenge in the 1980s will centre around the concept of integration. Population planning needs to become a more effective arm of over-all development planning, not only as an active sector in its own right, but also as a resource closely attuned to other realms of policy for actively affecting development. To these probable major areas of new substantive integrations should be added a variety of evolving novel integrations of a procedural administrative nature.

These developments entail periodic modifications in national as well as international population strategies. Activities related to migration, urbanization, aging, and integration of population and development are of current concern in many countries. While these activities clearly fall within the mandate of UNFPA, they have not yet figured prominently in the United Nations programme of assistance, but in the coming decades may prove significant.

President Brezhnev, in his address of April 1977 to the 25th Congress of the Communist Party of the Soviet Union, challenged Soviet economists to analyze the acute population problems prevailing in the world, noting that this was one of the important tasks facing the Soviet social sciences. Indeed, the conceptualization of population problems continues to be one of the most urgent global tasks that has to be faced in this and the next century.

Like others, we are already looking towards the twenty-first century. We envision that the decades ahead will bring about a global society that is secure and viable — where individuals develop fully their potential, free from the capricious inequalities of development and threats of environmental deterioration. As we broaden and deepen our understanding of the phenomenon of population, scientists will have an increasingly significant role in the realization of this vision.

THE POPULATION WAVE

Statement at the Western Hemisphere Conference of Parliamentarians on Population and Development, Brasilia, Brazil, 2 December 1982.

During the past thirty years the world has changed more, and more decisively, than in any comparable period in history. One remarkable feature has been the great wave of population growth which has been sweeping over the world. Thanks to the painstaking work of demographers and statisticians, we can see more clearly than ever before the dimensions of the population wave and judge its likely path and effects. We can see, for example, that the rate of growth is at its lowest point in nearly thirty years. But we can also see that it continues, and is likely to continue until well into the twenty-second century. We can see that growth is much faster in some regions than others and in some countries within regions.

Growth for the Latin American region is running at 2.4 per cent a year, compared with the world average of 1.7 per cent. The rate of growth is declining gradually, but we should pay attention to the increase in absolute numbers which it represents. Although rates of growth may be going down, the numbers of people added to national populations will continue to go up as the size of the base continues to increase. Percentages may be smaller, but numbers are larger.

Brazil, our host country, is a good example of expansion in both her economy and the numbers of her people in the last twenty years. But even Brazil is beginning to feel the pressure of rapid population growth. If it is true even of this vast and wealthy nation, consider the effects of population growth on other countries in the region, whose resources and therefore ranges of possible response are limited. I am thinking particularly of the island nations, where the constraints are easily visible. It is no surprise to find that these countries have been among the most successful in the world in bringing rates of population growth into balance with the demands of national development.

Elsewhere in the region, the effects of growth are expressed in different ways. Typically we find a steady exodus of people from the land into the cities, and from one country to another in search of a livelihood. Latin America's labour force was 55 million in 1950, 99 million in 1975 and will reach 197 million by the end of the century. It is projected to reach 314 million by 2025. In Mexico and Central America alone, roughly 1.2 million additional jobs will be needed each year until the end of the century.

Projections show that ten of the world's largest cities, with populations over 5 million, will be located in the region by the end of the century. These cities will be growing rapidly, creating immediate problems of food, water, housing, health and education. And the prospect of massive urban growth carries even more somber implications. Will the networks which support urban life and the shared standards which allow people to live together as part of a large and complex settlement be able to sustain such increases, or will they break down under the strain? Urban growth which is too rapid may be a threat to the values which we most desire to pass on to our children. For the sake of parents and children alike, and for the sake of the family which is the cornerstone of our societies, it is of the first importance that urban growth allow room for the growth of humanity as well as the growth of human numbers.

The projected increases in population as a whole and in urban numbers in particular are not inevitable. We are learning something about the dynamics of societies in a phase of rapid growth, thanks to the work of such institutions as the Latin American Demographic Centre. Purposeful interventions have helped to bring down death rates. Experience in many countries shows that there may be equally effective interventions to bring down birth rates and influence the rate and direction of population movements.

One such intervention is the redirection of urban growth, either to the countryside or to smaller cities. Our societies, though they may be powered by the cities, draw much of their strength from the land. The creation of secure and productive sources of income for rural populations, and the establishment of a network of services and support systems in the rural areas, can help to relieve pressure on the cities, and thus reduce the risk of breakdown of economic and political systems. The development of smaller urban centres has in many cases not only stimulated rural sector activity but simultaneously established alternatives for urban development.

In many countries of this region, the indicators are pointing to a need for lower national population growth rates. While countries in the process of economic and social development can often absorb the increases, there comes a point at which population growth begins to act as a brake on economic growth. This is especially true when populations grow very rapidly over a short period; the long-term effects may arguably be beneficial in providing a larger workforce and a larger market, but in the short term rapid growth makes excessive demands on the capital available for investment in development.

Population pressures, wherever they may be felt, poverty and underdevelopment threaten the well-being of individuals, the family and the nation. There is another dimension. The values which underlie all our societies depend for their survival on recognition of the importance of the individual, whether as worker, parent or child. It is now universally accepted that family size may affect individual development and that there is a fundamental right to choose the size and spacing of the family. It has been UNFPA's experience that if the policy adopted is in tune with the needs and aspirations of the people, and if it is promoted in a manner which is in accordance with religious belief and sensitive to cultural values, there need be no hesitation on the part of governments or local administrations in promoting, advising on and supplying the means of voluntary fertility control. Once started, it is essential that these programmes be maintained until the promise of stabilization is within sight of fulfillment, which in the case of Latin America will be towards the end of the next century.

We have found that in many countries the demand for such services has proved to be far greater than expected. Where fertility is already beginning to show signs of a downturn, as it is in many countries of this region, there is almost certain to be a large latent demand for acceptable means of fertility control. Awareness is spreading among parents that the future depends on more than the number of children in the family. Parents are concerned about giving their children the very best of which they are capable; more and more are realizing that increasing the size of the family may decrease the quality of what is available for each child. Governments may promote this concept and help educate and motivate couples to have only the number of children they are capable of bringing to adulthood as healthy, educated, aware members of society—human beings in the fullest sense.

To quote His Excellency General Figueiredo, President of Brazil:

"Under present conditions in Brazil, the outcome of social development programmes largely depends on family planning, subject to free decision by married couples. Meanwhile, the principles and methods of responsible parenthood are well known to the higher income classes but unknown precisely to the economically disadvantaged. The task of making such knowledge available to all families concerns the State."

The role of non-governmental organizations in this kind of work should not be underestimated. They can, especially in the early stages of a programme, do excellent work in testing the climate of opinion, promoting awareness, securing the support of the community and providing services in an acceptable way.

UNFPA is pledged to respect national, local and individual values, and never to attempt to impose any philosophy which runs counter to them. On this basis we have been able to help some 141 countries and territories, in all parts of the world, of all shades of political and religious beliefs and at all stages of development. We have not confined ourselves to assistance for fertility programmes; recognizing that in many countries other activities have equal importance, we have helped with population research, the collection and refinement of population data and with education and understanding of the dynamics of population. The all-important objectives of development are the health and well-being of the individual, the family and the nation; UNFPA was established to help in realizing them.

An interest in the composition, growth and dynamics of population is recognized today as an essential part of any government's approach to development. We have seen during the last decade a phenomenal increase in the share of national resources and the amount of international assistance devoted to population programmes. It is vital for the success of social and economic development efforts that this level of assistance is maintained and increased. Parliamentarians, entrusted by the electors with the guidance of national policy, are in a unique position to sustain the momentum. As the population wave rolls on into the next century, you can help to ensure that its effects are recognized and that due importance is given to programmes that will ensure that those effects are beneficial to humankind.

UNFPA AND THE ARAB WORLD

Statement at a Meeting on Co-operation between the
United Nations and the League of Arab States, Tunis, Tunisia,
29 June 1983.

The contributions of Arab culture, in particular to the development of the natural sciences, have helped to form the basis of our modern world.

It was one of the greatest of Arab thinkers and historians, Ibn-Khaldun, who introduced into his work the concept of cyclical population change which to this day guides social scientists in their work. The idea that awareness of population factors and demographic change is central to development planning therefore has its roots in the Arab World.

It was appropriate that action programmes in Tunisia and Egypt were among the first approved for support by UNFPA. Since that time, UNFPA has provided some $85 million in support of population programmes in Arab countries. We have been privileged to support, at government request, the conduct of censuses in Democratic Yemen, Somalia, Sudan, and Yemen, besides offering limited help in that area to nearly all Member States of the Arab League. We have assisted, again by government request, in the strengthening of maternal and child health programmes throughout the region. We have also provided support in the vitally important area of manpower planning and human resource management, as well as in education, information and activities for improving the status of women. We are pledged to continue this support to the extent we are permitted by availability of resources and by the interest of governments. Such interest is on the increase among Arab countries as it is among virtually all countries of the developing world. We have completed exhaustive surveys of the needs for population assistance of 11 members of the Arab League. On the basis of the recommendations of these needs assessments and, in accordance with the wishes of the governments concerned, programmes have been developed calling for UNFPA assistance in the amount of $110 million for the period up to 1986. According to our resource projections, UNFPA may be able to contribute a little over half this amount. We rely on bilateral and other programmes to make up the remainder, a process which is made easier by the existence of clearly identified needs in the area of population.

UNFPA's contact with the Arab League started at the very beginning of the Fund's active operations in 1969. A high point in our relationship was the League's convening of a Ministerial Conference on Population and Development held in 1975 in collaboration with UNFPA. At that Conference, various resolutions were adopted, including one urging the Member States of the League and the financial institutions of the League to contribute generously to UNFPA in order to permit the Fund to meet the additional requests of Arab countries for population assistance. It was with gratitude that we received contributions and pledges totalling $12 million, which have greatly assisted us in our work. Our specific connections with the League include a project for the establishment of a population research and study unit within the League's Social Affairs Department. That project is still operational and offers the possibility of further advancing co-operation between the League and UNFPA.

The role of UNFPA in national population programmes is necessarily a limited one. This is not merely a question of resources. The initiation and execution of population programmes is principally a matter for governments; they alone have the ability to assess their population situations, determine the need for action and assign priorities. By definition, the role of UNFPA is to assist governments in carrying out their declared aims, whatever they may be. UNFPA assistance is in money terms typically 20 per cent of total national resources set aside for population programmes. In conceptual terms, however, UNFPA assistance can be crucial. Through UNFPA assistance, vital expertise can be transferred at the very outset of a population programme. As the programme continues, UNFPA can help in structuring activities to make the best use of available resources, provide expert assistance in executing agreed projects, supply equipment and offer much-needed training facilities for local personnel at all levels. Thus, though small in amount, UNFPA assistance is conceptually unlimited in its extent and its impact.

This is important as members of the Arab League turn their interest towards intervention in population concerns. The particular problems of the region demand unique solutions, because the precise conditions existing in this region do not obtain anywhere else. It will be necessary to accelerate the building of national and regional resources for policy-making during the coming decades if positive and productive policies for population and development are to emerge. UNFPA stands ready as always to provide whatever help we can in this process.

UNFPA continues this effort in promoting co-operation with the Arab specialized organizations and Arab funds for development. We feel that UNFPA can share its experience with these organizations in the field of providing assistance to developing countries in the area of population. UNFPA has already contacted Arab funds with the intention of establishing joint financing in providing assistance to developing countries. UNFPA could also establish a working relationship with the Arab specialized organizations in that area to implement programmes and projects in the Arab World.

POPULATION – COMMON PROBLEMS, COMMON INTERESTS

Statement at the Regional Meeting on Population of the Economic Commission for Europe, Sofia, Bulgaria, 6 October 1983.

In our time, rapid population growth has been so much a feature of developing countries, that it has become part of the definition of underdevelopment. There is now firm evidence of a change. With constantly improving techniques of data collection and analysis at their command, an increasing number of countries are reporting declining growth rates. This reflects declining fertility, a trend made more impressive by concurrent improvements in life expectancy in many countries. The information gathered by the World Fertility Survey reveals a pattern of diminishing family size in countries of widely different ethnic, social and economic make-up.

This is a welcome transformation indeed, and is especially gratifying to those who have been actively involved in population programmes or who have supported them so generously over the years. We can look forward with some confidence to a steadily declining rate of world population growth, culminating in stability.

Having said this, it is proper to qualify our optimism. Present trends indicate that it will take more than a century for population to stabilize. Meanwhile, growth continues. It is important to remember that the annual average birth rate in the developing countries during 1975-1980 was twice as high as in the developed. In spite of the global decline in growth rates, annual net additions to world population will continue to rise during the rest of this century, from a current figure of 78 million to 89 million by the year 2000. Moreover, there are large areas — much of Latin America, for example, and most of Africa — where growth rates continue very high, and others, for example, parts of Asia, which do not follow the general declining trend despite, in some cases, a long history of population programmes. In many countries, the problems of growth are multiplied by concentration in urban areas.

There is a deepening consensus in developing countries that rapid growth and over-concentration are undesirable, and a growing determination to tackle the causes and effects of both. At the time of the Fourth Population Inquiry among Governments, it was found that some 80 per cent of the developing world's population lived under governments which considered their current rates of population growth unacceptable. The Fifth Inquiry, the results of which will be published later this year, are believed to show an even greater concern with growth.

In their determination to limit population growth, governments deserve the full-hearted support of the industrialized countries, both as a humanitarian act and as a sustained stimulus to development. Effective programming in population is possible, as we know from the experience and the gratifying trends of the last decade. Interest in population programmes and demand for resources are growing as never before. Much of the resources will come from within countries; national resources devoted to population are increasing as a percentage of development budgets and outstrip external assistance by a factor of two to one. External assistance has proved its value, however, where it has been given in accord with national policies, is appropriate to local conditions and needs, and is delivered where it can make the most impact.

The experience of the last decade has greatly improved our understanding of how population assistance can make its uniquely valuable contribution to national programmes. The continued interest and intensified co-operative action of the industrialized countries is very much needed to ensure the success of population programmes in developing countries.

There is another reason for concern on the part of developed countries about the future of population growth. The effects of growth cannot be isolated; they are felt far beyond the borders of the countries where growth is taking place. In former times, there were new frontiers to open, which represented new hope for populations threatening to overstrain resources. What are the avenues open today for the increasing numbers of people in developing countries? There are no easy answers to this difficult question; the search for an adequate response is one of the reasons for calling the International Conference on Population next year.

Discussions at the Conference will centre on four topics. Besides their interest in the future of population in the developing countries, members of the Economic Commission for Europe have their own concerns in each area.

The first topic is fertility and the family. Over the last two decades, a tendency towards lower birth rates and longer life expectancy has changed the age structure of industrialized countries. Numbers and the proportion of the elderly in the population have increased and will continue to do so. There are questions of the economic and social contributions which can be made by the elderly to the life of the family. This assumes a more serious aspect in times of economic stringency, and particularly in a static or shrinking job market. For those whose active life is coming to an end, there are questions of care and geriatric treatment to be considered. The elderly still hold an honoured position in traditional society. The tradition has been partly superseded by the demands of industrial development, but the increasing numbers of the elderly make it imperative that their contributions, needs and desires be taken at their proper worth.

Also of interest to your members are the consequences for social and economic policy of changing patterns of family formation and dissolution. Smaller families with a high proportion of mothers working outside the home create demands for care of children and the elderly. So do one-parent families, a phenomenon of growing importance in many countries of Europe.

The second topic is distribution and migration. The influx of immigrants, short and long-term, legal and illegal, create particular problems for industrialized countries. Most immigrants come from the developing world, and while there is an increasing flow to the oil-producing developing countries, most go to the industrialized. Some go for settlement, but a growing number intend to stay for a short time, until they have saved or sent home enough to return. These workers tend not to become part of the social fabric of their host country and sometimes their position and that of the host country become unduly difficult as a result.

A significant minority of immigrants have no proper documents. Many of them make a valuable contribution to the economic life of their host country, but remain in a twilight zone out of the sight of censuses and registration, and consequently of policy-makers. Social programmes cannot include them, and their contribution to the tax base remains unrealized. Nevertheless, they have rights and responsibilities. Equally, host country governments have responsibilities as well as rights regarding those within their borders, whether legally or illegally. Sending countries too have international obligations and a say in the future of their nationals.

It will be of prime importance to discuss these issues and to arrive at an international convention protecting the rights of individuals while safeguarding the interests of governments and establishing the responsibilities of both host and sending countries.

The third topic for discussion will be resources and the environment. It is a particular responsibility of industrialized nations to make careful use of limited resources and to ensure that their consumption contributes to the over-all balance of the environment. Recent activity, for example, co-operation in cleaning up the rivers and seas of Europe, has shown what can be done to rescue badly deteriorated natural systems. It is technically feasible to eliminate or at least limit such damage and the consequent cost to society of remedying its effects. The next stage is to ensure that the means are economical as well as effective and that they are used. Countries in the process of industrialization should be encouraged to take advantage of the available technology, with benefit to their own and the global ecosystem.

Post-industrial development is also a question for discussion, particularly its effect on population distribution and employment patterns. The question of employment is of course linked to that of migration.

The fourth and last topic is health and mortality. Longer life expectancy decreases the proportion of deaths from infectious and parasitic disease, and increases the proportion traceable to degenerative and environmental causes. The emphasis, particularly in an era when medical treatment is becoming more and more costly, must be on prevention. Diet, alcohol and drug abuse, air and water conditions, can all have strong influences on health patterns. Much progress has already been made—for instance, in improving diet in the United States, thereby reducing the toll of cardiovascular disease.

The interests of the members of the Economic Commission for Europe in all these four areas are more and more closely associated with those of the other regions. Next year's Conference offers a unique opportunity to establish the international consensus reached at Bucharest on an even firmer footing, to review and revise the World Population Plan of Action and to set out in broad terms the conditions and direction of co-operation in the future.

I would like to suggest that in your discussions at this meeting, you first consider the recommendations of the World Population Plan of Action as a whole, relating the four sectoral areas to the general objectives of the Plan, which remain valid and will not be revised.

Second, you may wish to consider which areas covered by the World Population Plan of Action need additional emphasis. There are also emerging areas of importance to the world community which are not fully covered by the Plan of Action and on which specific recommendations will be needed. Among these are urbanization, international migration and the balance between population, the use of resources and the protection of the environment.

Third, you should try to foresee the implications of your recommendations for the future. We are talking here not of the immediate future so much as the long time-frame in which population growth and movement evolve. The directions which are set by the International Conference on Population next year should remain valid for coming generations as well as for our own.

There are, of course, interests specific to your countries which apply to you all in common. I suggest that these interests be identified at this meeting, and explored insofar as possible for linkages to the concerns of other regions of the world. We know in a general way that the different manifestations of the population problem in different regions are related; the question now is to examine the nature of the relationships more closely and to come to conclusions on what action may be taken, nationally and internationally, to resolve, not only the problems of one group of countries, but the problems which are common to us all.

NATIONAL GROWTH, NATIONAL STRENGTH

Address at the Second African Population Conference, Arusha, United Republic of Tanzania, 8 January 1984.

I am deeply honoured to be asked to address this Conference, the sequel to the first such meeting in 1971. In the intervening 13 years, much that was forecast at that meeting has taken place.

The continent of Africa now presents to governments and international organizations some of the most serious issues of population in relation to development. Despite their urgency, many of these issues are still not immediately obvious; population densities are generally low throughout the continent and there is still a considerable area of potentially cultivable land. Yet attention has been drawn to population by the realization that Africa's population is growing faster than in any other region in the world.

Africa's population grew, according to the most recent United Nations figures, from 222 million to 476 million in the thirty years between 1950 and 1980. It is projected to grow to 877 million by the end of the century. Rates of growth in many African countries, and in the region as a whole, are actually rising. In the period 1950-1955 the rate was about 2.1 per cent. By the 1975-1980 period, it was 3.0 per cent, and may rise still further. With few exceptions birth rates in African countries have remained very high, in most cases over 45 births per thousand per year between 1950 and 1980.

Traditionally, the growth of population was identified with national strength, but as numbers have grown more and more rapidly this perception has been refined. It is now understood that demographic growth contributes to national strength only as long as numbers are matched by the development of the agricultural, industrial and social systems which support them.

The upsurge of population growth in Africa comes at a time when world growth rates, and the rates for all other regions of the world, have begun to decline. But growth itself is only one aspect of concern with population. Another and most important issue is the severe imbalance between resources and population which now exists in many African countries as the result of low levels of development and lagging utilization of natural resources, particularly for food production.

Sub-fertility still afflicts some countries, preventing them by lack of manpower from making full use of national resources for development. In the rest of the countries of the region, the increase in numbers of children has many implications for the family and the community. Some 45 per cent of Africa's population is now under 15.

At the same time, infant mortality rates remain very high, and the general level of life expectancy at birth is about 50 years. Population growth is accompanied by explosive urban growth in many centres, while international migration is also increasing, partly voluntary, partly under political or economic pressure.

A new emphasis on population questions in Africa invites consideration of new policy directions and reassessment of some old ones. It will be convenient to deal with these under the four subjects which will form the basis for the agenda at this year's International Conference on Population. These are mortality and health; fertility and the family; population distribution and migration; and population, resources, environment and development.

Mortality and health policy

Health, particularly the health of mothers and children, is one of the most important population issues in Africa. Reducing infant mortality is already a priority with African leaders, but it takes on new importance when considered as a contributor to population strategy. There is evidence in this region as elsewhere of a close connection between high birth rates and high infant mortality. Lower infant mortality increases the interval between births, making for smaller but healthier families. Parents, confident that children will survive, initiate fewer pregnancies.

African countries have taken determined action, especially in the past decade, to bring down death rates and improve health care generally. The effects can be seen today. But in order to make the impact which will be needed to reduce death and birth rates to levels compatible with development planning, a further sustained effort will be needed.

The traditional African approach has been to seek health care within the community. Traditional practices protected the health of families and were able, in many cases, despite the absence of modern medical science, to provide curative care. Today's practice is returning to the traditional concept of community care, because the origins of the vast majority of life-threatening health problems are nutritional or environmental and are found in the community itself.

Fertility and the family

Fertility and the family will be another major topic for discussion at Mexico City. It is the aim of every African government to strengthen the family and for this purpose to concentrate on the physical well-being of all family members. In African societies, one of the means of safeguarding the health of both mothers and children has been to ensure that births were well-spaced, giving both mother and child the opportunity to grow strong. In these days, modern means of birth-spacing have taken the place of traditional practices, but the aim remains the same.

The efficient delivery of advice about birth-spacing and the means to achieve it is thus as important a goal for the strength of the family as it is for the strength of the nation. This is underlined by the results of the World Fertility Survey which show that in the African countries covered, women were consistently having more children than they desired. The awareness of the need for birth-spacing is already there; it is now the responsibility of planners and technical experts to provide the means.

As in health, community concern has a most important part to play in delivering birth-spacing. Deciding to adopt modern techniques is a matter for individual decision, but is crucially affected by community attitudes. Once acceptance is secured, the community can provide through its own means many of the channels for providing essential supplies and services. In modern population programmes, community commitment has come to be seen as an essential element in translating government policy into local action.

Along with health, other elements of social development are coming to be seen as vital for population programmes which intend to affect fertility.

A connection which could be crucial for Africa is between education, particularly for women, and birth rates. Not only are the children of literate parents more likely to survive, but the intervals between births tend to be longer and completed family size smaller.

Population distribution and migration

A third most important element of population policy which will be discussed at the International Conference on Population is population distribution and migration. As urban growth becomes increasingly an African phenomenon, close attention is being paid to the movement of population, along with the vital statistics of births and deaths and the causes of death. With improved knowledge of their population structures, African governments are giving increased importance to the development of population policy and its integration into wider development policies at local and national levels.

Population, resources, environment and development

A fourth topic for discussion at Mexico City will be population, resources, environment and development. Rapid growth of population without accompanying economic structures for developing resources is one of Africa's most pressing problems. The opportunity now exists for a determined attempt to emphasize the importance of population for development planning. There are no simple equations – population, on the one hand, and resources, on the other – but understanding of the complexity of the relationship between population, the resource bases on which it depends and the natural environment in which it thrives can only have beneficial effect on development efforts.

Renewed emphasis on population as an aspect of development is seen increasingly to be an essential component of the wider framework. The networks of information and communication are as necessary a part of the infrastructure as roads and bridges; the development of a healthy and educated workforce is as vital as the establishment of an industrial base.

Emphasis on population calls for an extension of understanding on the part of donor countries in international population assistance. Industrial countries understand the desire of developing countries for economic development. But frequently the social structure on which all else rests is neglected.

One of the functions of UNFPA is to act as a channel of communication between the developing countries which need assistance for social development and the industrialized countries which possess the financial resources to assist them. UNFPA has been successful in mobilizing some of those resources on behalf of developing countries – for censuses of population in

22 African countries, for example, and now increasingly for support in policy-making and for programmes aimed at attacking the causes of high mortality and fertility. Africa is a key area for increased UNFPA assistance in the future, with 33 out of 53 of the countries designated as priority countries for population assistance.

There are certain specific areas on which this Conference might find it profitable to concentrate. First is how to achieve the acceptance of population as a priority for governments and communities concerned with development. Second is the question of spreading the awareness of population concerns through the whole of society. Third is effective programmes by which policy and awareness are transformed into action.

There are many fundamentally important problems, not the least of which are physical and human resources. The infrastructure of transport and communications, education services and health care on which population programmes rely does not exist in many parts of Africa. A realistic population policy cannot wait until they are established; programmes are needed which take these deficiencies into account and, where possible, take advantage of existing networks. One possible approach is to turn the management of population programmes over to the community, securing maximum popular involvement with minimum supervision. Effective programmes can be established in Africa despite many obstacles. It is part of the function of this Conference to recommend ways in which this can be done.

The International Conference on Population offers the opportunity for the nations of the world to exchange experiences and information and to agree on a plan of continued common action for the benefit of all. This meeting is an important stage in the preparations for the International Conference, but it is also important in itself as a forum for the discussion of uniquely African problems and achievements in the past decade and agreement on approaches which are appropriate in the African context. As such, it has a vital part to play in the path which African nations and peoples are taking to development.

LIST OF
MAJOR STATEMENTS
SINCE JANUARY 1979

Editors' note: Listed below are the major statements given by the Executive Director of UNFPA from the beginning of 1979 (since the issuance of *International Population Assistance: The First Decade*), from which the excerpts in the *Excerpts from Statements* sections in Chapters II-VII have been culled. Unless otherwise indicated, all statements have been printed and are available from UNFPA.

29 January 1979
Statement to the United Nations Population Commission at its Twentieth Session, United Nations, New York (not printed).

13 February 1979
Statement at Cairo University, Cairo, Egypt (not printed).

10 April 1979
Statement at a Meeting of Population Concern, London, England (not printed).

10 May 1979
The Relationship Between Development Planning and Population. Statement at the Latin American Conference on Development Planning and Population, Cartagena, Colombia.

14 May 1979
Statement at University Federico Villarreal, Lima, Peru (not printed).

18 June 1979
UNFPA: Past, Present, Future. Statement to the UNDP Governing Council at its Twenty-sixth Session, United Nations, New York.

19 June 1979
Population and the New International Development Strategy. Statement to the Preparatory Committee for the New International Development Strategy at its Second Session, United Nations, New York.

28 August 1979
Population and Development: The Challenges for the Future. Statement at the International Conference of Parliamentarians on Population and Development, Colombo, Sri Lanka.

29 August 1979
The Ethic of Restraint. Statement at Special Convocation of the University of Colombo, Colombo, Sri Lanka.

31 October 1979
The UNFPA: First Decade, Next Decade. Statement to the Second Committee of the United Nations General Assembly at its Thirty-fourth Session, United Nations, New York.

15 January 1980
The World Population Crisis. Statement to the National Press Club, Washington, D.C. Speech Series No. 50.

13 May 1980
Population and the 1980s. Statement at the Media Conference on Population in Development, Sarpsborg, Norway. Speech Series No. 51.

19 May 1980
The Expanding Nature of the Population Field. Statement at the International Seminar on Planned Population Distribution for Development: The Hokkaido Experience, Sapporo, Hokkaido, Japan. Speech Series No. 53.

9 June 1980
Statement at the Romanian Academy for Economic Sciences, Bucharest, Romania (not printed).

16 June 1980
Resources and the Future. Statement to the UNDP Governing Council at its Twenty-seventh session, United Nations, Geneva. Speech Series No. 52.

7 July 1980
The World Fertility Survey: A Basis for Population and Development Planning. Statement at the World Fertility Survey Conference, London, England. Speech Series No. 54.

12 July 1980
UNFPA and the Resident Representatives: A Continuing Relationship. Statement at the Global Meeting of UNDP Resident Representatives, Tunis, Tunisia. Speech Series No. 55.

15 July 1980
Women, Population and Development. Statement at the World Conference of the United Nations Decade for Women: Equality, Development and Peace, Copenhagen, Denmark. Speech Series No. 56.

21 July 1980
Population and the Global Future. Statement at the First Global Conference on the Future: Through the '80s, Toronto, Canada. Speech Series No. 57.

1 September 1980
Population and the Urban Future. Statement at the International Conference on Population and the Urban Future, Rome, Italy. Speech Series No. 58.

3 October 1980
The Need for a Global Commitment. Statement to the Second Committee of the United Nations General Assembly at its Thirty-fifth Session, United Nations, New York. Speech Series No. 59.

25 October 1980
The Food, Population and Development Equation. Statement at the Southeastern Dialogue on the Changing World Economy, Atlanta, Georgia.

20 December 1980
International Co-operation for Global Development. Commencement address at the University of Maryland, University College, College Park, Maryland. Speech Series No. 60.

29 January 1981
Statement to the Population Commission. Statement to the United Nations Population Commission at its Twenty-first Session, United Nations, New York. Speech Series No. 61.

14 February 1981

The Indonesia Experience. Statement at Special Convocation, University of Indonesia, Jakarta, Indonesia. Speech Series No. 62.

16 March 1981

The True Spirit of International Co-operation. Statement at a Meeting of the National Population Council of the Government of Mexico, Mexico City, Mexico. Speech Series No. 63 (Spanish/English).

27 April 1981

Family Planning in the '80s: Requisites for the Future. Statement at the International Conference on Family Planning in the 1980s, Jakarta, Indonesia (English/French/Spanish).

3 May 1981

Technology for Humanity. Statement at Spring Commencement, The George Washington University, Washington, D.C. Speech Series No. 64.

12 May 1981

Global Population Trends. Statement at the International Development Conference, Washington, D.C. Speech Series No. 65.

12 June 1981

Report to the Council: Present and Future Programme. Statement to the UNDP Governing Council at its Twenty-eighth Session, United Nations, New York. Speech Series No. 66.

2 July 1981

Report to ECOSOC. Statement to the United Nations Economic and Social Council at its Second Regular Session of 1981, United Nations, Geneva. Speech Series No. 67.

6 July 1981

Population and Development in Africa. Statement at the Parliamentary Conference on Population and Development in Africa, Nairobi, Kenya. Speech Series No. 68.

18 August 1981

Population and the Role of Communication. Statement at Special Ceremony, Faculty of Humanities, Universidad Autonoma de Santo Domingo, Santo Domingo, Dominican Republic. Speech Series No. 70 (Spanish/English).

6 September 1981

Aging Population and Development. Statement at the European Follow-up Forum on Aging, Castelgandolfo, Italy. Speech Series No. 69.

8 September 1981

Notes for the Nobel Symposium on Population Growth and World Economic Development sponsored by the Norwegian Nobel Committee, Oslo, Norway (not printed).

2 October 1981

Report to the General Assembly. Statement to the Second Committee of the United Nations General Assembly at its Thirty-sixth Session, United Nations, New York. Speech Series No. 71.

27 October 1981

Population and Development in Asia. Statement at the Asian Conference of Parliamentarians on Population and Development, Beijing, People's Republic of China. Speech Series No. 72.

7 December 1981

Labour and Demography—A Global Perspective. Statement at the Fourth National Population Welfare Congress, Manila, Philippines. Speech Series No. 74.

9 December 1981

Vision and Adaptability—Demography in the Twenty-First Century. Statement at the 19th General Conference of the International Union for the Scientific Study of Population, Manila, Philippines. Speech Series No. 73.

14 April 1982-A

Statement to the Faculty of Economics, Catholic University, Quito, Ecuador (not printed).

14 April 1982-B

Statement to the Faculty of Economic Sciences at Central University of Ecuador, Quito, Ecuador (not printed).

11 June 1982

Report to the Council: The future of the UNFPA programme. Statement to the UNDP Governing Council at its Twenty-ninth Session, United Nations, Geneva. Speech Series No. 75.

8 July 1982-A

Report to ECOSOC on the work of the UNFPA. Statement to the United Nations Economic and Social Council at its Second Regular Session of 1982, United Nations, Geneva. Speech Series No. 76.

8 July 1982-B

Report to ECOSOC on preparations for the 1984 International Conference on Population. Statement to the United Nations Economic and Social Council at its Second Regular Session of 1982, United Nations, Geneva. Speech Series No. 77.

27 July 1982

Aging—A Matter of International Concern. Statement to the World Assembly on Aging, Vienna, Austria. Speech Series No. 78.

20 September 1982

Population in Asia: the Cresting Wave. Statement at the Third Asian and Pacific Population Conference, Colombo, Sri Lanka. Speech Series No. 79 (also in French).

29 September 1982

Population Problems and International Co-operation. Statement at a Meeting of the Scientific Council of the Moscow State University, Moscow, Union of Soviet Socialist Republics. Speech Series No. 80.

2 October 1982

Population in Development Planning. Statement at Special Convocation of the Quaid-i-Azam University, Islamabad, Pakistan. Speech Series No. 81.

5 October 1982

Report to the General Assembly. Statement to the Second Committee of the United Nations General Assembly at its Thirty-seventh Session, United Nations, New York. Speech Series No. 82.

28 October 1982

CELADE: The First Twenty-Five Years. Statement at the Ceremony Commemorating the Twenty-Fifth Anniversary of the Establishment of the Latin American Demographic Centre, Santiago, Chile. Speech Series No. 83 (Spanish/English).

24 November 1982

Aging: The Universal Phenomenon. Statement at the International Symposium on An Aging Society: Strategies for 21st Century Japan, Nihon University, Tokyo, Japan. Speech Series No. 85.

2 December 1982

The Population Wave. Statement at the Western Hemisphere Conference of Parliamentarians on Population and Development, Brasilia, Brazil. Speech Series No. 84 (Spanish/English).

5 January 1983
Fertility and the Family: Operational Responses Since Bucharest and for the Future. Statement at the Expert Group Meeting on Factors Relating to Fertility and Family, New Delhi, India. Speech Series No. 86.

7 March 1983
Defining Population Education. Statement at the University of Nevada, Reno, Nevada. Speech Series No. 87.

21 March 1983
Distribution, Migration and Development. Statement at the Expert Group Meeting on Population Distribution, Migration and Development, Hammamet, Tunisia. Speech Series No. 88 (also in French).

25 April 1983
Issues on Inter-relationships. Statement at the Expert Group Meeting on Population, Resources, Environment and Development, Geneva, Switzerland. Speech Series No. 89.

31 May 1983
Concerning Mortality and Health. Statement at the Expert Group Meeting on Mortality and Health Policy, Rome, Italy. Speech Series No. 90.

13 June 1983
The Population Factor in Trade and Development. Statement at UNCTAD VI (United Nations Conference on Trade and Development), Belgrade, Yugoslavia. Speech Series No. 91.

17 June 1983
Report to the Council—1983. Statement at the Thirtieth Session of the UNDP Governing Council, United Nations, New York. Speech Series No. 92.

29 June 1983
UNFPA and the Arab World. Statement at a Meeting on Co-operation between the United Nations and the League of Arab States, Tunis, Tunisia. Speech Series No. 93.

8 August 1983
The Philippines— Towards the Year 2000. Statement at Honorary Degree Conferment Ceremony at the University of the Philippines, Quezon City, Philippines. Speech Series No. 94.

5 September 1983
Integrating Population Programmes. Statement at 10th Asian Parasite Control Organization/Family Planning Conference, Tokyo, Japan. Speech Series No. 95.

13 September 1983
The Creative Role of Non-Governmental Organizations in the Population Field. Statement at the International Consultation of Non-Governmental Organizations on Population Issues, Geneva, Switzerland. Speech Series No. 96.

14 September 1983
Population Trends and Issues. Statement at Meeting of the Netherlands Association of Demographers, The Hague, Netherlands. Speech Series No. 97.

19 September 1983
Confronting the Population Problem. Statement at 1983 Editors' Seminar at the United Nations, sponsored by the United Nations Association of the United States of America, United Nations, New York. Speech Series No. 98.

26 September 1983
Health, Mortality and Population. Statement at the National Council for International Health, Washington, D.C. Speech Series No. 99.

6 October 1983
Population—Common Problems, Common Interests. Statement at Regional Meeting on Population of the Economic Commission for Europe, Sofia, Bulgaria. Speech Series No. 100.

7 October 1983
The Bulgarian Experience. Statement at Special Convocation, Sofia State University, Sofia, Bulgaria. Speech Series No. 101.

22 November 1983
The Family—The Basis of Society. Statement at the Seminar for Women Leaders on Population and Development in the English-speaking Caribbean, Basseterre, Saint Christopher and Nevis. Speech Series No. 102.

26 November 1983
Population, Development and Human Rights. Commencement address at the University of the West Indies, Mona Campus, Jamaica. Speech Series No. 103.

29 November 1983
The Role of the University in Population. Statement at a Special Convocation at the University of Panama, Panama City, Panama. Speech Series No. 104 (Spanish/English).

8 January 1984
National Growth, National Strength. Address at the Second African Population Conference, Arusha, United Republic of Tanzania. Speech Series No. 105.

23 January 1984

Progress Report on the Preparations for the 1984 International Conference on Population. Statement to the Preparatory Committee for the 1984 International Conference on Population, United Nations, New York. Speech Series No. 106.

17 February 1984

Parliamentarians and Population — Asia. Statement at the First Conference of the Asian Forum of Parliamentarians on Population and Development, New Delhi, India. Speech Series No. 107.

INDEX

SPECIAL INDEX TO CONCEPTS IN THE WORLD POPULATION PLAN OF ACTION* AND THE RECOMMENDATIONS FOR THE FURTHER IMPLEMENTATION OF THE WORLD POPULATION PLAN OF ACTION**

Editor's note: In the following index, references are to paragraph and recommendation numbers, not page numbers. The paragraphs of the World Population Plan of Action and the Recommendations for the Further Implementation of the World Population Plan of Action are indicated by their number, while the recommendations proper of the Recommendations are identified by their number preceded by R. Sub-paragraphs are identified by a letter immediately following a number: ex. 74c). The occurrence of an entry in both the heading of a paragraph and in a subsequent sub-paragraph is indicated by a space between the two references: ex. 74 c). An asterisk denotes an indirect reference to the concept.

This index is a revised version of one originally prepared by the Population Division of the United Nations Department of International Economic and Social Affairs, whose work is gratefully acknowledged.

Report of the United Nations World Population Conference, 1974, Bucharest, 19-30 August 1974 (United Nations publication, Sales No. E.75.XIII.3), chap. I.

**Report of the International Conference on Population, 1984, Mexico City, 6-14 August 1984* (United Nations publication, Sales No. E.84.XIII.8), chap. I. sect. B.